# STEVEN SCOTT



ESSAY BY **ROBERT C. MORGAN**

LUMINOUS ICONS

# STEVEN SCOTT

1999–2011

FOREWORD BY OLE NØRYNG

ESSAY BY **ROBERT C. MORGAN**

HIRMER

LUMINOUS ICONS

# OLE NØRLYNG

FOREWORD

**THE THEATRE IS IMAGINATION'S BOUNDLESS PLAYGROUND.** That's true not just for playwrights, composers and choreographers – but also for the person who lights the stage. Stage designers are like little gods, revealing the unseen, creating art from darkness.

Steven Scott is deeply rooted in the theatre. His father was a stage master while Scott himself trained as a theatre technician at the Royal Court Theatre in London during the early seventies. It was here that two lighting wizards, Andy Philips and Rory Dempster, put the 17-year-old on a path towards light. The two mentors, who were lighting designers at a time when the concept barely existed, were exceptionally gifted. They developed new techniques from which they could create entirely new experiences from light. A seed was planted in the young Steven Scott.

Later, Scott became a theatre technician at the Royal Opera House in Covent Garden before joining the experimental London arts centre Riverside Studios, an important milestone in his early career. It was here he honed his craft, collaborating with some of the artistic giants of the day – singers and dancers as well as ambitious directors and angry young playwrights intent on revolutionising the world. It was a powerhouse, and it entered his bloodstream.

Ever since, Steven Scott has used light to reveal, enhance and create productions of breathtaking beauty. From daylight to moonlight, cathedrals as well as concentration camps.

> **"… And the most spectacular stage design to date: an engineered prison-hell**
> **by Steven Scott executed by steel with bars and hatches which can be lowered from the ceiling…"**
> **Anne Middelboe Christensen on *MIDNIGHT EXPRESS*, Peter Schaufuss Ballet**
> **Information newspaper, 10 March 2000.**

In the 1960s and 1970s, the physical and visual aspects of theatre went through rapid developments. The entire concept of stage design was re-examined thanks to the influence of practitioners such as Edward Gordon Craig, the English theorist, and Oscar Schlemmer of the Bauhaus. Theatre could be seen holistically from the point of view of 'the empty space', a term coined by the great English director Peter Brook. The empty space was also the black box.

In this environment, space could be revealed through the conscious and artistic use of light, unfolding over time like a narrative. Light could allow the viewer to perceive for the first time, or see things that weren't even there.

The prerequisite for such magic is the empty space and the black box. A space however is defined by its proportions, which have to be seen and experienced in relation to the human form. This is where sacred geometry and the golden section play a fundamental role.

A constant thread in Steven Scott's work has been a concern with dance and the human form, and although he has created stage designs for all theatrical disciplines – including for operas such as Peter Greenaway's *Rosa: A Horse Drama* with De Nederlandse Opera (1994) – it is dance that has primarily benefited from Scott's ideas.

 As soon as the empty space and black box are justly proportioned, the designer creates a light box, defining light within an undefined darkness. The designer is faced with an immense breadth of possibilities, ranging from extreme minimalism to extreme complexity. A simple pool of light may be all that is required for the space to come to life and for the right mood to be established.

Among Steven Scott's simplest yet most complex designs was the arrangement for Peter Schaufuss Ballet's *HC Andersen* (Holstebro 2000). Physically, it consisted of five rectangular and rotating panels arranged in a rectangular frame, while a shifting play of light created countless modulations, colours and reflections. From bright red to dreamy blue. From oppressive darkness to ethereal brightness.

The light box within a black box is a central motif in Stevens Scott's work. The theme was explored in all its shimmering optical complexity in *The Shakespeare Suite,* choreographed by David Bintley for Birmingham Royal Ballet in 1999, where light appeared to suck the viewer in one moment only to build an impenetrable wall the next.

In contrast to the op art-inspired staging of *The Shakespeare Suite,* Tim Rushton's *Requiem* with the Royal Danish Theatre and the Royal Danish Ballet (Copenhagen, 2006) set a calmer, more architectural tone. Here, Scott developed light in ways that seemed almost to break the bounds of physics. Taking a strictly minimalist approach, he built an enclosed courtyard space

# LUMINOUS ICONS

# FOREWORD

on three levels. Dancers populated the ground-floor level while an opera chorus was arranged on the upper floors. A series of identically proportioned light boxes created subtle flows of slowly changing light.

In 1996, Steven Scott created a remarkable staging for the Royal Danish Theatre's production of *Hamlet,* performed with the Royal Danish Ballet as part of the Copenhagen City of Culture, at the Kronborg castle in Elsinore, Denmark. Here, Scott created a spectacular installation on a large floating stage on the moat, while the walls of the Renaissance castle formed a dramatic backdrop.

In staging this open-air dance version of Shakespeare's existential drama, Scott's main allies were the four elements: air, earth, fire and water. As part of the staging, Scott created a wailing wall of water, animated by colour and varying intensities of light. Along the edge of the stage platform were elements of fire as well as flames from torches positioned on the castle's fortifications. The seductive combination of elements combined to form a magnificent whole. Silent, intimate light art became a total theatre of unimaginable dimensions.

The performance took on a very different form when it was transferred to the Old Stage at the Royal Danish Theatre in Copenhagen. In this more confined space the spectator came closer to the core of both the Shakespearean drama and Stevens Scott's own universe. Light, colour and texture were distilled into a dense fusion of visual effects.

Steven Scott also created for Peter Schaufuss a *Tchaikovsky Trilogy,* in which an overarching stage design helped to link the three ballet classics *Swan Lake, Sleeping Beauty* and *The Nutcracker* into one continuous narrative. A significant development in the staging of this kaleidoscopic performance was the use of mirrors, an effect that Scott had already used in collaboration with the English avant-garde choreographer Michael Clark during the 1980s.

In 1999, Scott incorporated photographic projections into a design for William Tuckett's ballet *Turn of the Screw,* performed by the Royal Ballet at Covent Garden. After the premiere, dance critic Judith Mackrell wrote in *The Guardian:*

**"... in the light of Steven Scott's set, which quite simply advances ballet design by years. Scott has realised the ballet's country house setting entirely through the projection of photographic transparencies [...] These give the ballet the freedom to change scene, to pass from night to day, summer to autumn as seamlessly as a film.**

**Yet the effect isn't of dancers performing within picture postcards, for the images are layered so subtly over each other that they seem like the inner geography of the characters' souls as much as their physical location. The effect is genuinely haunting."**

This cinematic dimension in the overall scenographic expression has been a major factor in Stevens Scott's collaboration with the Danish choreographer Kim Brandstrup, which came to the fore in a sublime production of the ballet *Ghosts* performed by the Royal Danish Ballet (Copenhagen 2007). Returning to his use of cinematic projections, Scott created an eerie, ghostly form of light – pale and shadowless. This light created the effect of apparitional dancers emerging and disappearing from nowhere.

A highly unusual visual experience ensued when Steven Scott collaborated with choreographer Steen Koerner to create a hip-hop, breakdance version of the romantic ballet *Sylfiden* (The Sylph, Copenhagen 2009). Here, moonlit romance was replaced with an ultramodern, abstract staging. Zigzags of colour created a labyrinth of light, which evolved to form back-drops for a church, a forest or a city. Etching itself powerfully into the mind's eye, this offbeat design was Scott's most ambitious light work and a distinct counterpoint to the tranquility and harmony that otherwise characterise his pieces.

Scott's techniques may be modern but his concerns are largely ancient. His thinking is not only with the ancient teachings of proportion but also the medieval and spiritual perception of light. If just proportions have a harmonising and centreing effect on human beings, then light has a definite healing effect. Light penetrates deep into our consciousness, and at the same time positively influences our physical well-being.

Even when Steven Scott's light installations occur in the empty space or the black box of the theatre, they still strive to amplify the thoughts that Bernard of Clairvaux, the founder of the Cistercian Order, articulated when he declared:

**"There must be no decoration, only proportion."**

According to Saint Bernard, light is comparable to the Holy Spirit, and the result of this revelation is the wondrous luminous scenes we see in the stained-glass windows of medieval cathedrals. Not all light art is spiritual. Much is certainly not spiritu-ally conceived. But it cannot be denied that we feel something spiritual when encountering the floating, shifting light that pours from the works of Steven Scott, and the magnificent harmony of time, light and proportion he creates.

# LIGHT WORKS IN THEATRE

**REQUIEM**
CHOREOGRAPHER    TIM RUSHTON | COSTUMES    MIA STENSGAARD
ROYAL DANISH BALLET & OPERA CHOIR
WORLD PREMIERE MARCH 2005
ROYAL THEATRE
OPERAEN    COPENHAGEN    DENMARK

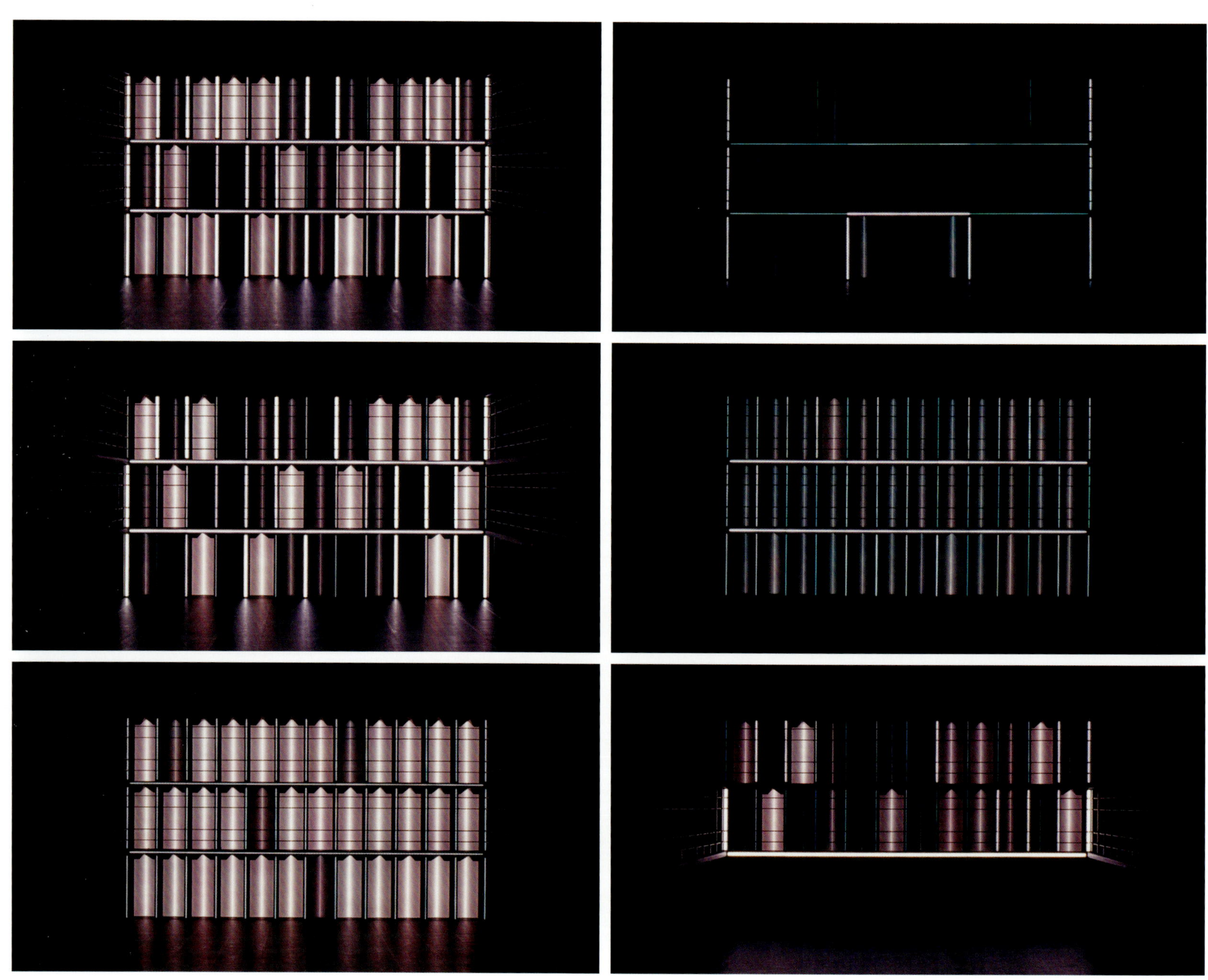

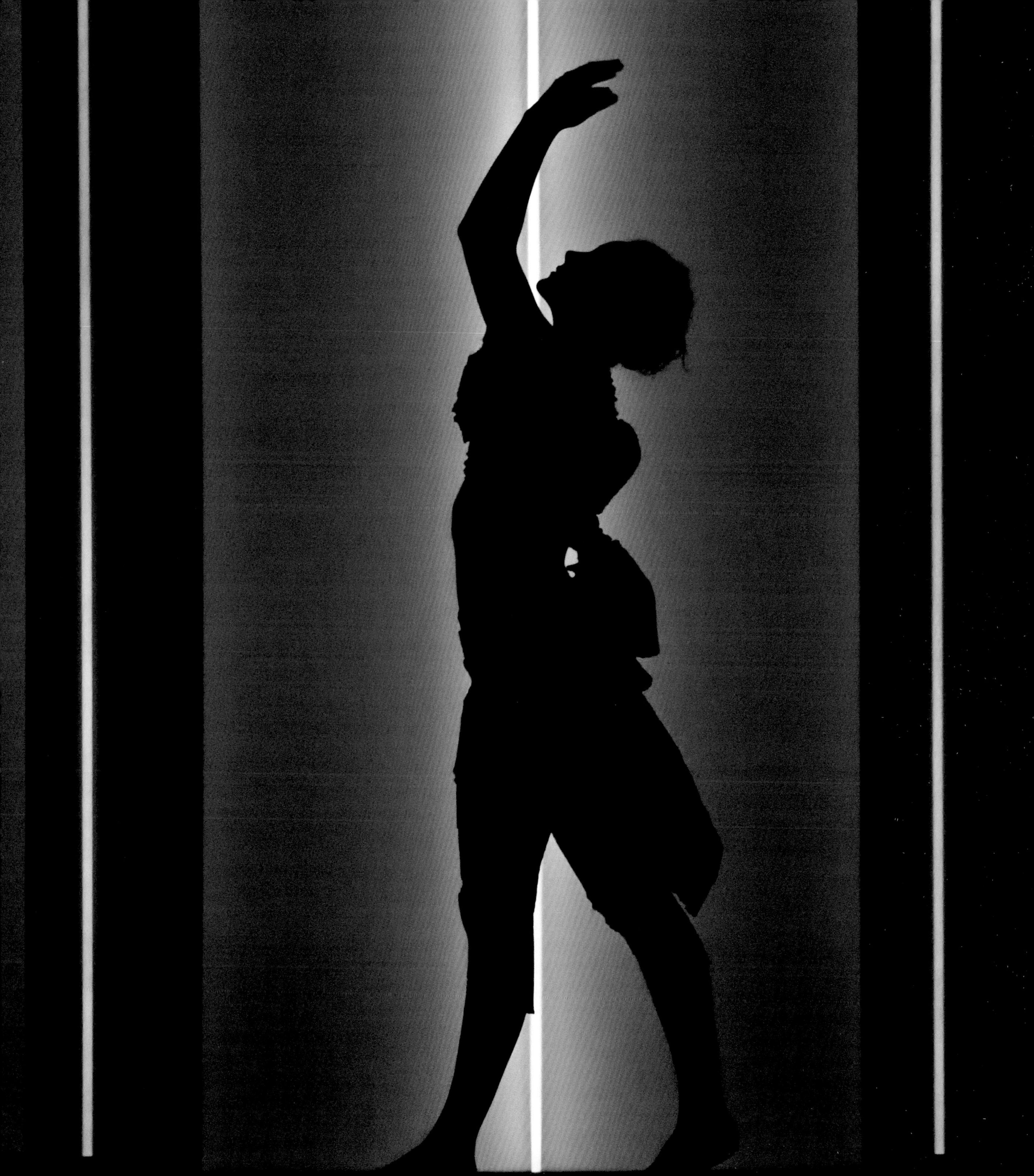

**REQUIEM**
CHOREOGRAPHER   TIM RUSHTON | COSTUMES   MIA STENSGAARD
ROYAL DANISH BALLET & OPERA CHOIR
WORLD PREMIERE MARCH 2005
ROYAL THEATRE
OPERAEN   COPENHAGEN   DENMARK

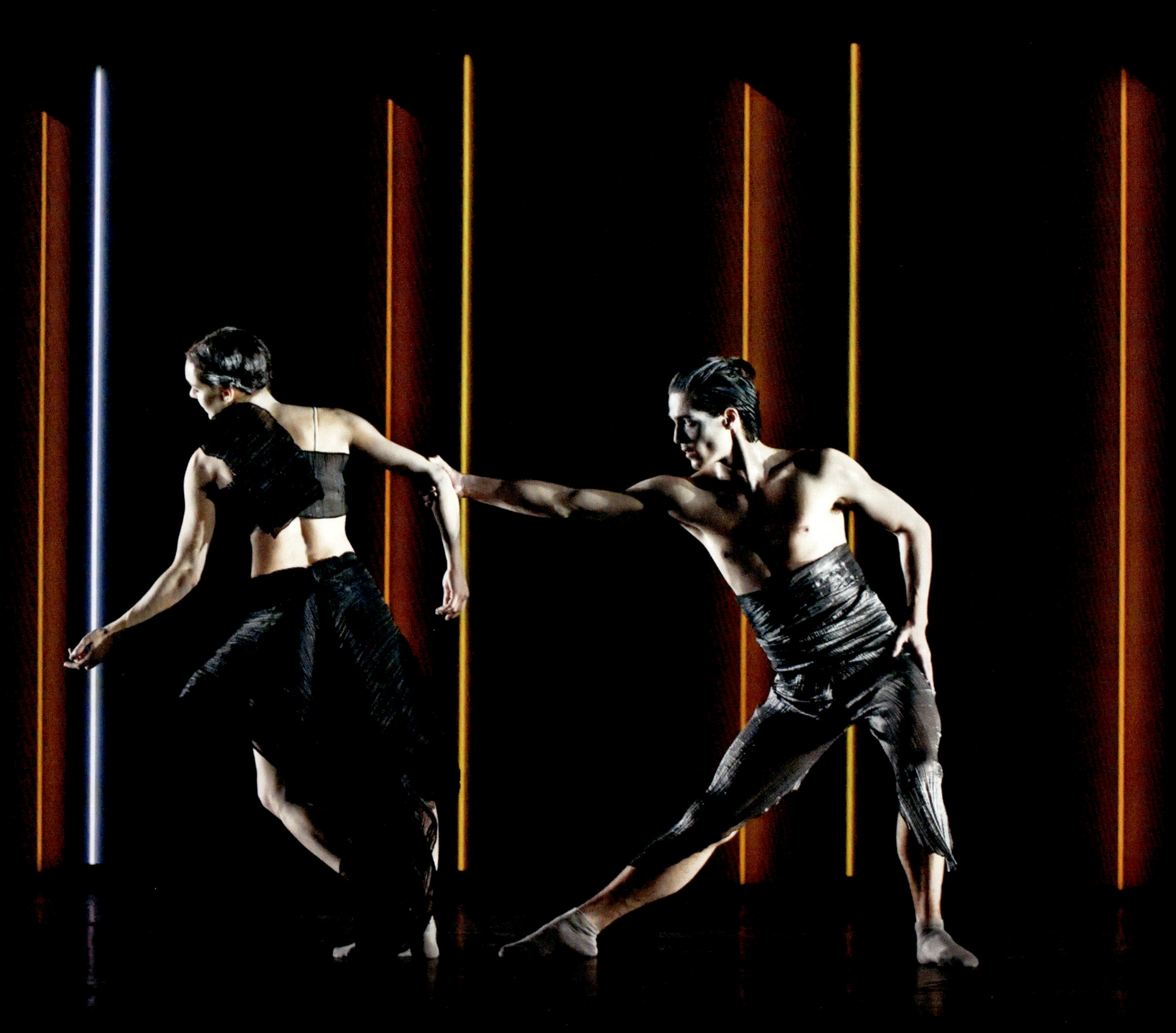

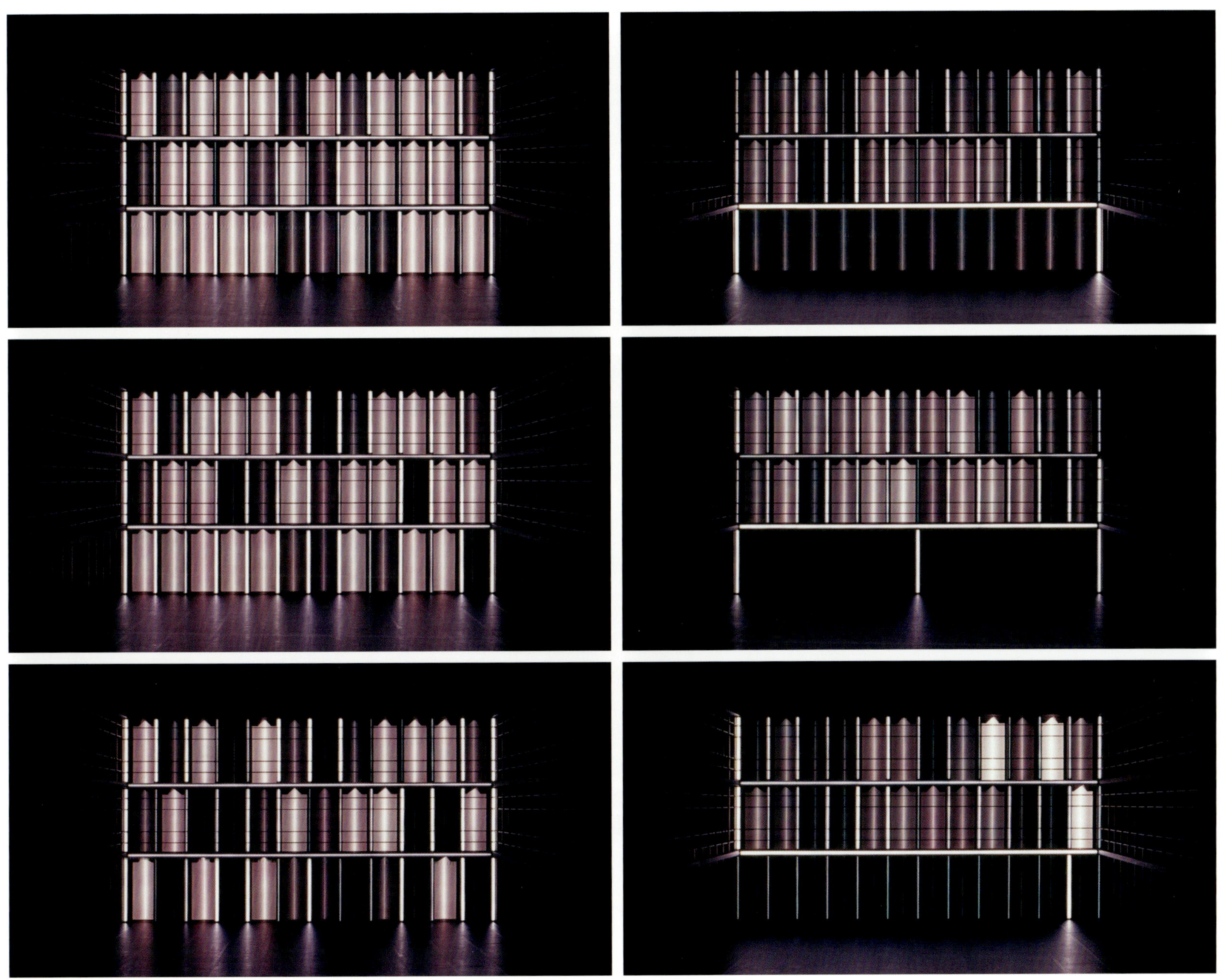

**REQUIEM**
CHOREOGRAPHER   TIM RUSHTON | COSTUMES   MIA STENSGAARD
ROYAL DANISH BALLET & OPERA CHOIR
WORLD PREMIERE MARCH 2005
ROYAL THEATRE
OPERAEN   COPENHAGEN   DENMARK

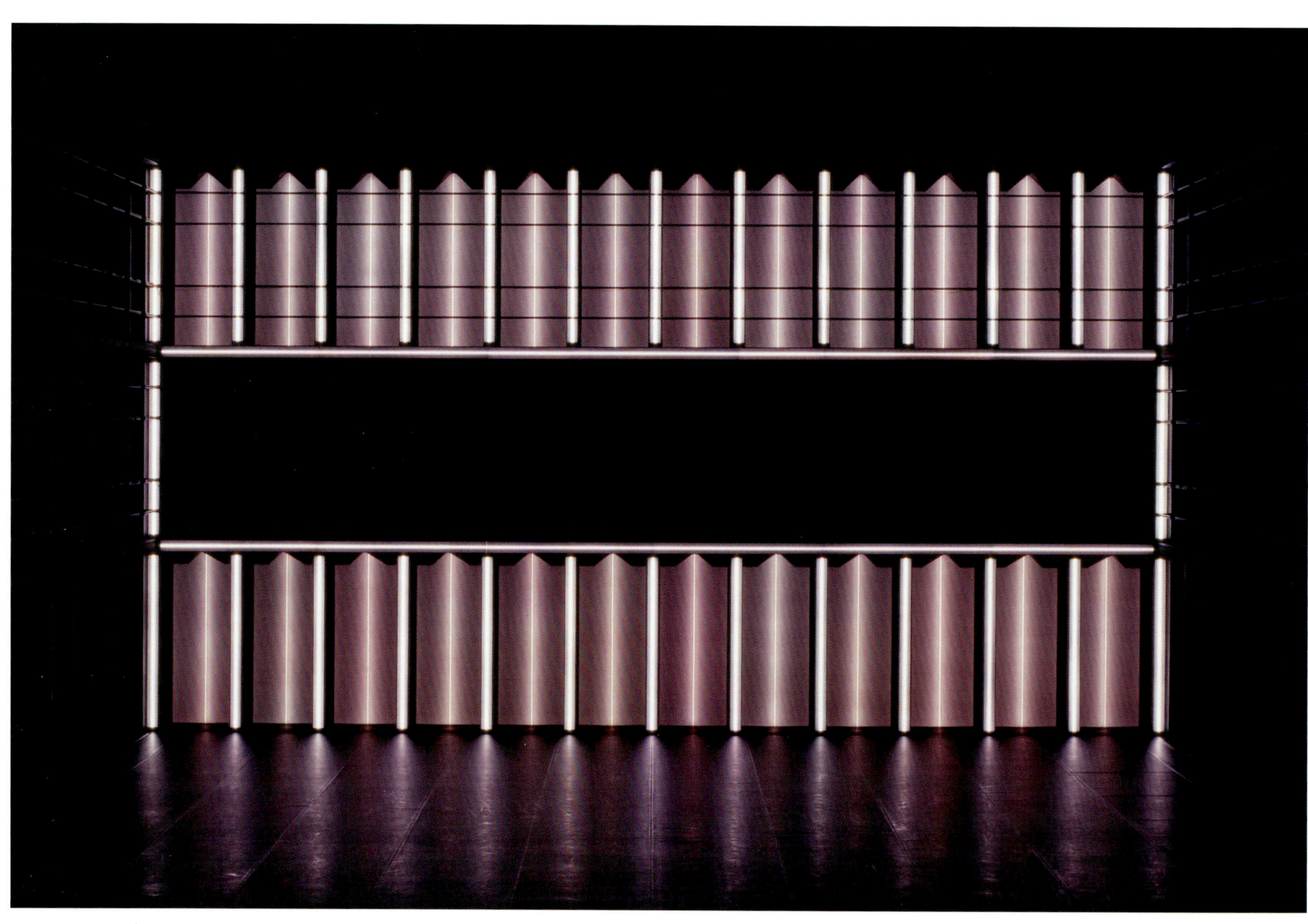

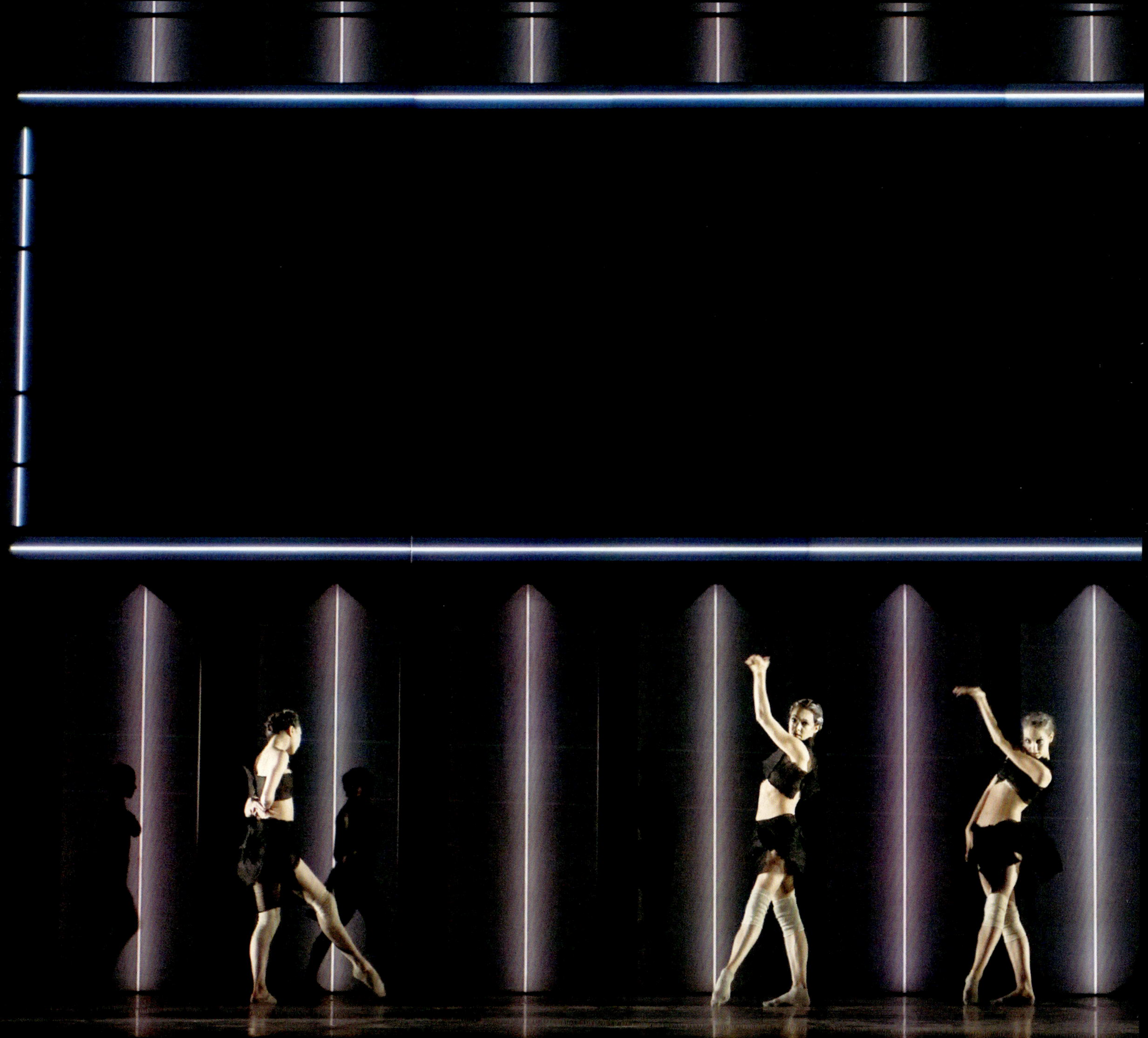

**REQUIEM**

CHOREOGRAPHER   TIM RUSHTON  |  COSTUMES   MIA STENSGAARD
ROYAL DANISH BALLET & OPERA CHOIR
WORLD PREMIERE MARCH 2005
ROYAL THEATRE
OPERAEN   COPENHAGEN   DENMARK

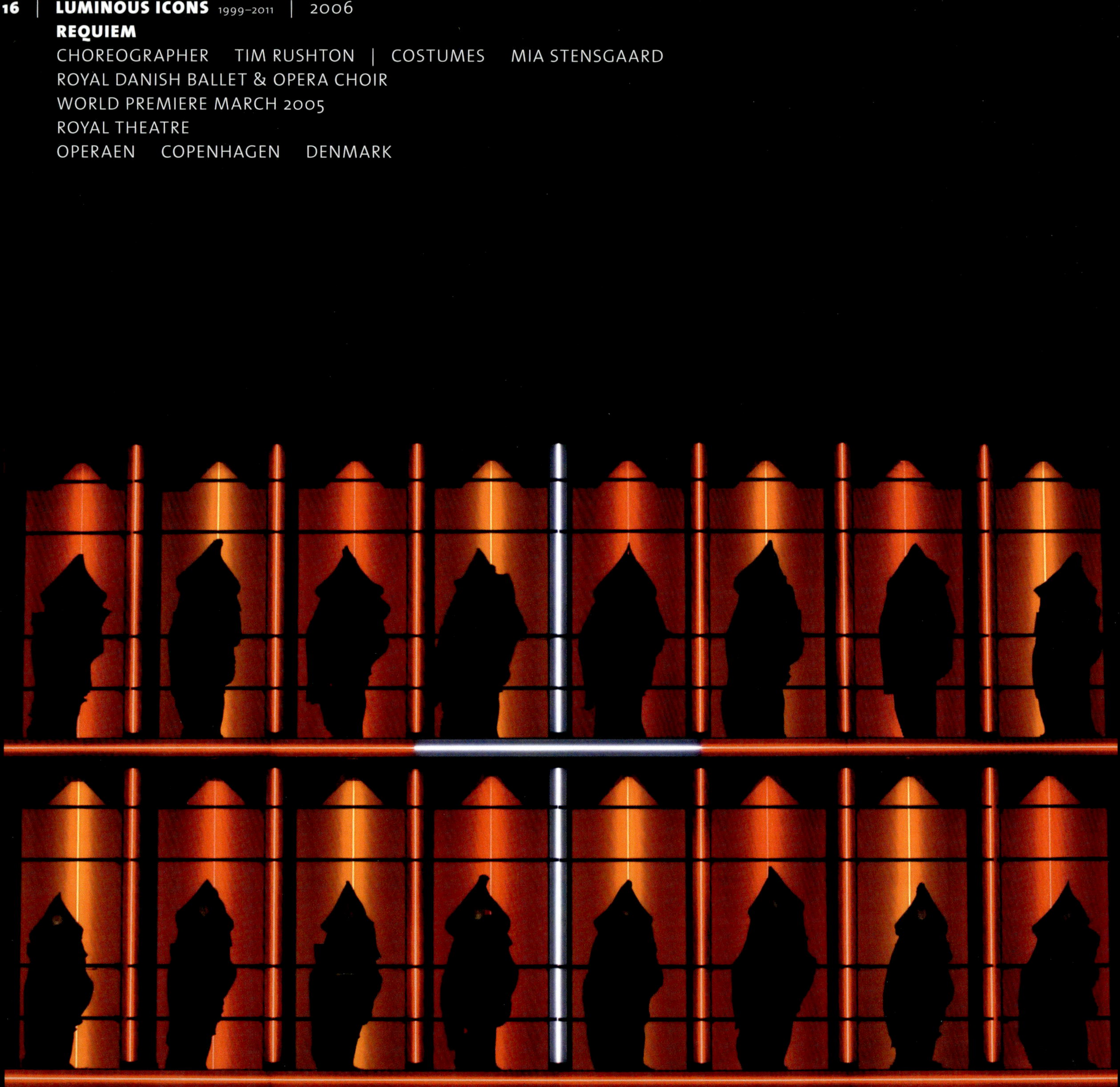

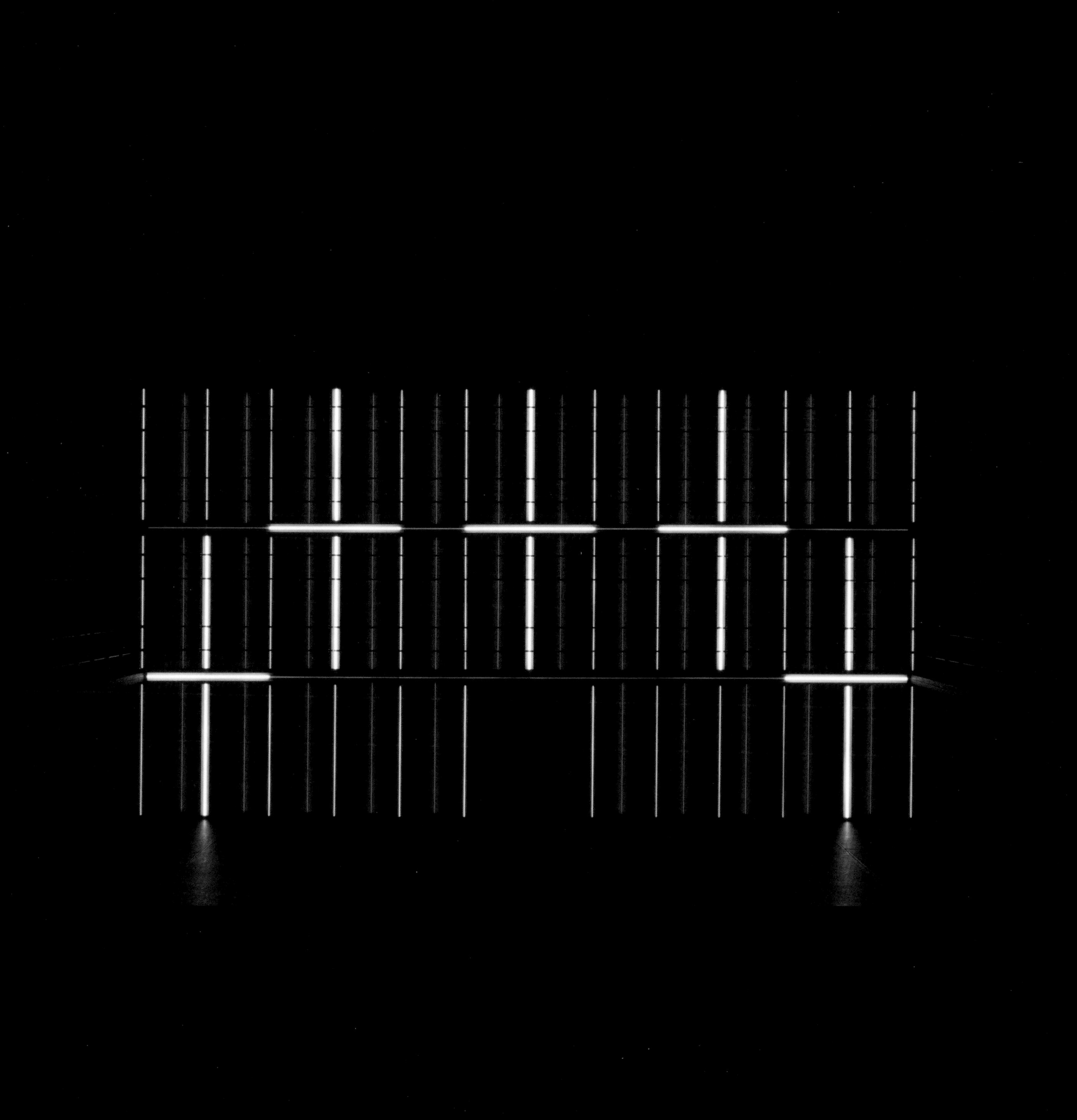

**SYLPHIDE**
CHOREOGRAPHER   STEEN KOERNER | COSTUMES   HENRIK VIBSKOV
INTERNATIONAL FREELANCE THEATRE ENSEMBLE
WORLD PREMIERE OCTOBER 2005
AVENY-T   COPENHAGEN   DENMARK

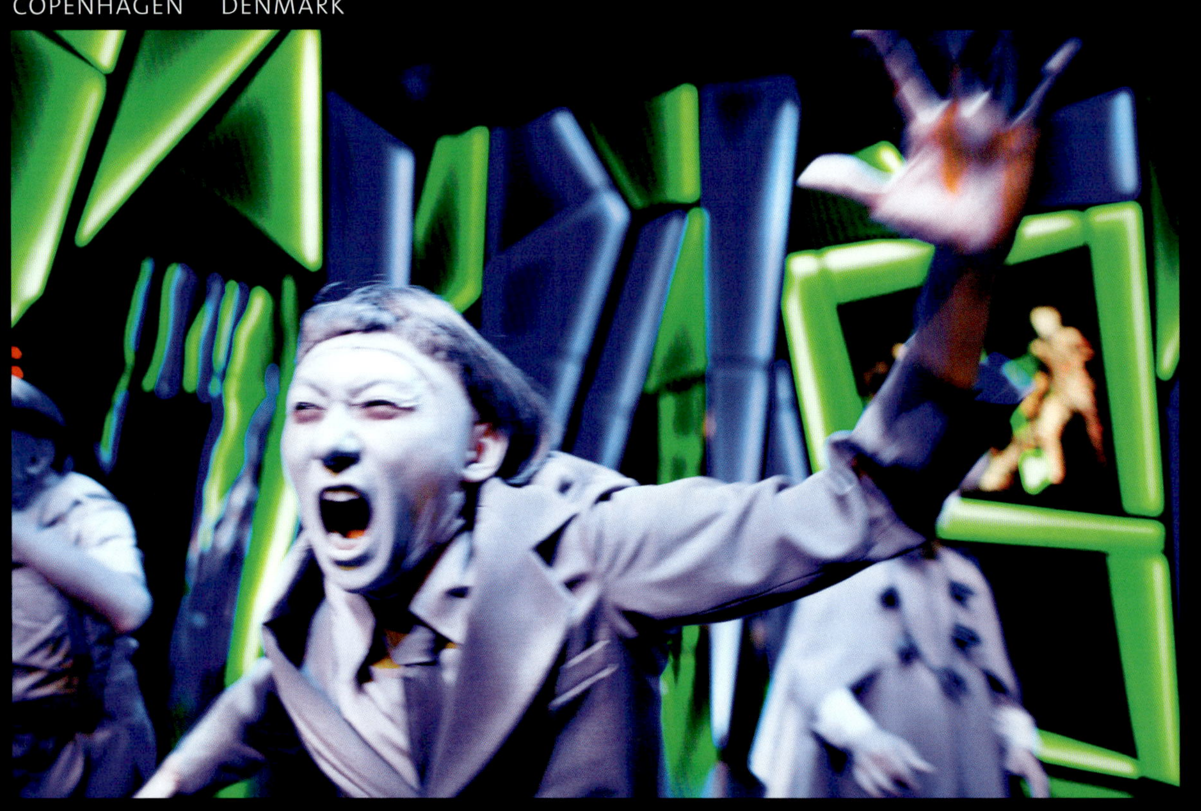

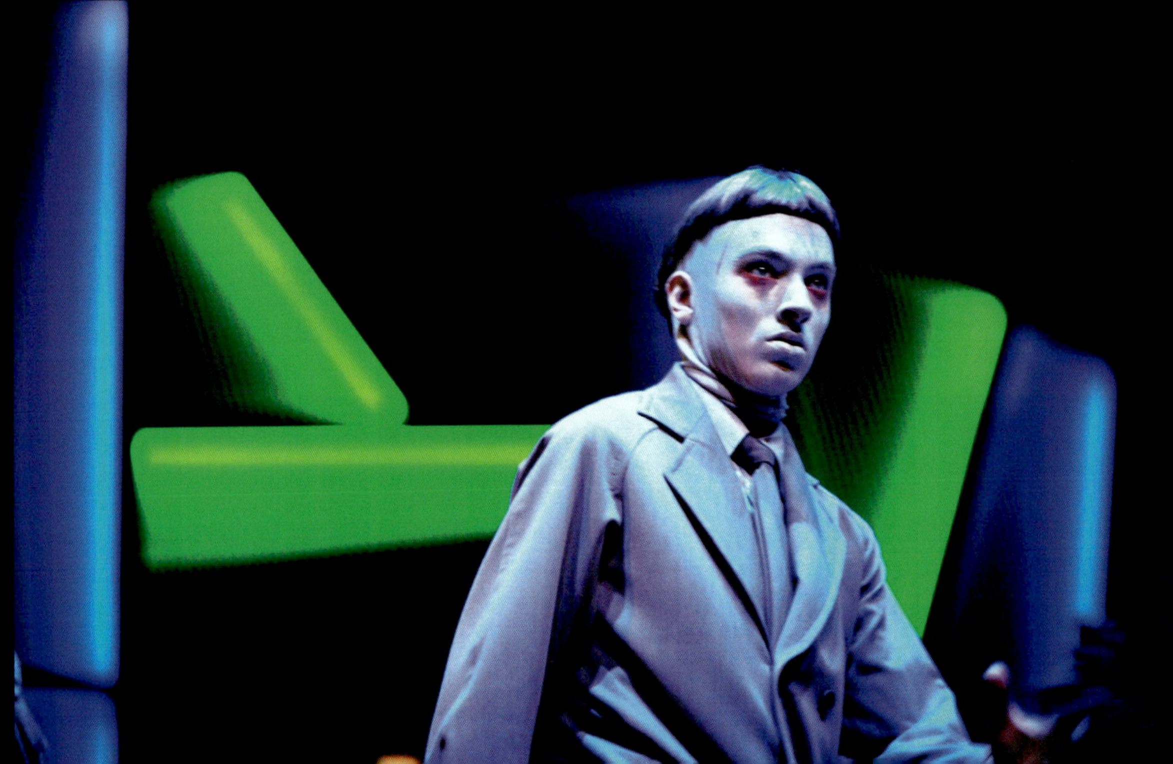

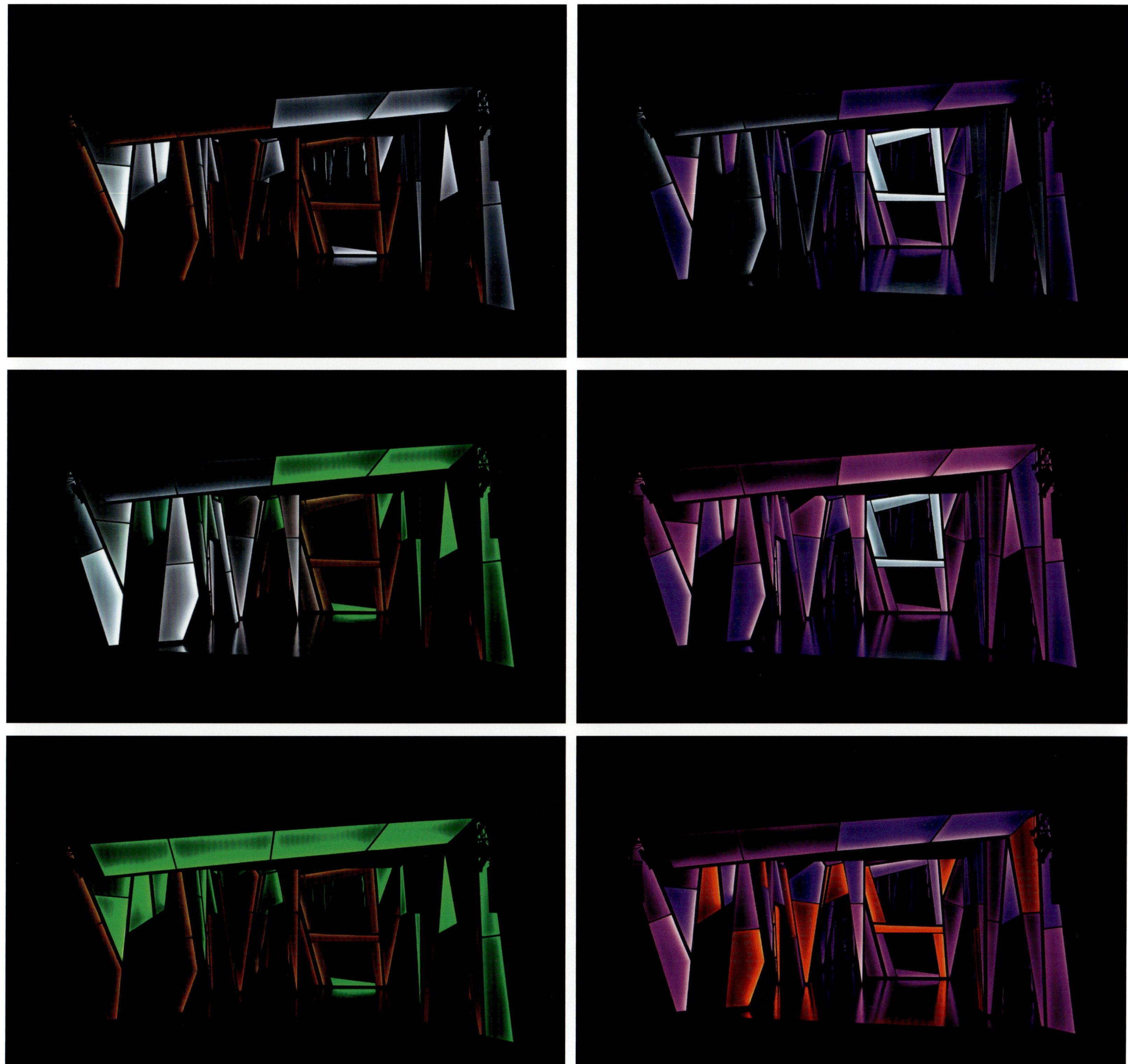

**SYLPHIDE**
CHOREOGRAPHER STEEN KOERNER | COSTUMES HENRIK VIBSKOV
INTERNATIONAL FREELANCE THEATRE ENSEMBLE
WORLD PREMIERE OCTOBER 2005
AVENY-T COPENHAGEN DENMARK

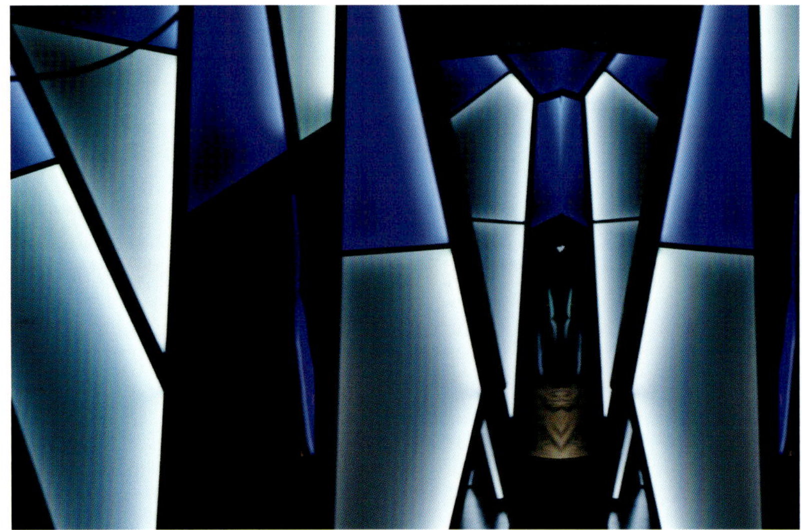
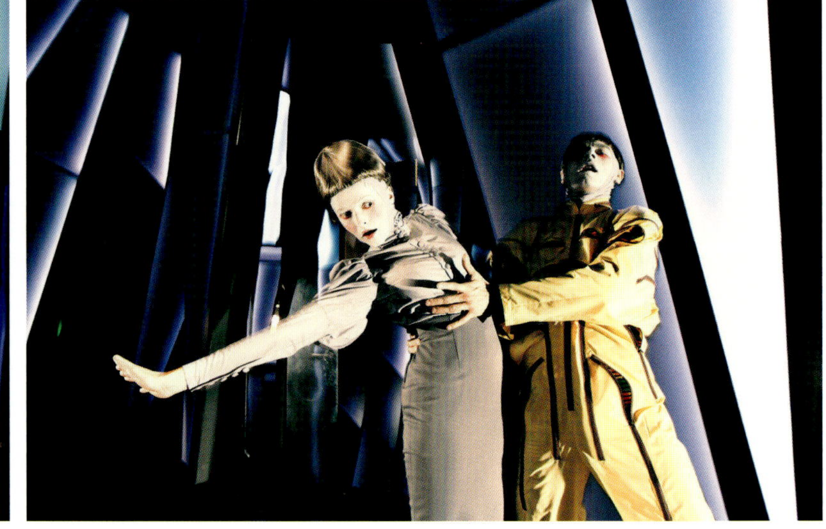

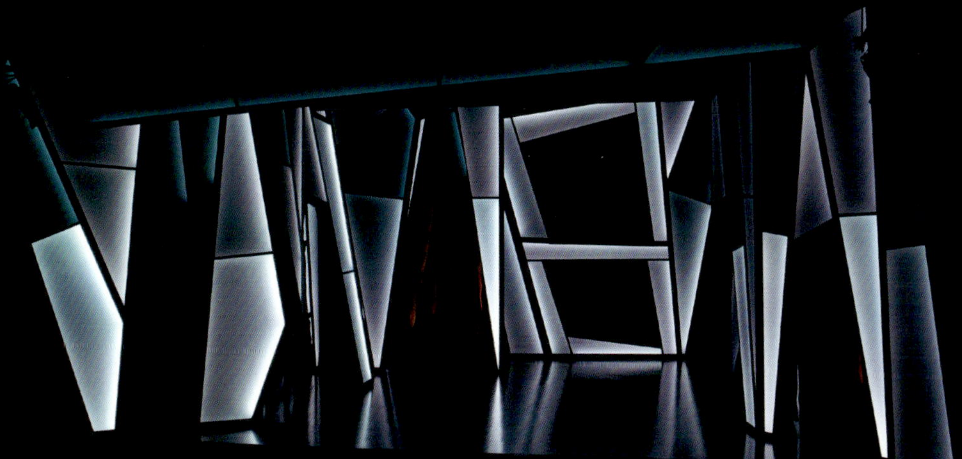

**SYLPHIDE**
CHOREOGRAPHER   STEEN KOERNER  |  COSTUMES   HENRIK VIBSKOV
INTERNATIONAL FREELANCE THEATRE ENSEMBLE
WORLD PREMIERE OCTOBER 2005
AVENY-T   COPENHAGEN   DENMARK

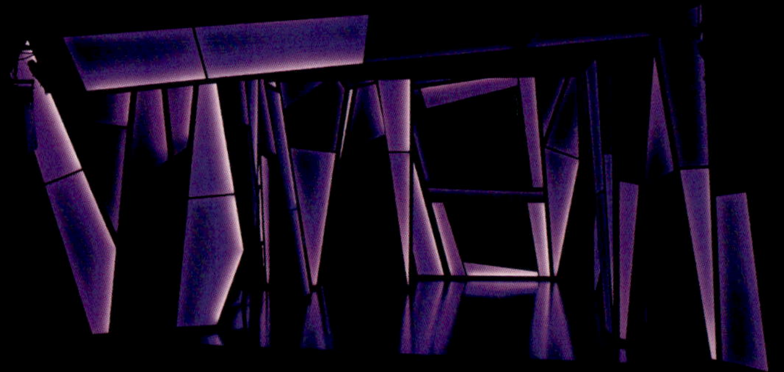
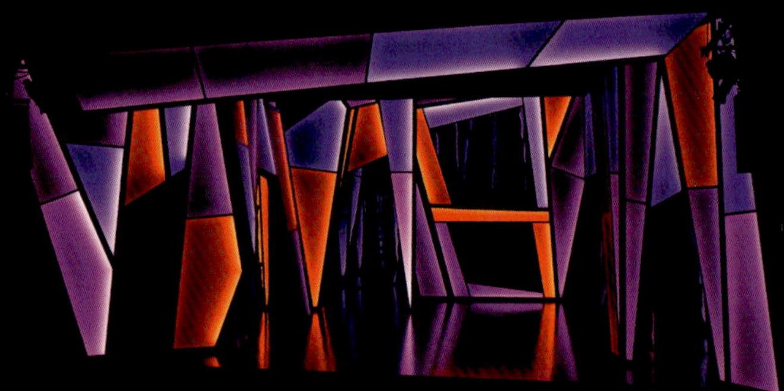
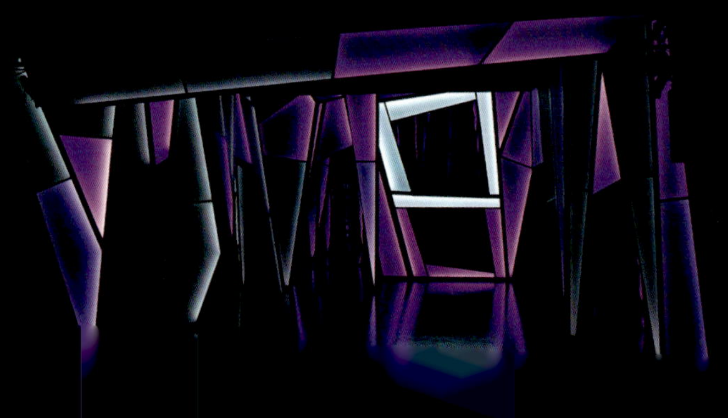
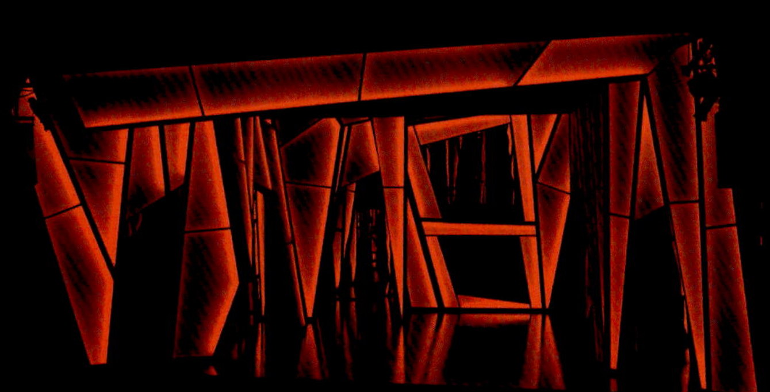

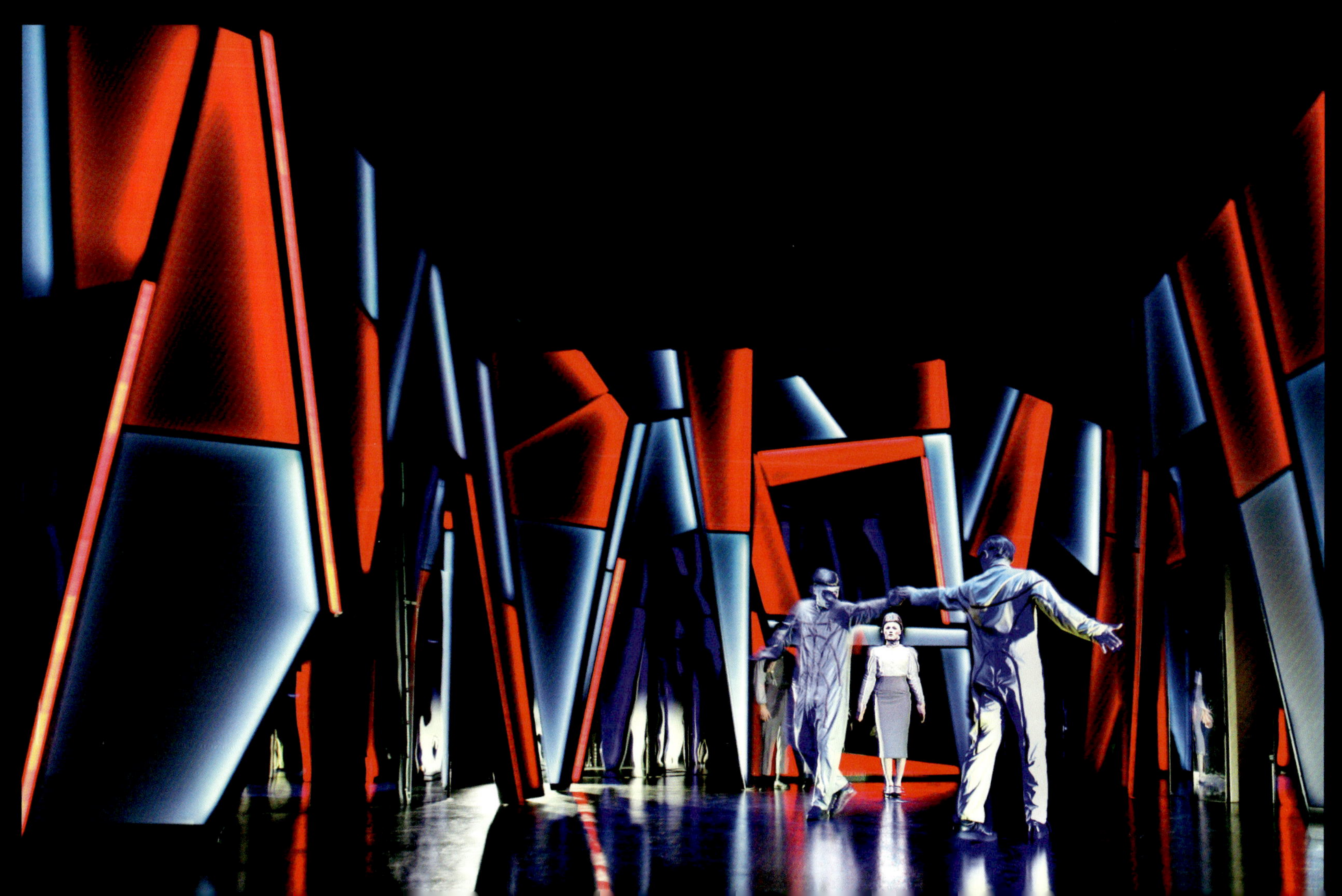

LUMINOUS ICONS
# ROBERT C. MORGAN
INTRODUCTION

**ALTHOUGH HE BEGAN HIS CAREER AS A PAINTER,** Steven Scott has emerged over the past decade as a highly original artist who is persistently opening new doors, trying out new theories and experimenting with new materials that cross over between the fine and applied arts. As a maker of luminous icons, Scott has been involved in testing the virtual and physical potential of the illimitable threshold of visual creativity. He applies his empirical and aesthetic knowledge of colour through the use of the latest software in programming the display of subtle graduations of light. At the same time, he gives precise attention to the material components that further enhance the transmission and operation of his light boxes and modules of colour. Scott understands his light art as a form of communication capable of functioning in private collections alongside paintings, in public atriums, on building facades, or on auditorium walls, such as the magnificent Walls of Light at the Contemporary Music Concert Hall in Amsterdam (1999–2005). In this regard, he further acknowledges the need to move art into a broader, public context without losing a sense of the work's intimacy. The overarching triadic subject matter in Scott's forms includes light, time, and the permutation of colour. In analyzing his recent work over the past twelve years, it becomes clear that Scott has redefined not only the function but also the meaning of colour through our sensory and cognitive input. Upon realising that colour is fundamentally an extension of light, and that light, in turn, becomes an extension of colour, the artist introduced the omnipresence of time into the mix. Through time, tempi and temporality – as noted by the philosopher Eugene Kaelin in his book *Art and Existence* (1970) – we engage with relative variations of time in relation to interactive modalities of colour and light. Kaelin's properties of time, which include relative motion, rhythm, and duration, function one way when colour is transient through light and another way when colour exists as material pigment. Whereas pigment gives a static representation of light, the programming of colour changing through time offers a completely different kind of phenomenological experience. By adhering to all three variations of time – in this case, light being observed as it moves through extended rhythms – we see colour not as a static entity but as an evolving permutation of form as it functions in relation to the space that encompasses it, whether in a domestic, public or natural environment.

Relative to Scott's installation of light works, one might argue that they offer some form of intimacy, whether they are placed on the wall of someone's private collection or in the atrium of a public office building. To comprehend this phenom enon, we may consider that intimacy in art is not dependent on scale so much as it is dependent on context and content. In Denmark, for example, the feeling of an intimate space is different from that in the United States. Each culture differs in terms of what this means – perceptually, socially and psychologically. Often there are practical reasons as to why a small space is capable of appearing intimate and functional whereas a larger space may falter on both counts.

In that most art is conceived without utility, the sense of intimacy may communicate differently from the way it does in relation to architecture. For example, there are small works, such as jade carvings from the Zhou Dynasty (1100–221 B.C.E.) in China, and large mural-scale paintings, such as Jackson Pollock's *Autumn Rhythm* (1950) in the collection of the Metropolitan Museum of Art in New York. In either case, there is a quality about these works that invites intimacy within the process of viewing them. We are not detached from the artist's feeling or intention. Instead, we are connected to the work on another level. Of course, not all art operates the same way. For example, I have seen both marvellous hunting scenes by Rubens at the Alte Pinakothek in Munich and pensive guild portraits by seventeenth-century Dutch artists hanging on the high walls of the Rijksmuseum in Amsterdam. In either case, I would hesitate to call these works intimate. I mention this only to clarify the logic of the installations I have seen in the light works of Steven Scott. In fact, their intimacy – whether public or private – is often disarming to the extent that one is welcomed by them rather than pushed away. Scott has understood that content emanating from his colour modulations can be pleasurable if they are placed in the right context, where they afford a visibility appropriate to the space.

As with any new or different point of view in art, there are always subjective differences in terms of its reception. Some observers may initially find Scott's light installations cool or distant as opposed to intimate. Such responses often have

# LUMINOUS ICONS

## INTRODUCTION

more to do with expectations than actuality. Scott's early *Horizons* or *Black Light* boxes are not the kind of art that will immediately satisfy the anxious viewer in search of a narrative or emblematic abstract painting. These works are neither trendy nor Pop. This is to suggest that Steven Scott is not merely appropriating the data that he sees around him. Rather he recreates what he feels in response to that data. He employs his imagination in order to reset the dials between internal and external realities. His biomechanical awareness of what goes on around him is exemplary. The phenomenological basis of his art evolved from his primary engagement with the act of seeing. As the twentieth century philosopher and novelist Aldous Huxley reminds us, the act of seeing is implicitly and inexorably connected to memory. Therefore, the eyes are literally the windows to the brain – a point introduced by Huxley.

Seeing without cognisance of memory might be considered aberrant if our global societies were less divisive in their opposition between desire and control, as Freud reminds us. Yet most citizens of the global community may not possess this awareness. Stated simply, the act of seeing instigates memory. One might say that Steven Scott's work reminds us of this coalescence – that we see and we think, and concomitantly, we think and we see. Conception and perception are not intrinsically opposed, but quite the opposite. The duality from a human biomechanical premise is, in fact, a unified whole. To engage in the world of the twenty-first century is about finding this connection, and it is the work of Steven Scott that is helping to move in this direction: a readaption to the world, a salutary acknowledgement of how to become who we are in the world.

Because Scott's light works, whether situated in domestic or public spaces, involve the movement of colour sequences through time, instigated by the artist's complex programming, one may detect the generation of slow, nearly invisible transitional changes that reveal subtle shifts and nearly indiscernible nuances. Viewers who are willing to spend time with Scott's work will generally reap the rewards. The experience is both sensual and arbitrarily physical in the sense that the optic nerve reaches out to the light and pulls it through the mind's eye, inciting an experience comparable to something between the psychic automatism of the Surrealist André Breton and the intense, phenomenal and vibratory power of a Mark Rothko chromatic abstract painting from the 1950s. Yet the experience of Scott's light works is less about a rush or an external pulsation than it is about harmony derived from contemplation where slow-moving passages of colour are in a continual state of transition. The fact of time comes to the forefront of consciousness. The rarified experience of Scott's shifting colour sensations exceeds the limits of one's everyday temporal routines. Therefore, to see one of Scott's light works for a few minutes may incite a kind of restoration of balance within the deluge of data that normally races through our minds as we engage in the diurnal cause and effect relationships between the reality of virtual software and the impact of these virtual transmissions on the emotional structure of our Being within our unconscious material existence.

Put another way, to experience the perception of moving colour and light constitutes the normative standard of material existence in today's digitally saturated urban complexes. Even so, most of these lights are commercially directed and therefore focus on the tyranny of the logo, rather than contemplative experience. In Scott's work, we catch the light in a different way that transcends the normative assault of urban logos. I believe this is what Scott is aiming for – an experience that relaxes our sensory input; that is, our ability to open Huxley's windows of the brain so that we can breathe again. In being aware of our breathing selves, we may reduce the anxieties and empty aggression. Just as the early Modernist painters Kandinsky and Frantisek Kupka (and later, Mark Rothko and Agnes Martin) understood the spirituality of colour in their abstract paintings, Steven Scott continues to amplify the same idea. In Scott's case, he is placing his idea squarely within life in the twenty-first century.

LUMINOUS ICONS PART ONE

# ROBERT C. MORGAN

FROM THE HORIZONS TO THE BLACK LIGHT SERIES 1999–2006

**WHETHER FROM THE EASTERN OR WESTERN HEMISPHERES,** there is no art that comes entirely out of the void. In this case, I refer to the void not in the Zen sense of emptiness of mind (*wu-nien*) but rather according to its Western usage, which is more vernacular, thereby suggesting that nothing came before it. In any advanced form of art, there are always antecedents, traces, links, histories, tendencies, influences and affinities that emerge from various directions, various points on the compass, various cultural references, experiential dimensions and states of mental persuasion. While this may sound obvious to many, the overwhelming force of commercial media tries to convince us otherwise, either by implication or assertion that significant works of art are always "new" and that artists exist in isolation from everything happening around them. This may have been plausible in a prelinguistic culture, but not in the media-saturated environment of the present. In addition, one might argue that originality in art is not always new (in the sense that media makes it "new") and it is less apparent in the objects themselves – whether painting, sculpture, or mixed media – than in the syntax; that is, the manner in which artists are capable of discovering originality by reconfiguring and contextualising their chosen mediums. I would say the latter method is clearly the one that Steven Scott has chosen to employ in his work. Beginning in the 1970s, with a background in theatre design and painting, it was only a matter of time before the artist would synchronise his energies into an innovative form of light art. There were many stops and starts along the way, but somehow Scott was able to find the path through his acute organisational skills and his ability to work with diverse synthetic materials and with advanced technologies in manoeuvring a clear symbiotic relationship between natural and artificial light. Much of this was acquired during his years at the Riverside Studios in Hammersmith (London), where he was deeply engaged in theatre, painting and the multimedia arts. Scott continually refers to his beginnings there as being both tenuous and highly inspirational. Working and conversing with various artists from various disciplines and fields of endeavour, who were each involved in the early stages in the evolution of their careers, the excitement and pulsation of these exchanges and interactions through multimedia and experimental forms of art were for Scott both authentic and unforgettable and are still indelibly embedded in his spiritual, aesthetic and pragmatic understanding of advanced art.

As a result, Scott has no trepidation in acknowledging the sources and paradigms that have influenced his work and from which his original approach to light over the years has come to evolve. In discussing these influences, Scott holds a particular reverence for the achievements of the great Bauhaus artists, specifically the light works of Moholy-Nagy, the spatial concepts of theatre in the *Triadic Ballets* and *Bauhaus* Dances conceived and executed by Oskar Schlemmer, and finally the *Gestalt* notion of a "total architecture" advanced by the Bauhaus founder, Walter Gropius. One cannot ignore the important kinetic light works of Thomas Wilfred and Earl Rieback, both of whom used low-tech analogue systems as a means to generate swirling patterns of coloured light. In addition there are works by the Hungarian artist György Kepes, and important contributions by Minimal artist Dan Flavin and the light installations of American artist James Turrell. Each of these figures has contributed to the historical and aesthetic development of light art in the twentieth century and therefore substantiates the important direction in which Steven Scott continues to work. These will be cited further in relation to Scott's large-scale, site-specific light works, designed to function in the context of architecture and public spaces. But, for the moment, it will be necessary to address the initial phases of Scott's works in his early *Horizon* pieces and the evolution of his *Black Light* concept, for which he is widely known, particularly in Denmark, Sweden, Germany, Austria, Netherlands and the United Kingdom.

While Scott began working on the *Open Box* and *Horizon* light works in 1999, it was in 2001 that these works came to fruition and were first exhibited at Galleri Weinberger in Copenhagen. In *Open Box,* Scott employs a horizontal repetition of

## LUMINOUS ICONS PART ONE

## FROM THE HORIZONS TO THE BLACK LIGHT SERIES 1999–2006

contrasting inertly gaseous tubes of light, stacked vertically in an open box placed on the wall. In the *Untitled* piece, three tubes are also aligned horizontally so that the light emanating from the tubes appears to move from one to another. In *Horizon One*, also shown in 2001 at the Vaerket cultural centre in Randers, also in Denmark, Scott juxtaposed the synthetic light with a window filter installation on an adjacent wall so that the natural light played a key role in relation to shifting colours in the darkened space.

In 2003, Scott began working on another prototype, *Glass and Light Study*, for the University of Southern Denmark's Alsion building, designed by 3XN architects. Here, the square modular boxes conceal the source of light on the inside as the hues modulate separately, while appearing to pass from one to another.

In the works, commissioned by the ING-DiBa bank for their headquarters in Frankfurt, Vienna, Hanover and Nuremberg, Scott becomes more involved in the programming of the light modules, contained within the framed compartments. In these installations, the process of composing white light from two varying but complementary colours is made evident. In fact, the ING-DiBa commission should be cited as the beginning of what would eventually become the *Black Light* studies in 2005, again shown at the Galleri Weinberger that year.

Concurrent to the evolution of the *Black Light* series, Scott was commissioned by the Hans Christian Andersen Foundation at the Kunstforeningen Gammel Strand (Denmark) to produce a labyrinthine installation for six interrelated spaces. For *The Childhood Room*, Scott designed a large, three-panelled triptych using sound and light; for *The Society Room*, he developed a four-wall installation, which also incorporated sound into the changing light patterns; and finally, in *Room of Letters*, a video installation was projected in which a palimpsest based on actual letters written by Andersen was shown in perpetual vibratory motion, culminating in a vortex in which the video script folds into the centre of the screen. The Kunstforeningen installations proved important for Scott in promoting his work to corporate clients outside the art world, thus opening the door for further public art commissions, such as Deloitte's major new offices in Copenhagen in 2005, where seventy-seven light panels were installed in a systemic architectural relationship to the bridges and zigzag stairways, running on a program lasting twenty-seven hours and twenty minutes, and which illuminate the colossal interior of the building's atrium.

In the same year, the *Black Light* editions were unveiled at Galleri Weinberger in two versions, a triptych titled *Black Light One* and a quadtych titled *Black Light Two*. In each work, the surface, when unilluminated, reads as matt black. When lit, the translucent blacks reveal a sequence of colour permutations either in three or four horizontal blocks. The use of the golden section of a quadrant is evident in *Black Light One* with related permutations in *Black Light Two*. In each case, the forms suggest a serial progression of space related to the sculpture of American Minimal artist Donald Judd. Curiously, in 2006, Scott pays homage to another American Minimal artist and close colleague of Judd in a work titled *Corner for Dan Flavin,* installed in the Kulturrum Hammenhog in Ystad, Sweden. While Flavin was known for his installations involving fluorescent light and his ability to manipulate colour and thus to transform architecture into ethereal spaces, Steven Scott took the concept of the horizontal bar of light – something he shared in common with Flavin – and brought it back into his work. *Corner for Dan Flavin* also conceals the source of light like many of Scott's works do, and, at the same time, reiterates the *Black Light* theme, whereby the process of slow looking allows the viewer to become involved phenomenologically in the work for a duration that exceeds the normative "quick take" given to much static art that is subjected to the virtual age of the present.

# FROM THE HORIZONS TO THE BLACK LIGHT SERIES 1999–2006

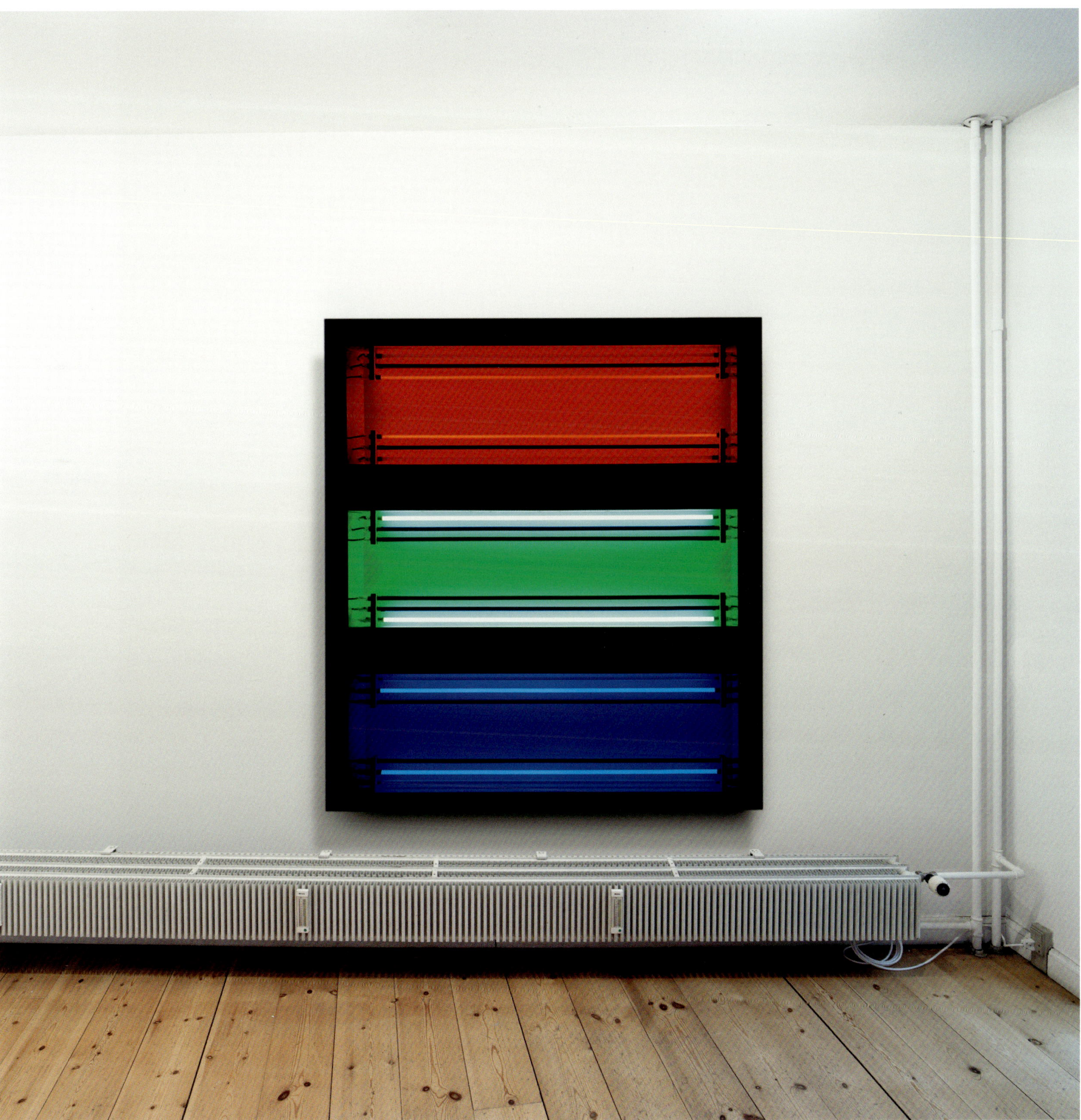

**OPEN BOX** | 210 x 130 x 15 cm
GALLERI WEINBERGER    COPENHAGEN    DENMARK

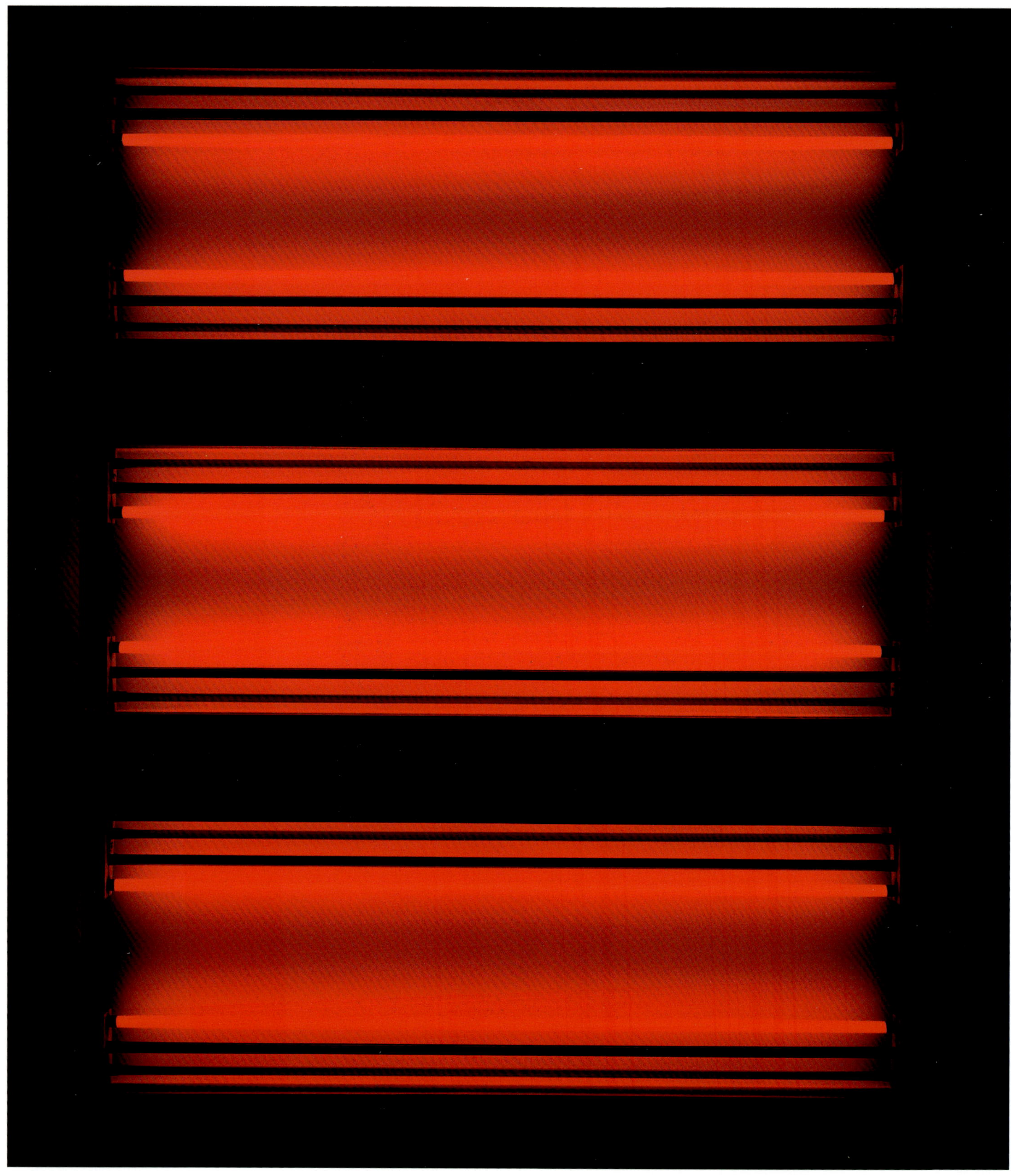

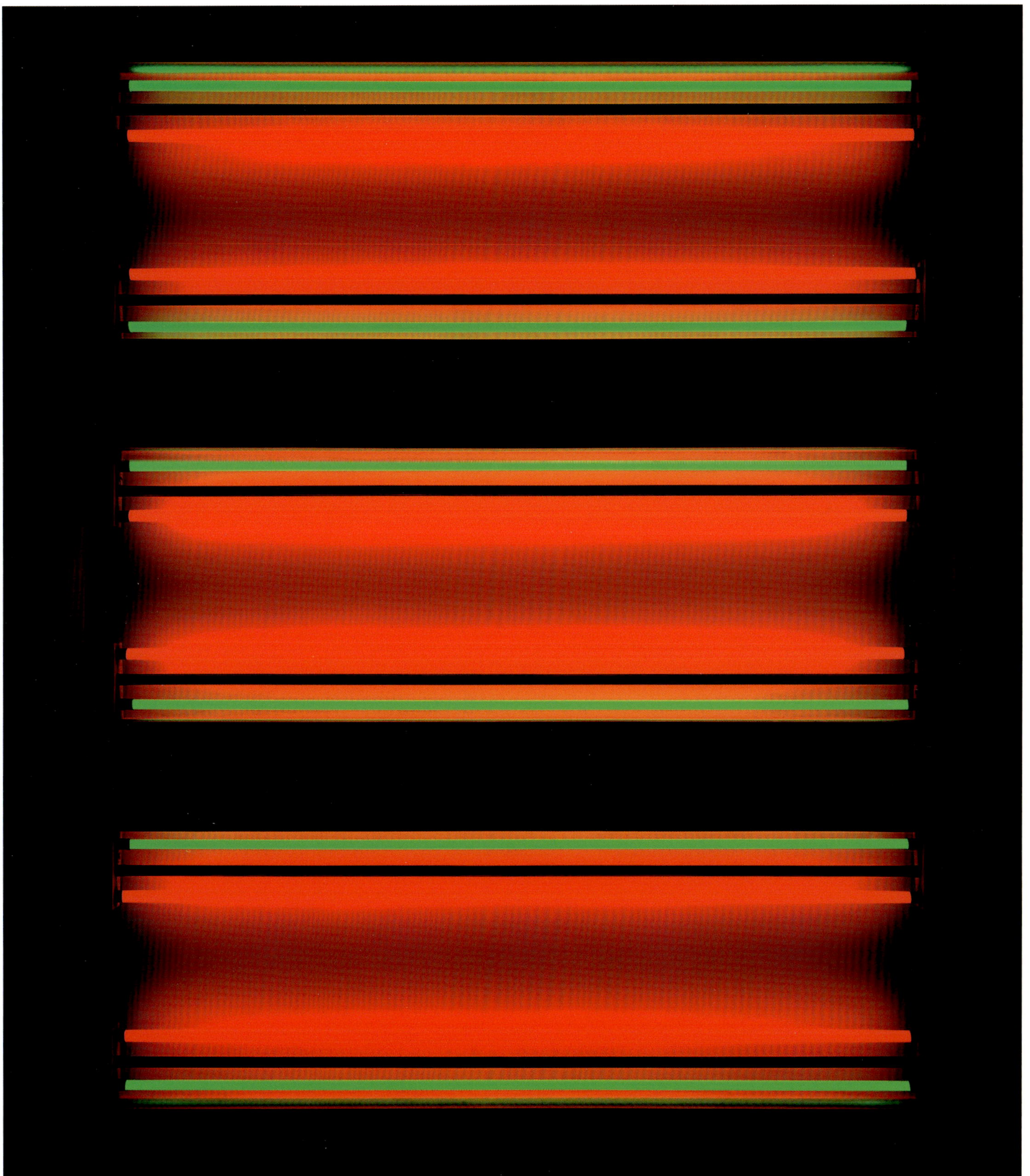

**OPEN BOX** | 210 x 130 x 15 cm
GALLERI WEINBERGER    COPENHAGEN    DENMARK

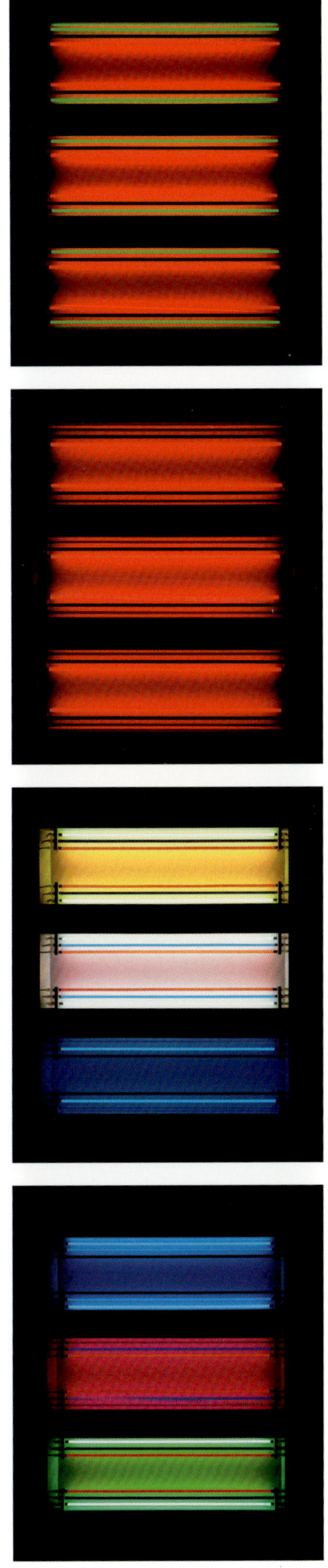

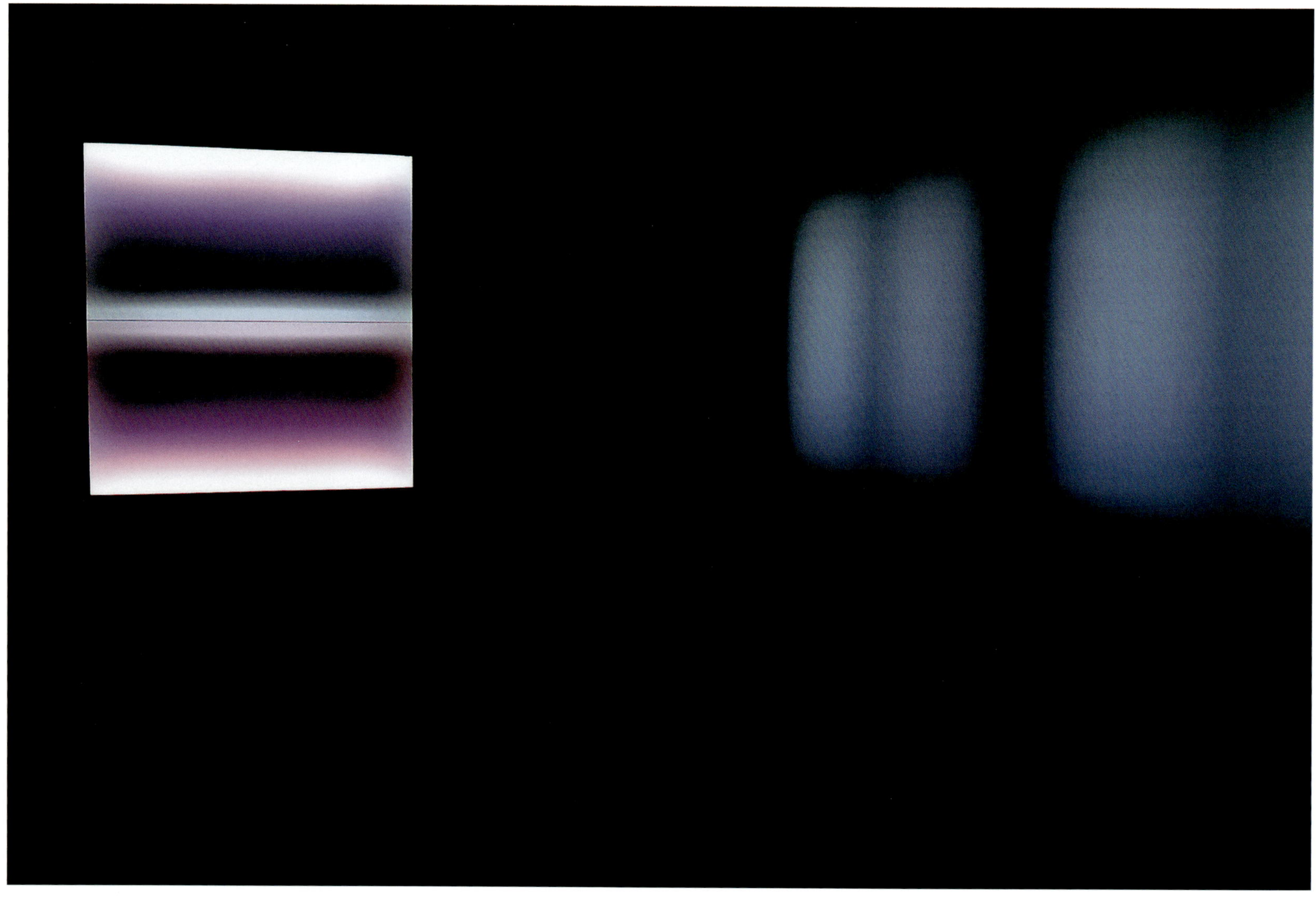

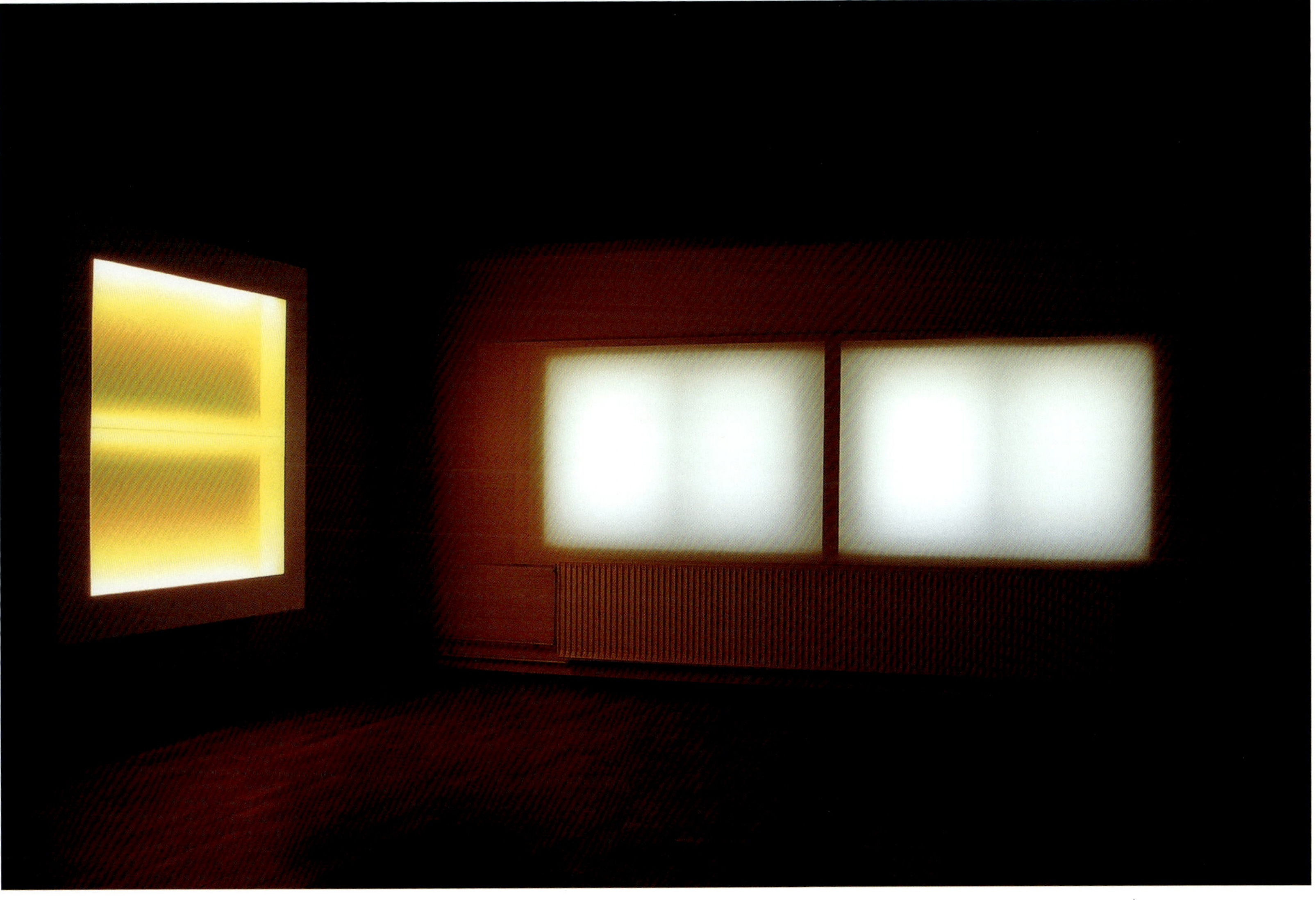

**HORIZON ONE** | 200 x 200 x 20 cm
VÆRKET ART CENTRE   RANDERS   DENMARK

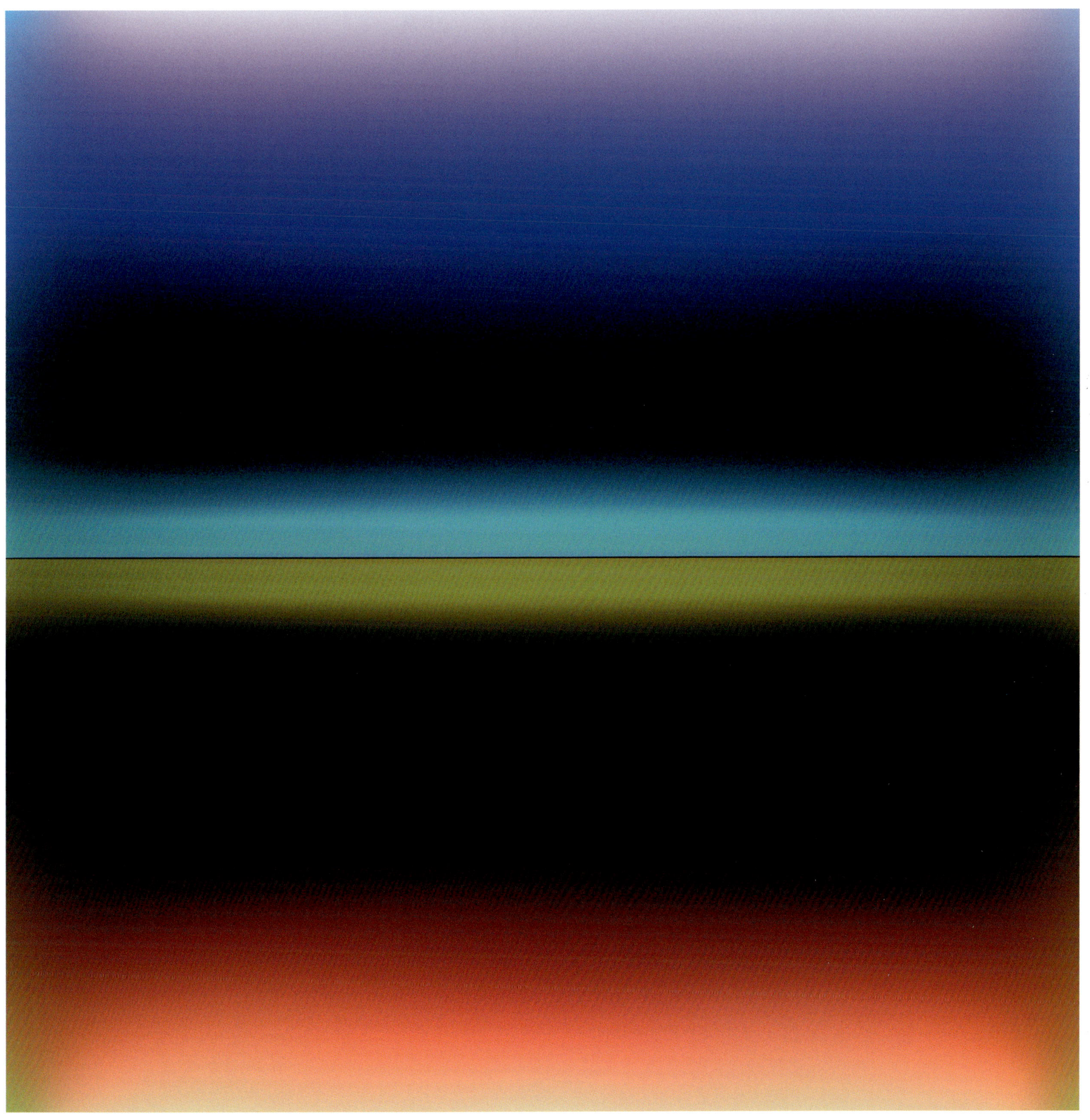

**HORIZON ONE** | 200 x 200 x 20 cm
VÆRKET ART CENTRE RANDERS DENMARK

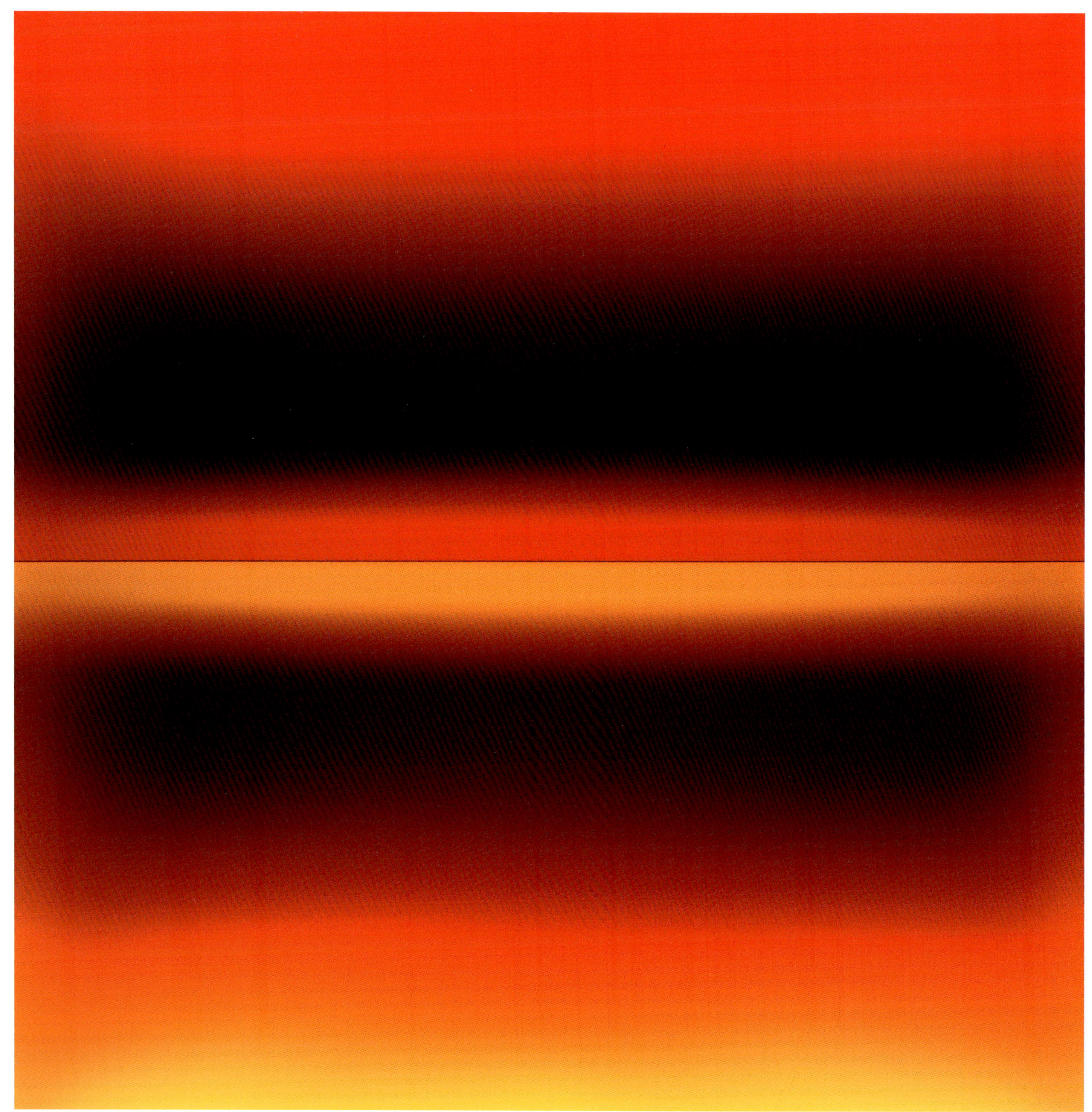

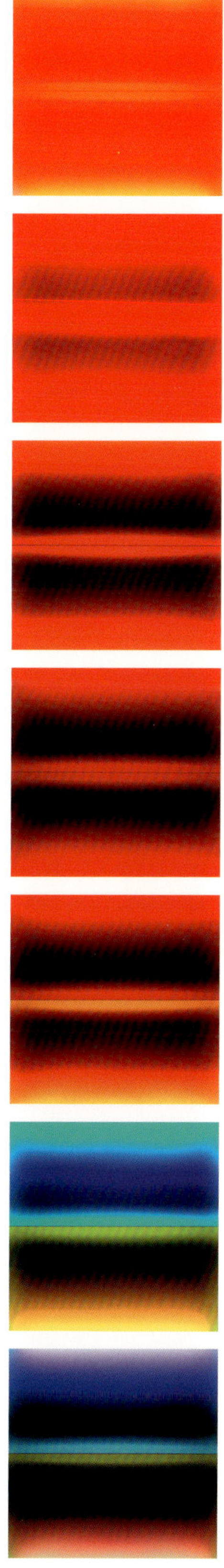

**CEILING OF LIGHT** | 5000 x 600 cm
3XN OFFICE INSTALLATION   2008   COPENHAGEN   DENMARK
PAGE 51   DETAIL   CEILING OF LIGHT

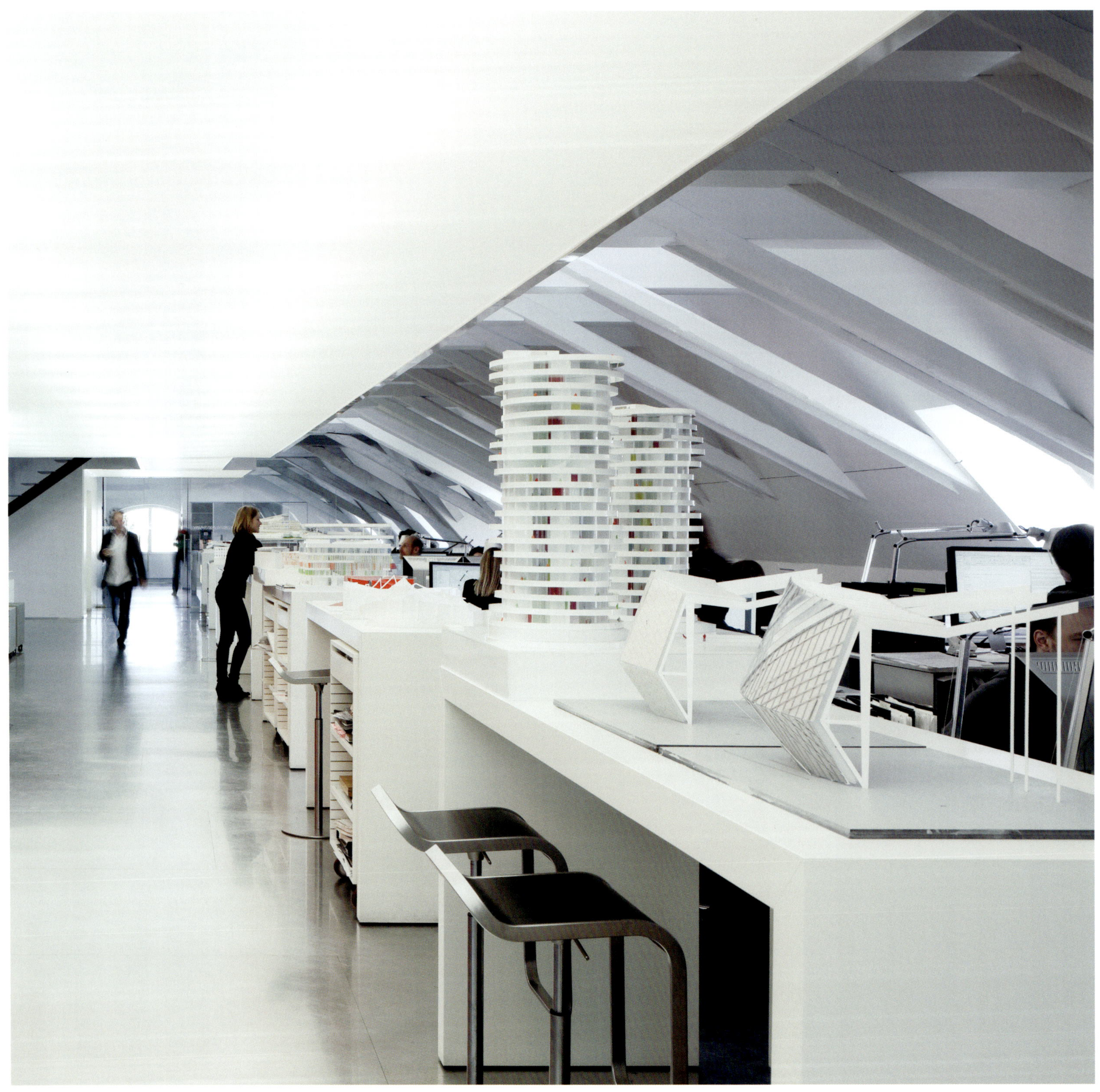

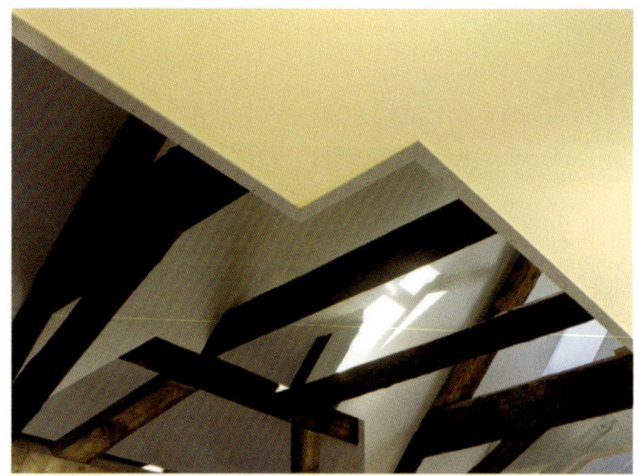

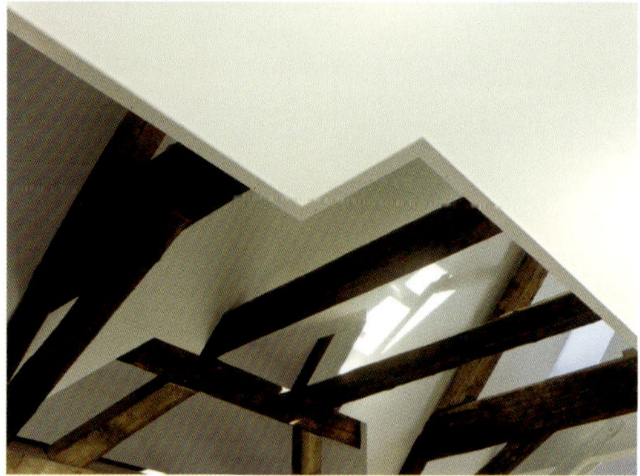

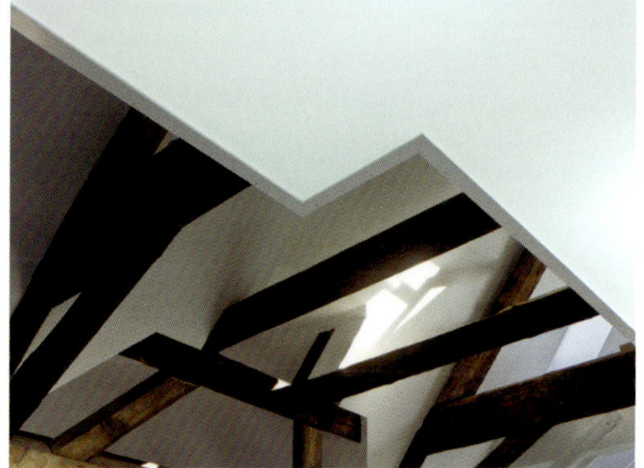

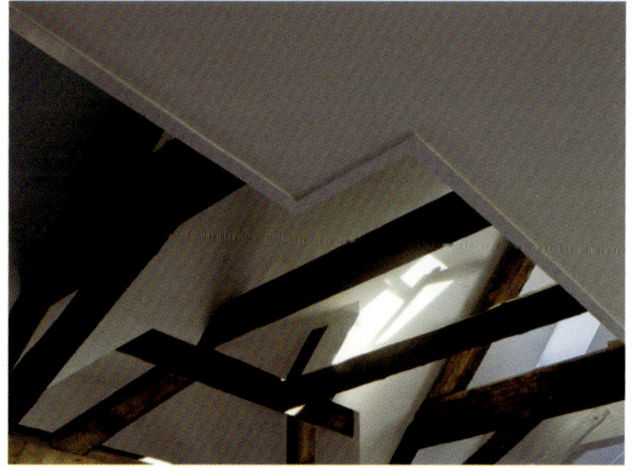

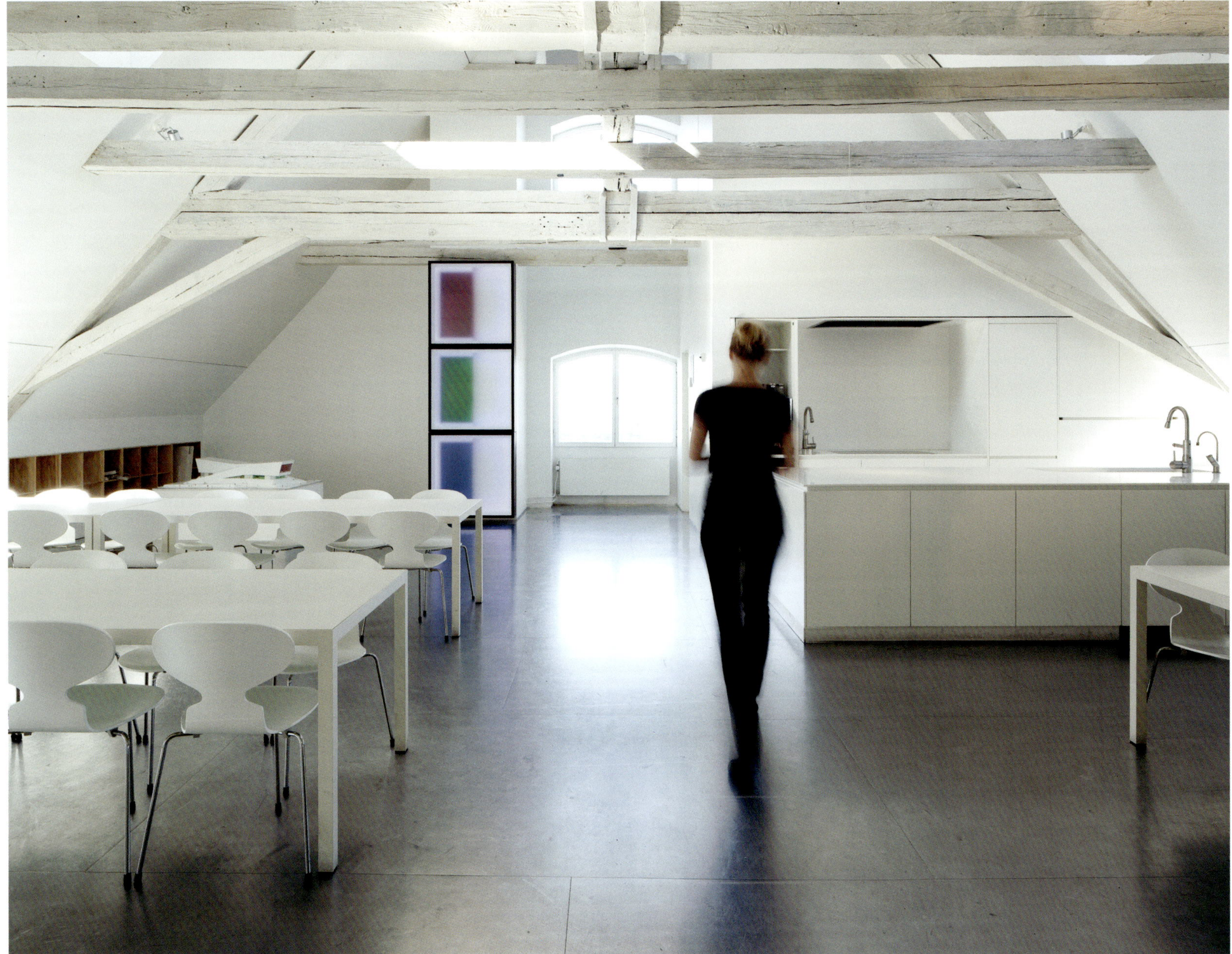

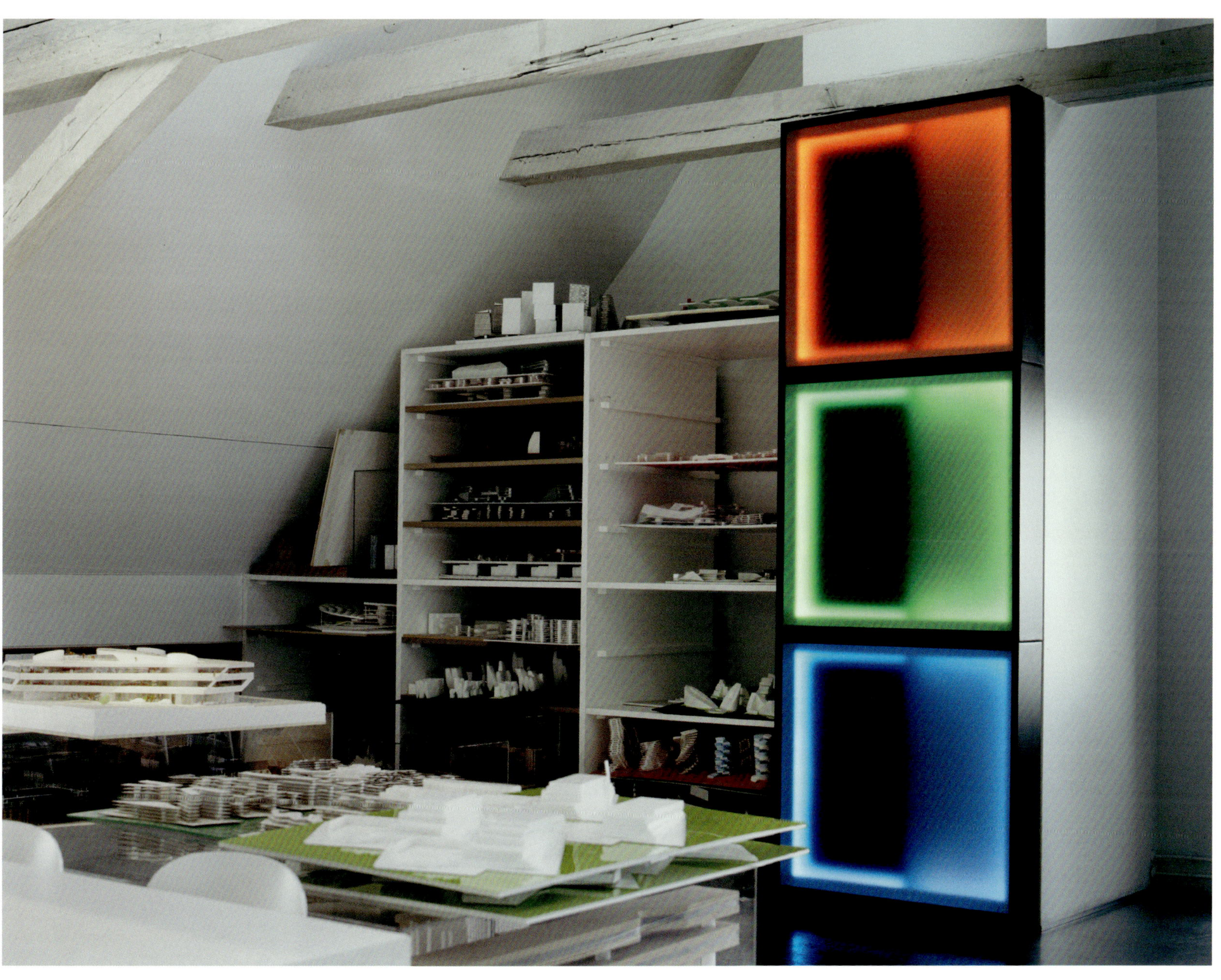

**COLOUR STUDY** | 225 x 100 x 10 cm
FOUR LIGHT WORKS FOR ING-DiBa BANK
HQ FRANKFURT   GERMANY | HQ VIENNA   AUSTRIA
REGIONAL HQ HANOVER   GERMANY | REGIONAL HQ NUREMBERG   GERMANY
COLLECTION OF ING-DiBa BANK

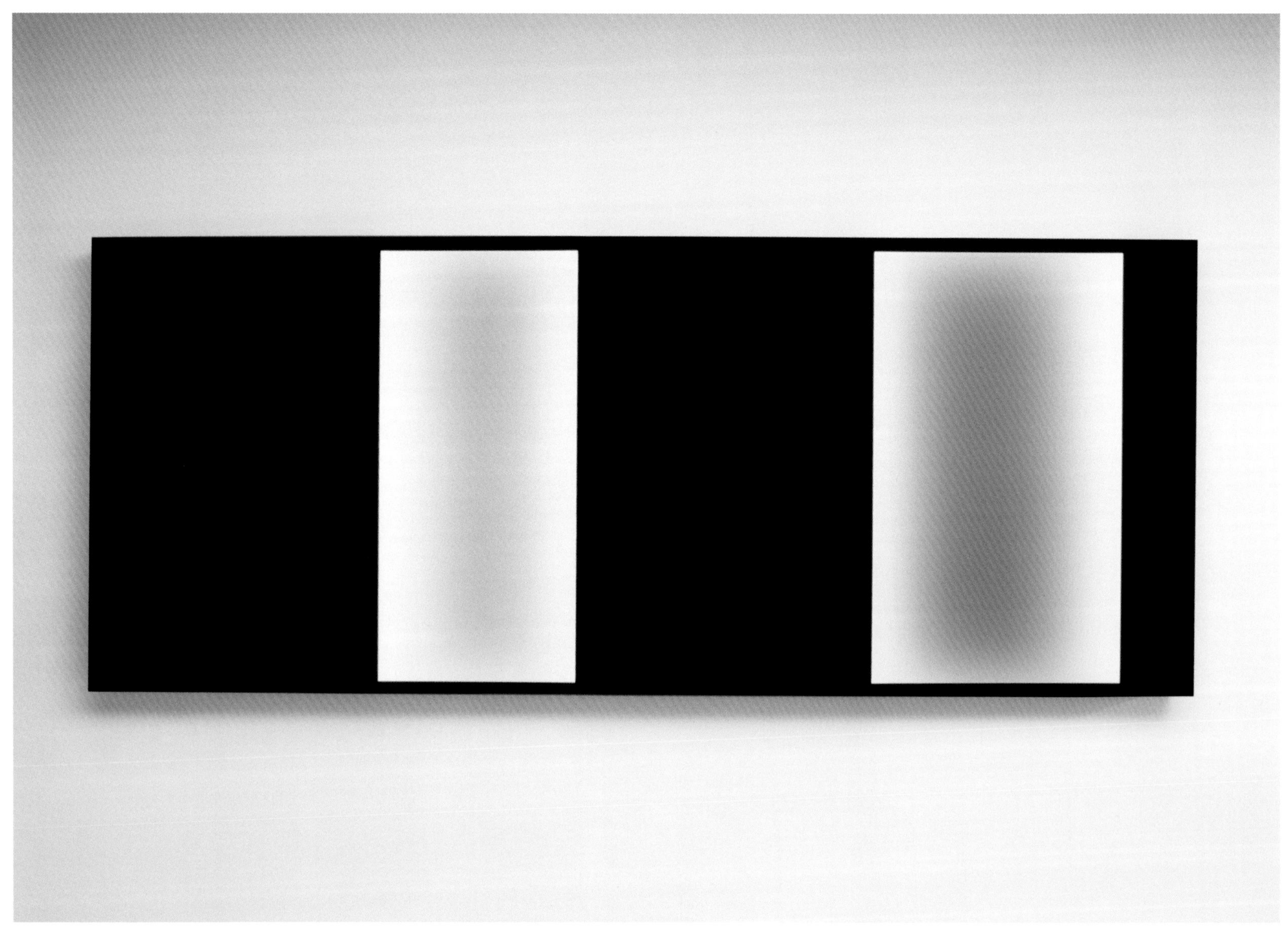

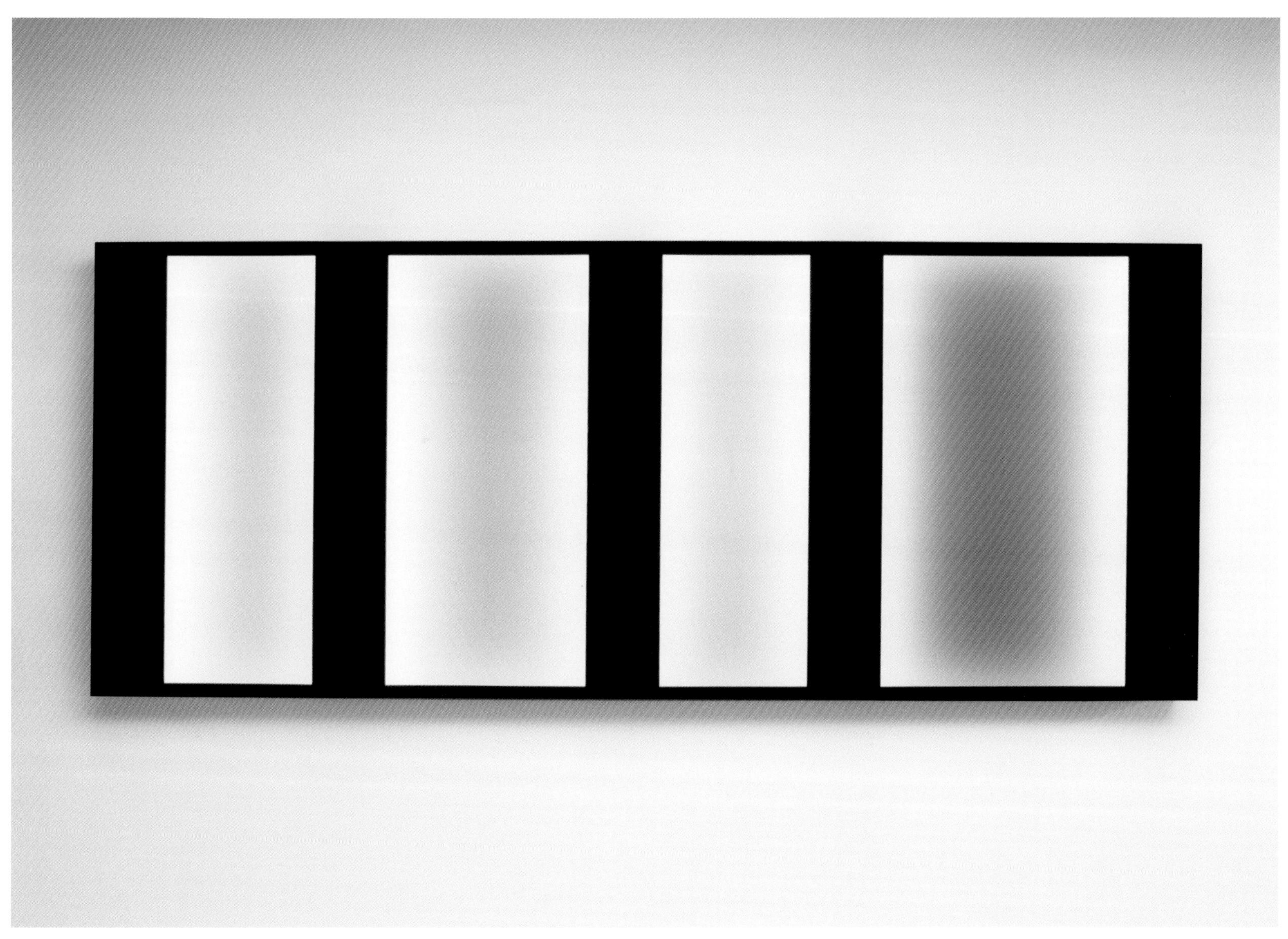

**COLOUR STUDY** | 225 x 100 x 10 cm
FOUR LIGHT WORKS FOR ING-DiBa BANK
HQ FRANKFURT   GERMANY | HQ VIENNA   AUSTRIA
REGIONAL HQ HANOVER   GERMANY | REGIONAL HQ NUREMBERG   GERMANY
COLLECTION OF ING-DiBa BANK

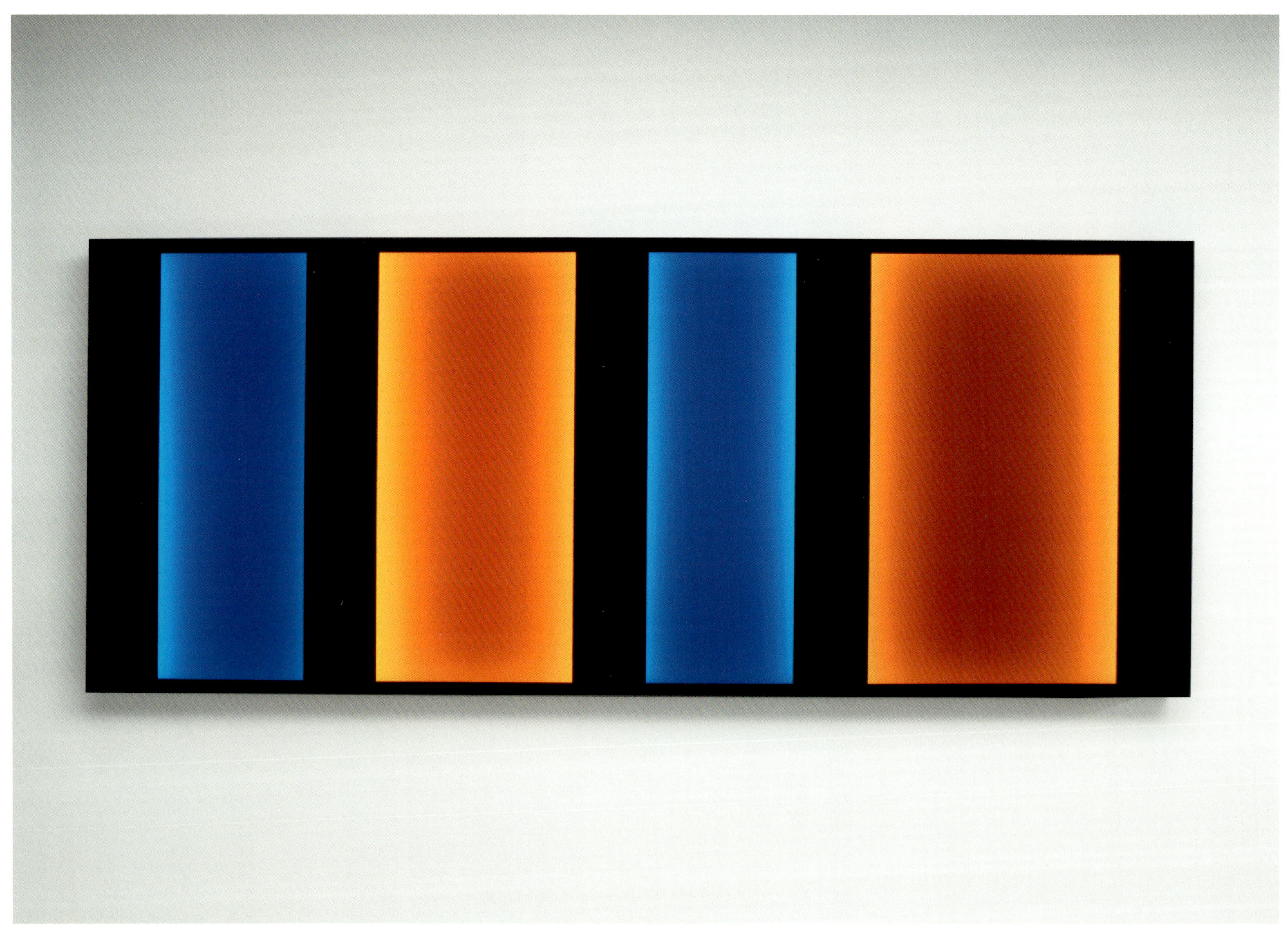

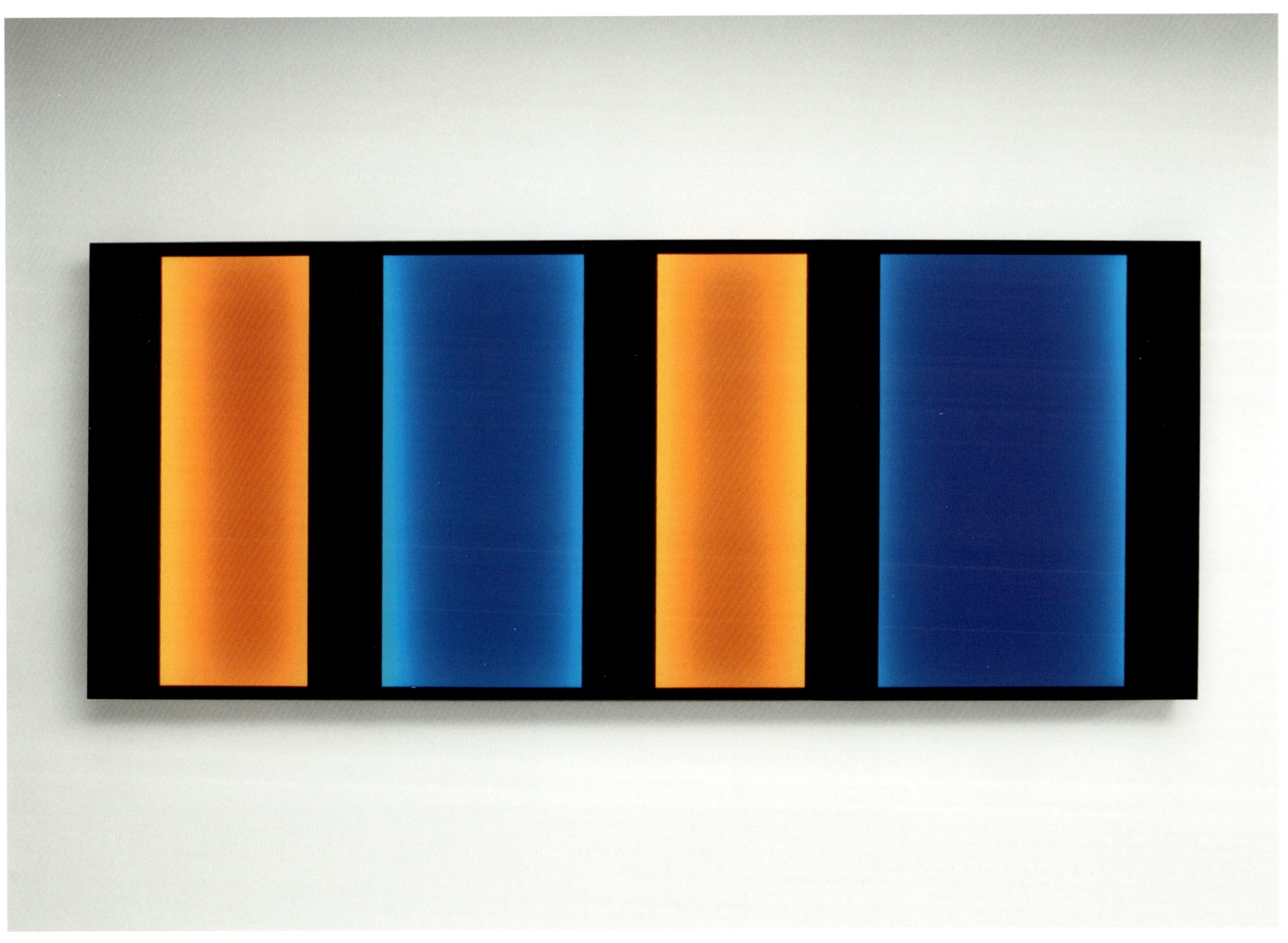

**THE CHILDHOOD ROOM** | 500 x 300 x 10 cm
AN INSTALLATION IN LIGHT AND SOUND
KUNSTFORENINGEN GAMMEL STRAND    COPENHAGEN    DENMARK

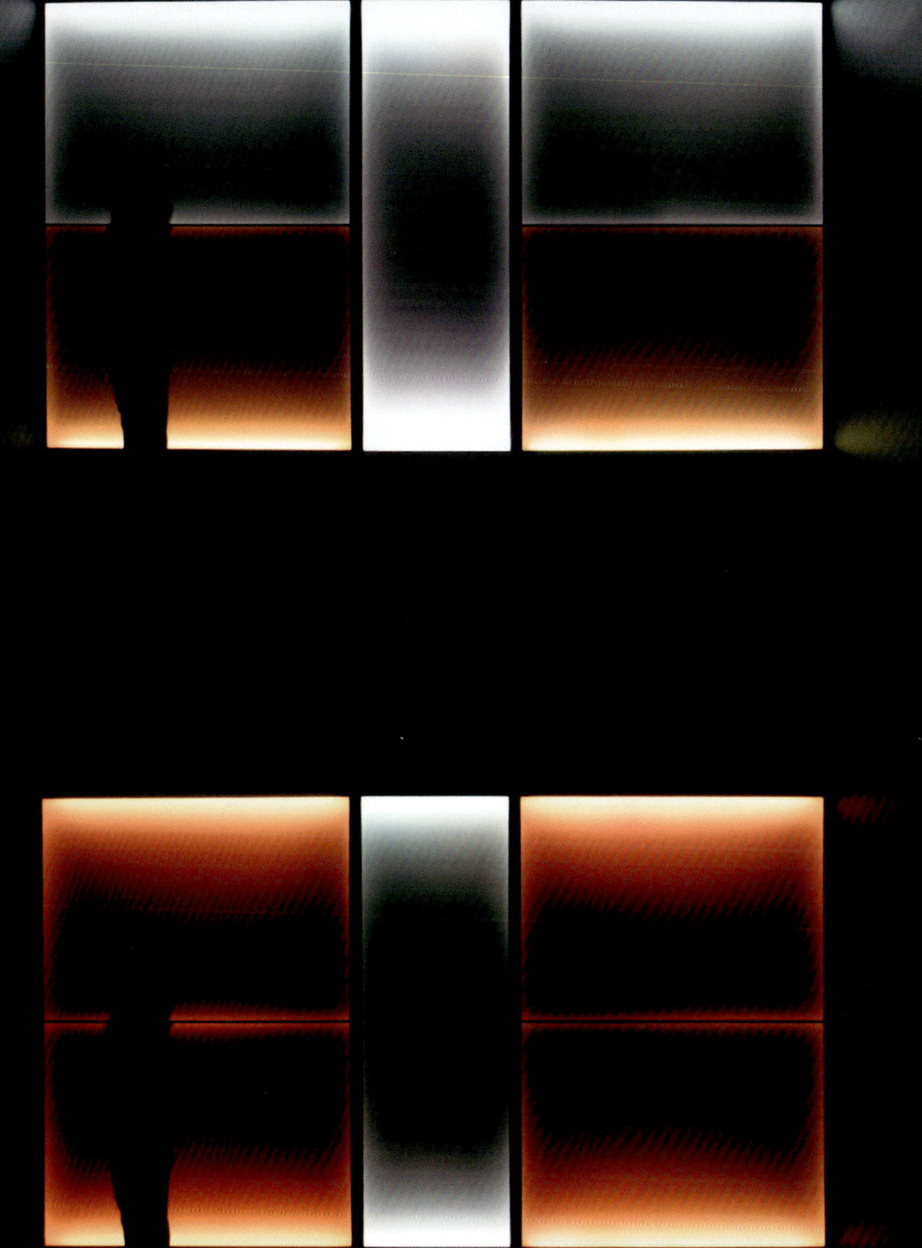

**60** | **LUMINOUS ICONS** 1999–2011 | SOLO EXHIBITION | HANS CHRISTIAN ANDERSEN'S LABYRINTH | 2005
**THE SOCIETY ROOM**
FOUR-WALL INSTALLATION | 300 x 200 x 10 cm | CENTRAL SCULPTURE | 290 x 290 x 200 cm
AN INSTALLATION IN LIGHT AND SOUND
KUNSTFORENINGEN GAMMEL STRAND   COPENHAGEN   DENMARK

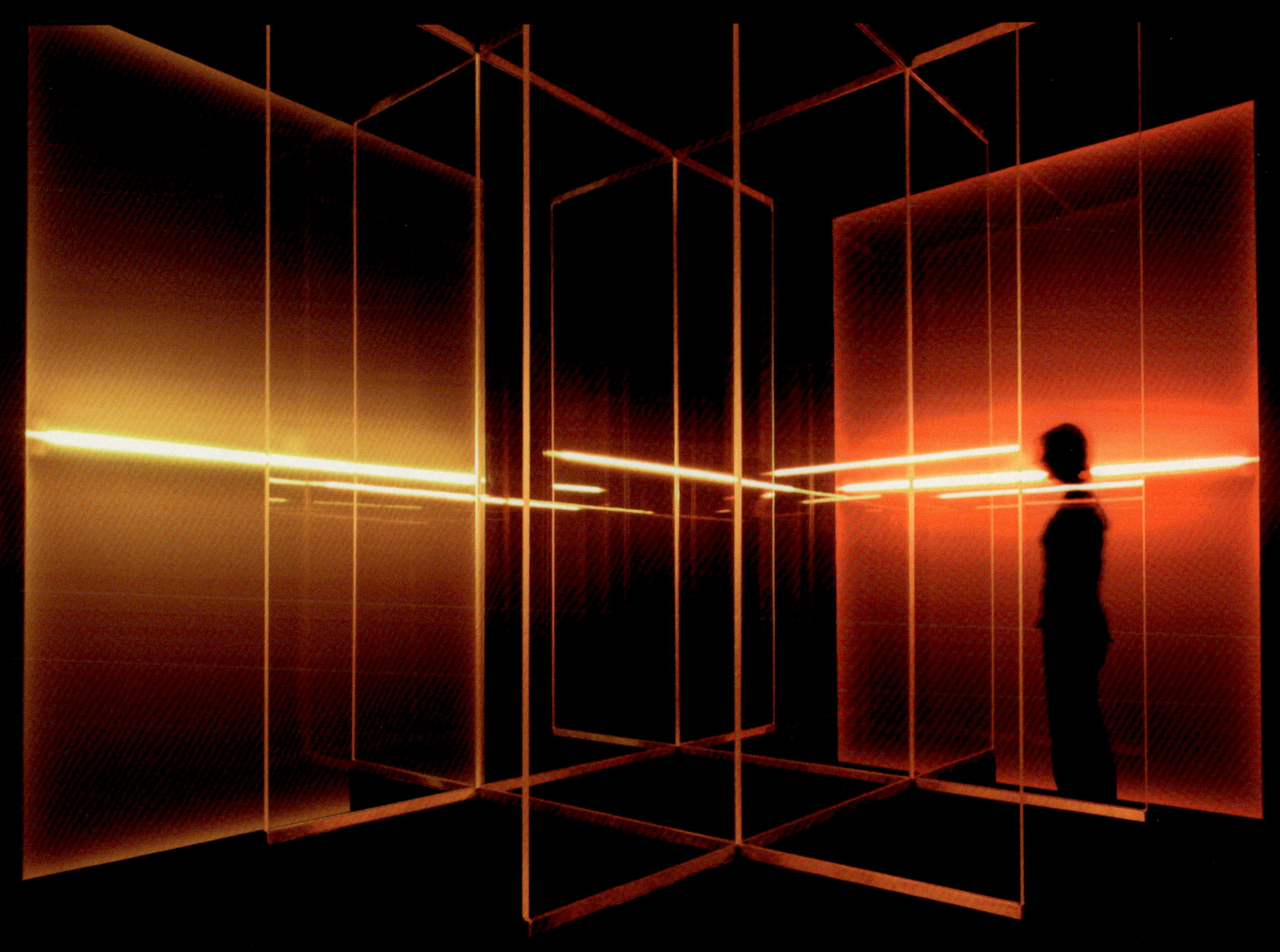

**THE SOCIETY ROOM**
FOUR-WALL INSTALLATION | 300 x 200 x 10 cm | CENTRAL SCULPTURE | 290 x 290 x 200 cm
AN INSTALLATION IN LIGHT AND SOUND
KUNSTFORENINGEN GAMMEL STRAND   COPENHAGEN   DENMARK

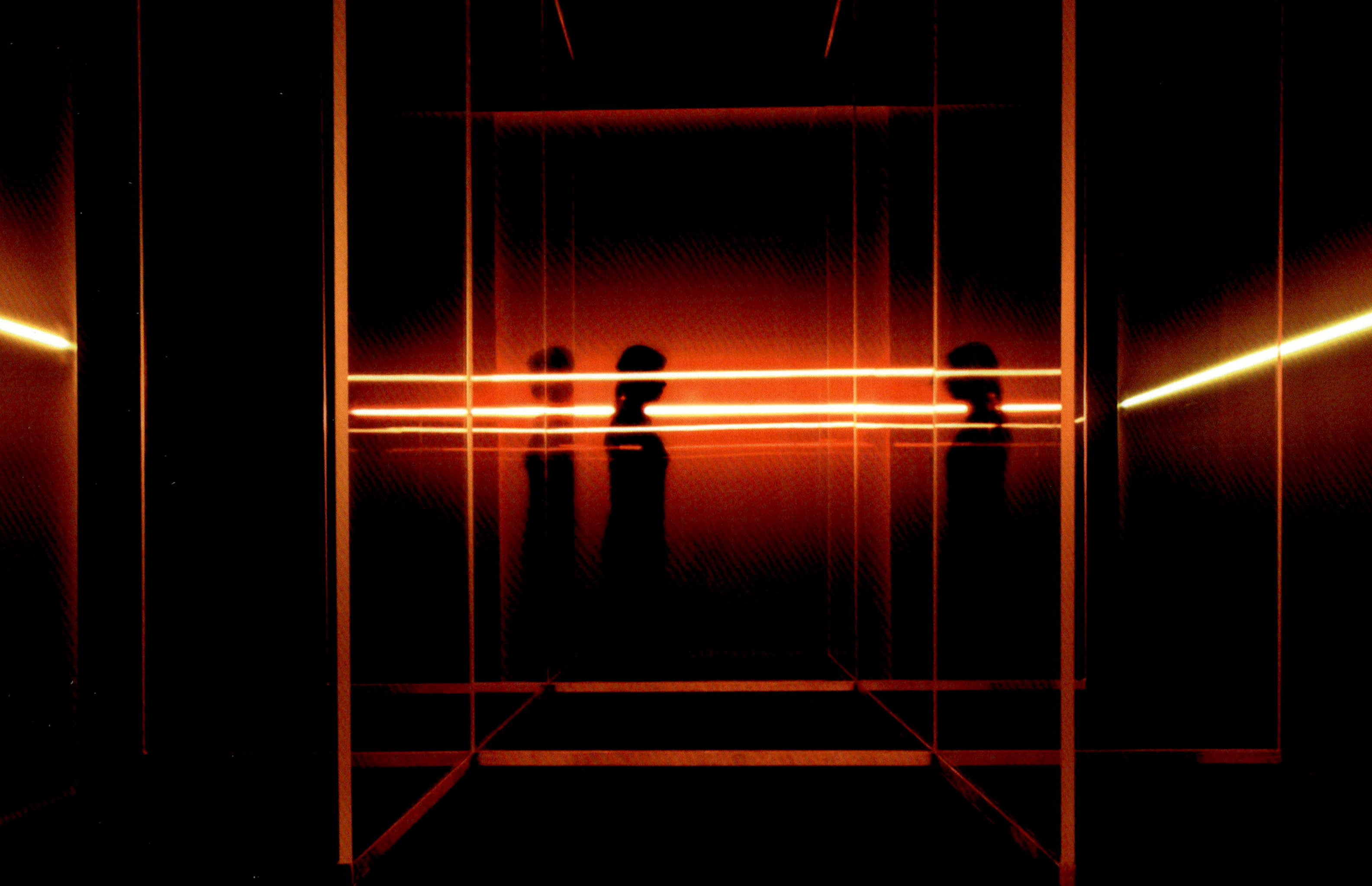

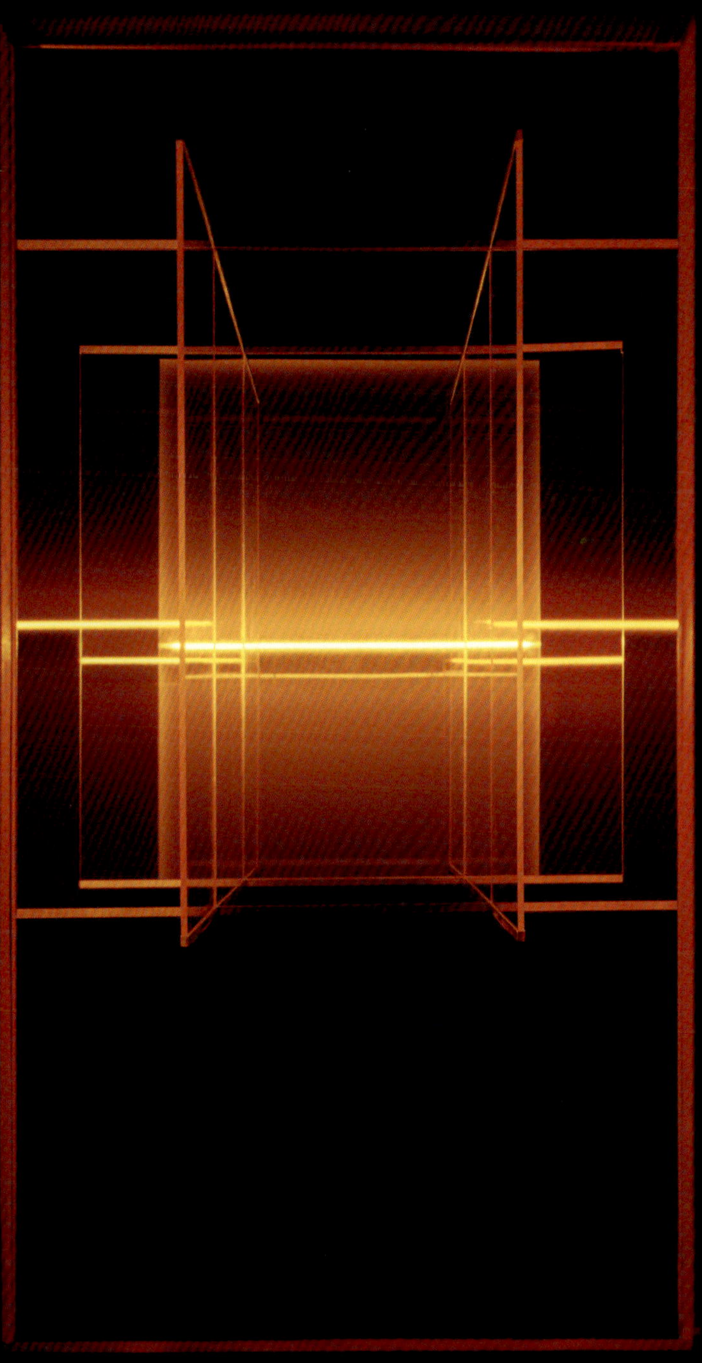

**ROOM OF LETTERS** | VIDEO PROJECTION | 500 x 500 x 300 cm
AN INSTALLATION IN LIGHT AND SOUND
KUNSTFORENINGEN GAMMEL STRAND   COPENHAGEN   DENMARK
PAGE 65   DETAIL   POET AND SHADOW   PALLE SIGSGAARD

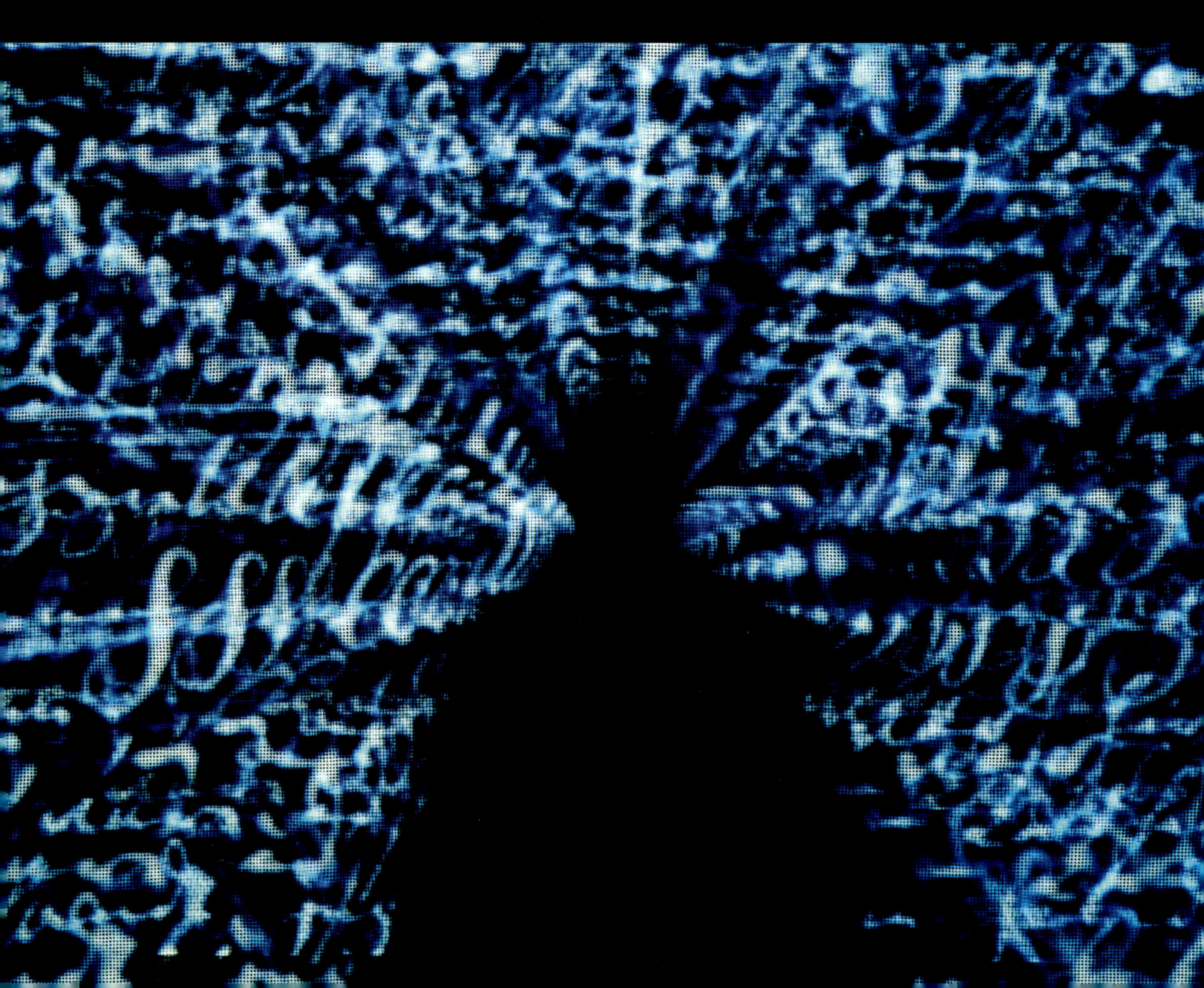

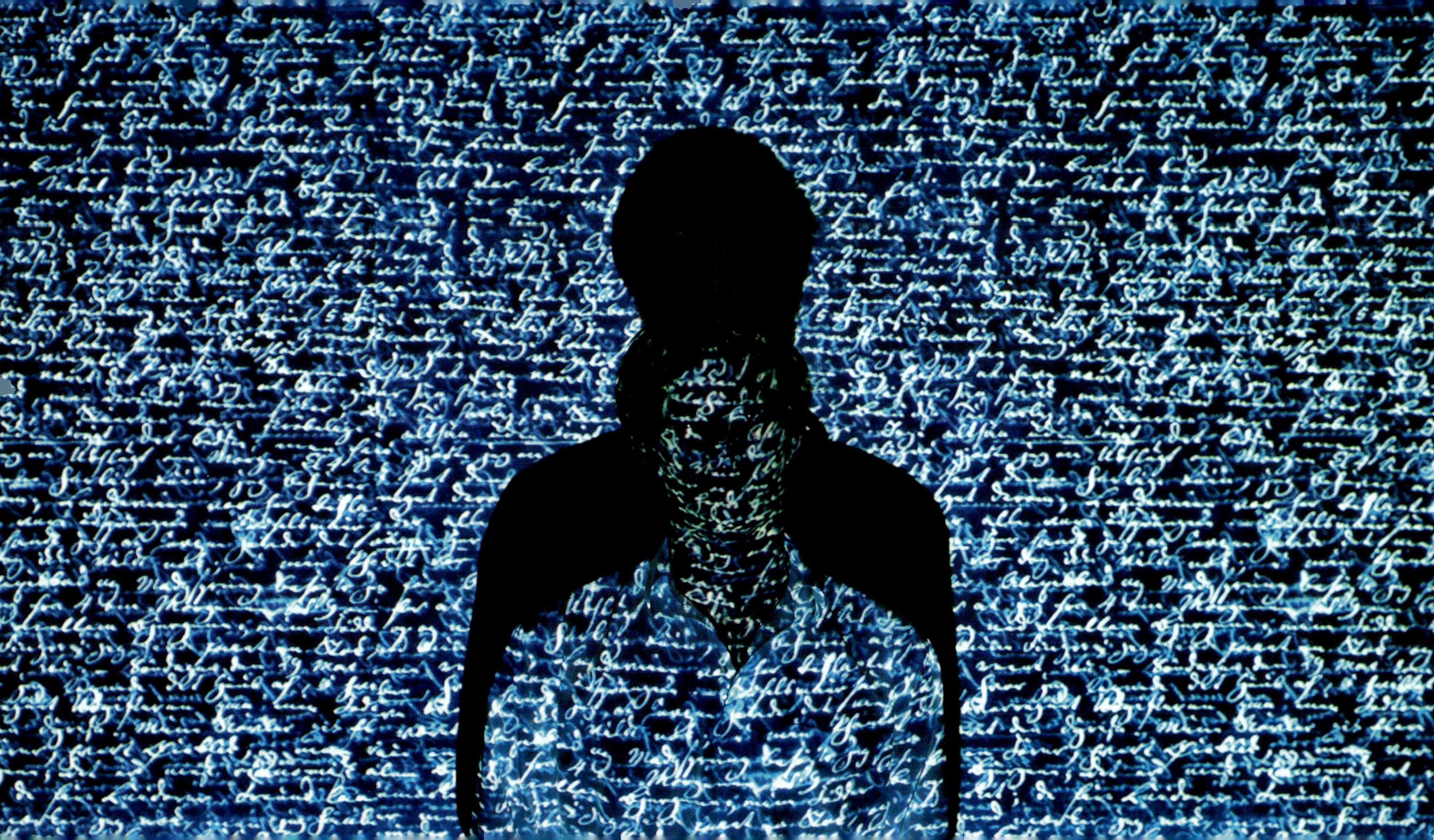

**BLACK LIGHT THREE** | 94 x 19 x 8 cm | **BLACK LIGHT THREE** | 94 x 19 x 8 cm | **BLACK LIGHT TWO** | 122 x 34 x 8 cm
BLACK LIGHT THREE EDITION OF TEN | BLACK LIGHT TWO EDITION OF FIVE
GALLERI WEINBERGER    COPENHAGEN    DENMARK
PRIVATE COLLECTIONS | UNITED KINGDOM, GERMANY & DENMARK

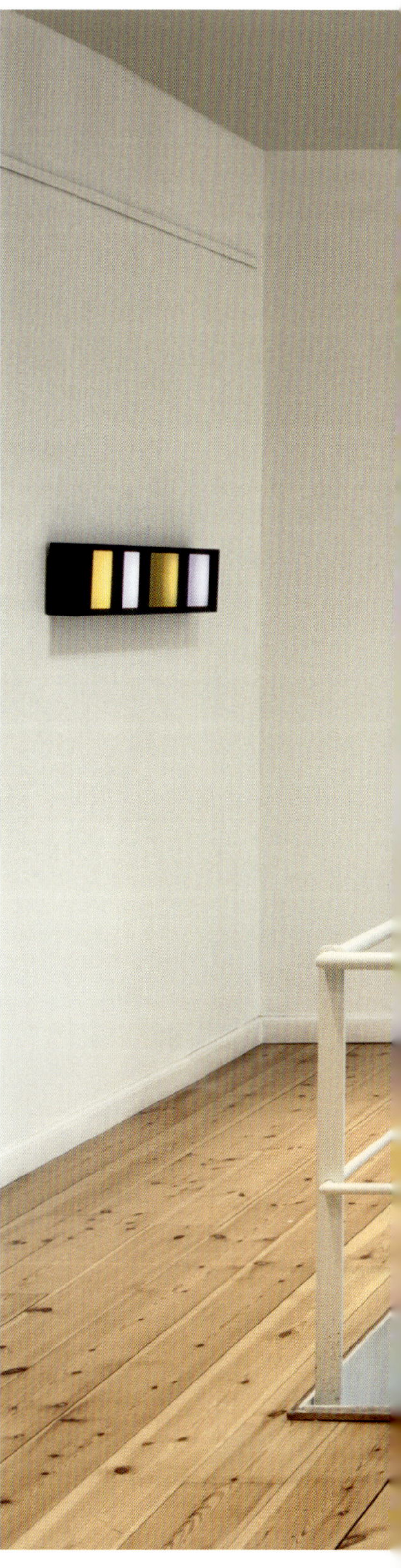

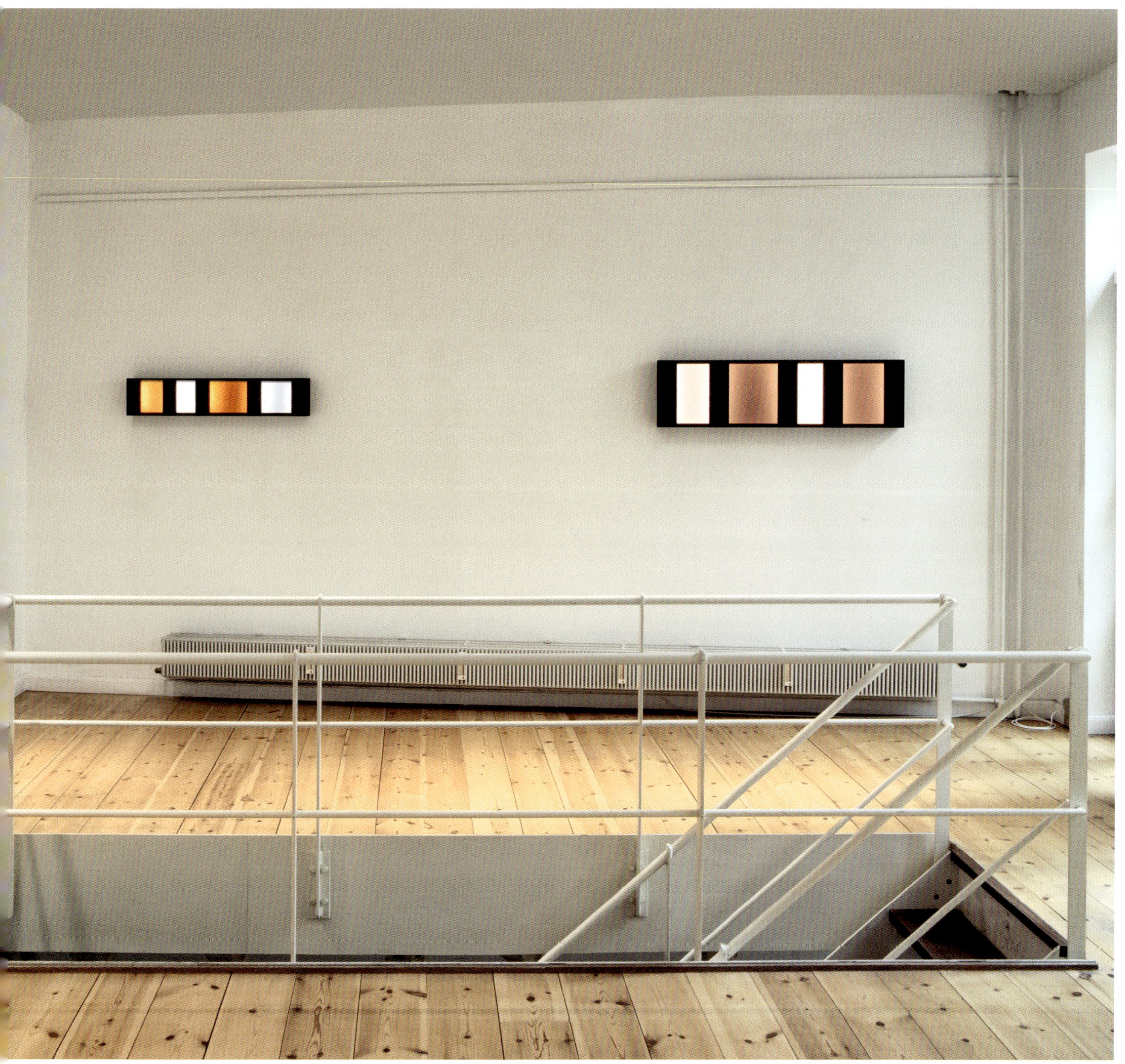

**BLACK LIGHT ONE** | 140 x 34 x 8 cm
BLACK LIGHT ONE EDITION OF FIVE
GALLERI WEINBERGER  COPENHAGEN  DENMARK
PRIVATE COLLECTIONS | UNITED KINGDOM, GERMANY & DENMARK

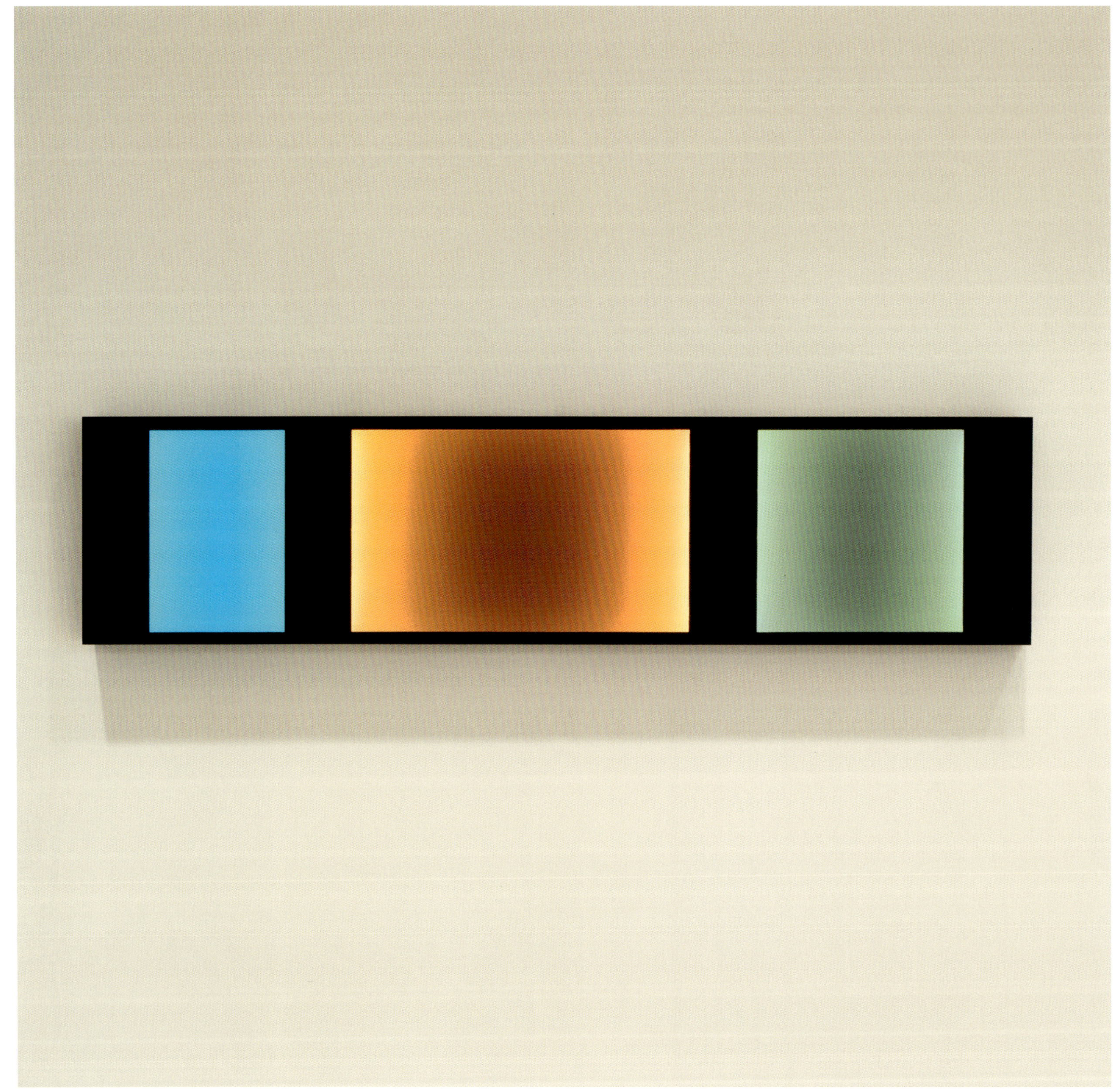

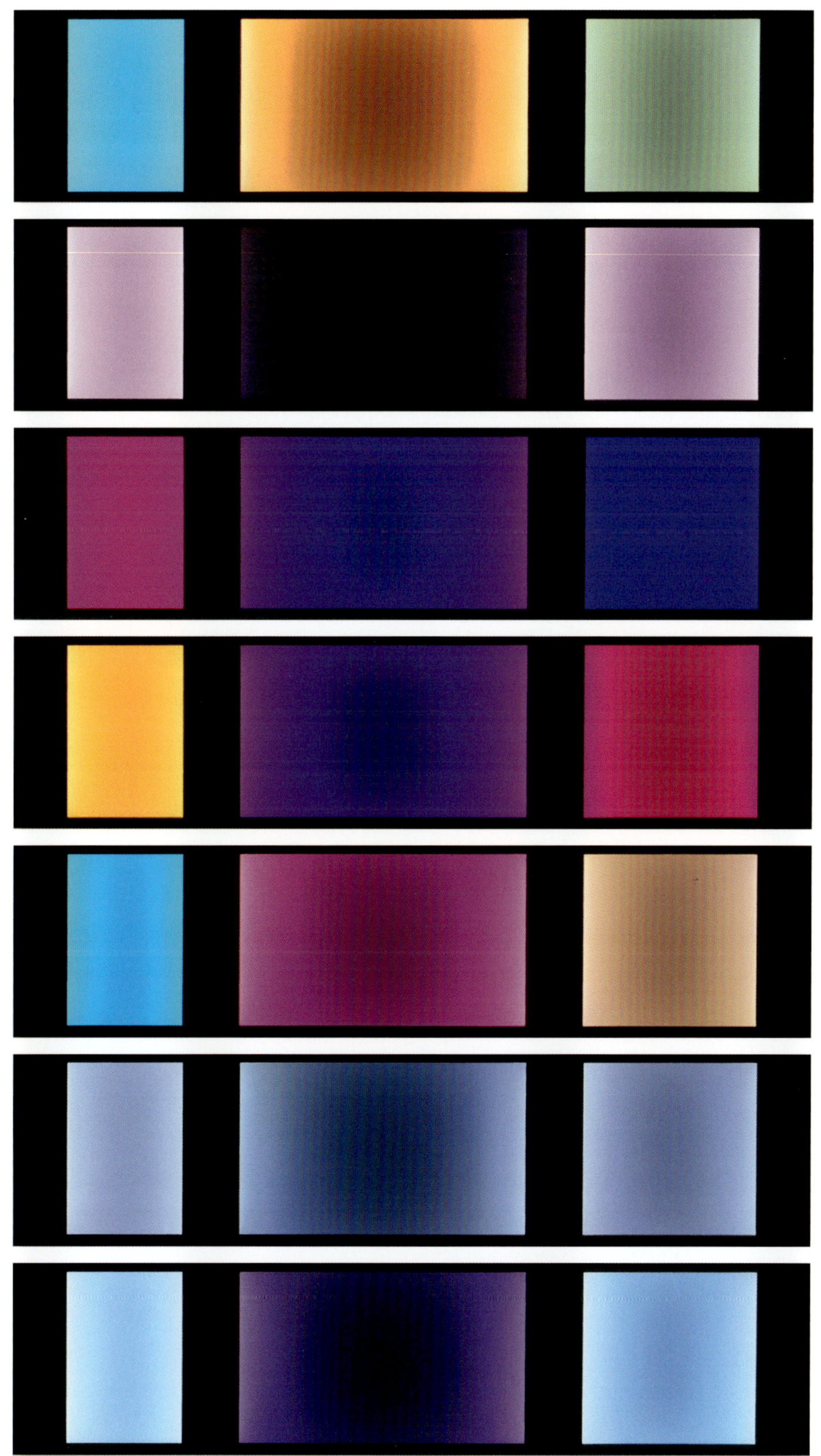

**BLACK LIGHT TWO** | 122 x 34 x 8 cm
BLACK LIGHT TWO EDITION OF FIVE
GALLERI WEINBERGER   COPENHAGEN   DENMARK
PRIVATE COLLECTIONS | UNITED KINGDOM, GERMANY & DENMARK

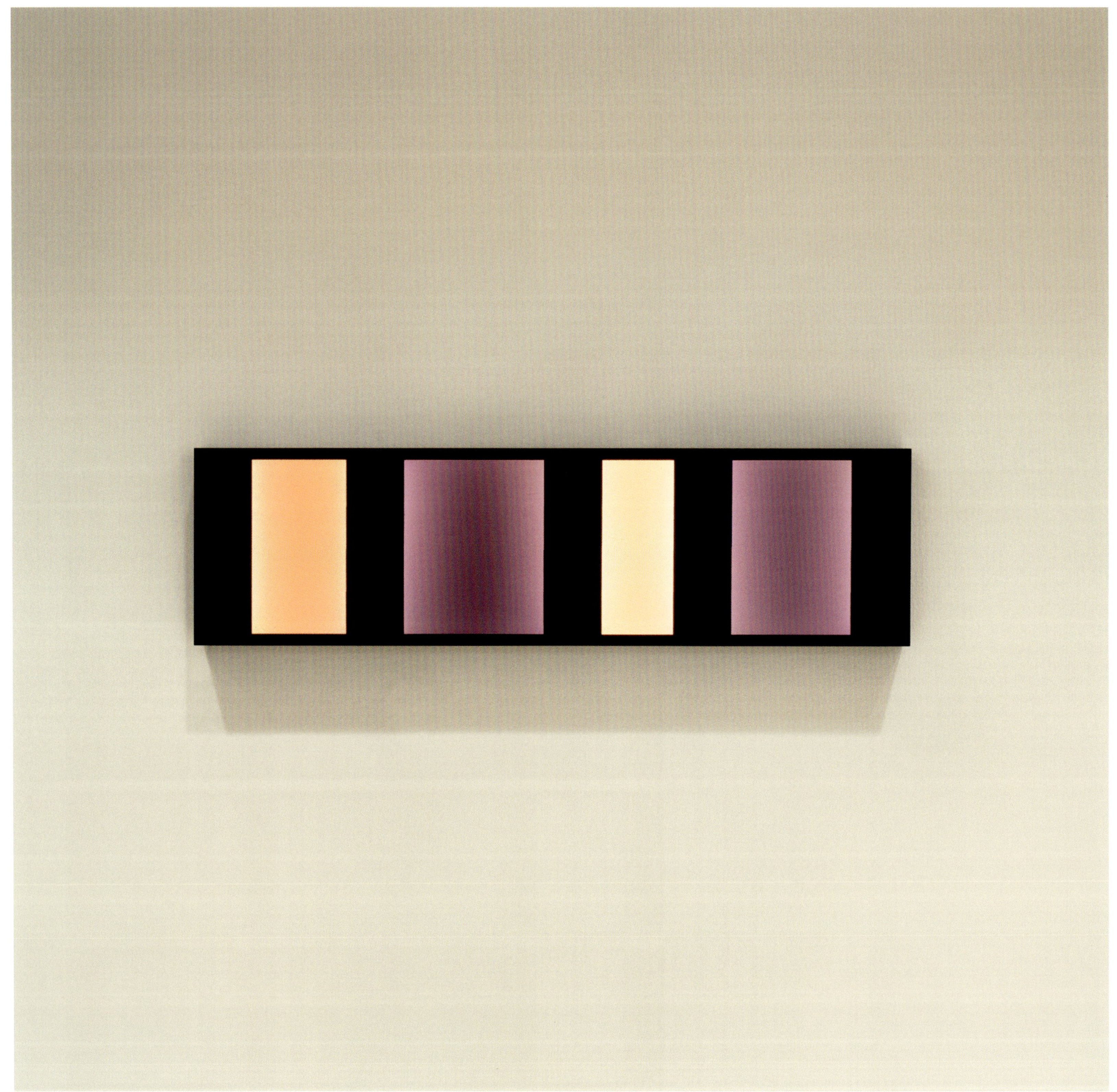

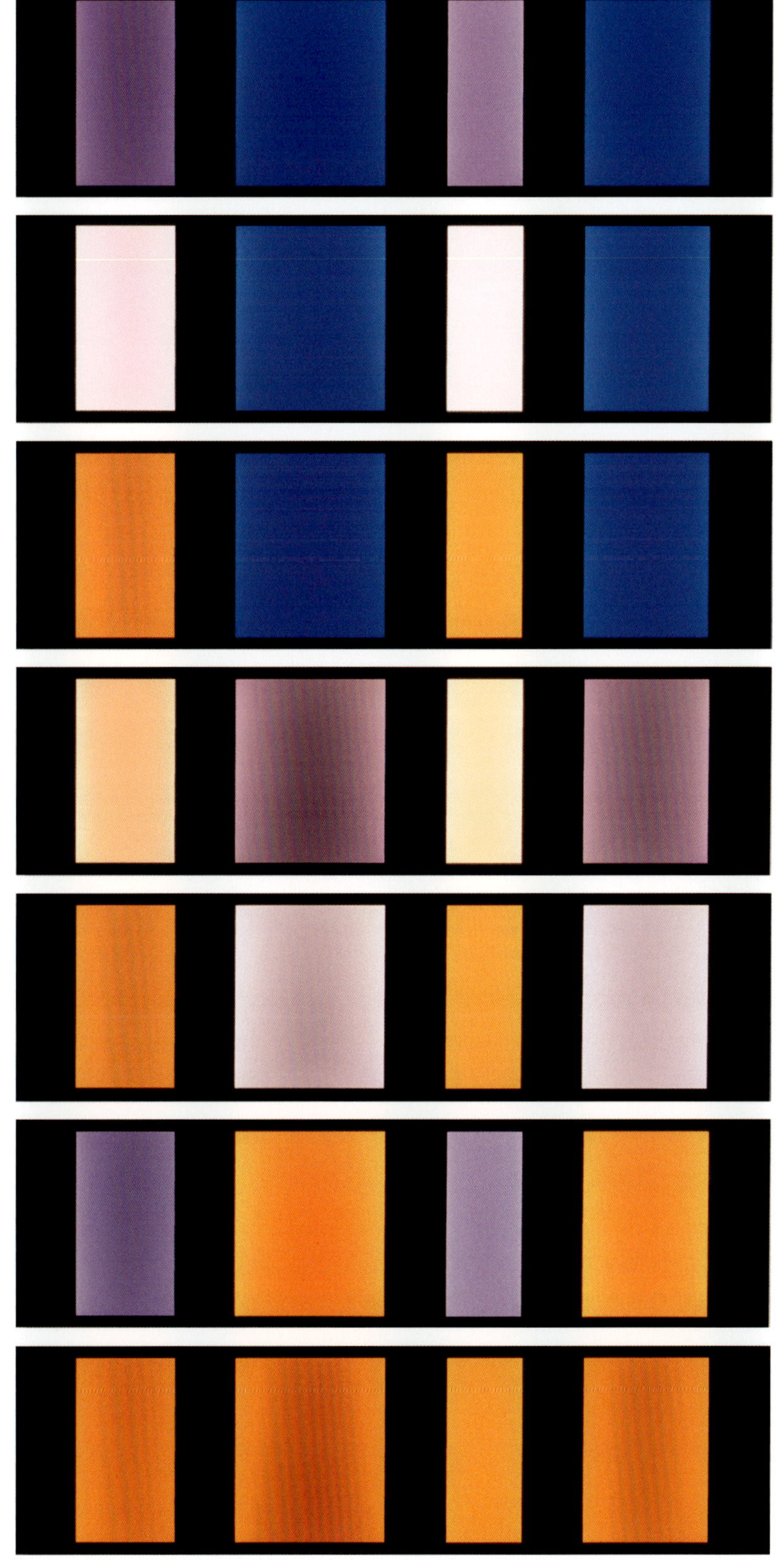

**CORNER** | 200 x 30 x 8 cm
CORNER INSTALLATION | KULTURRUM HAMMENHOG   YSTAD   SWEDEN
COLLECTION OF ARTIST

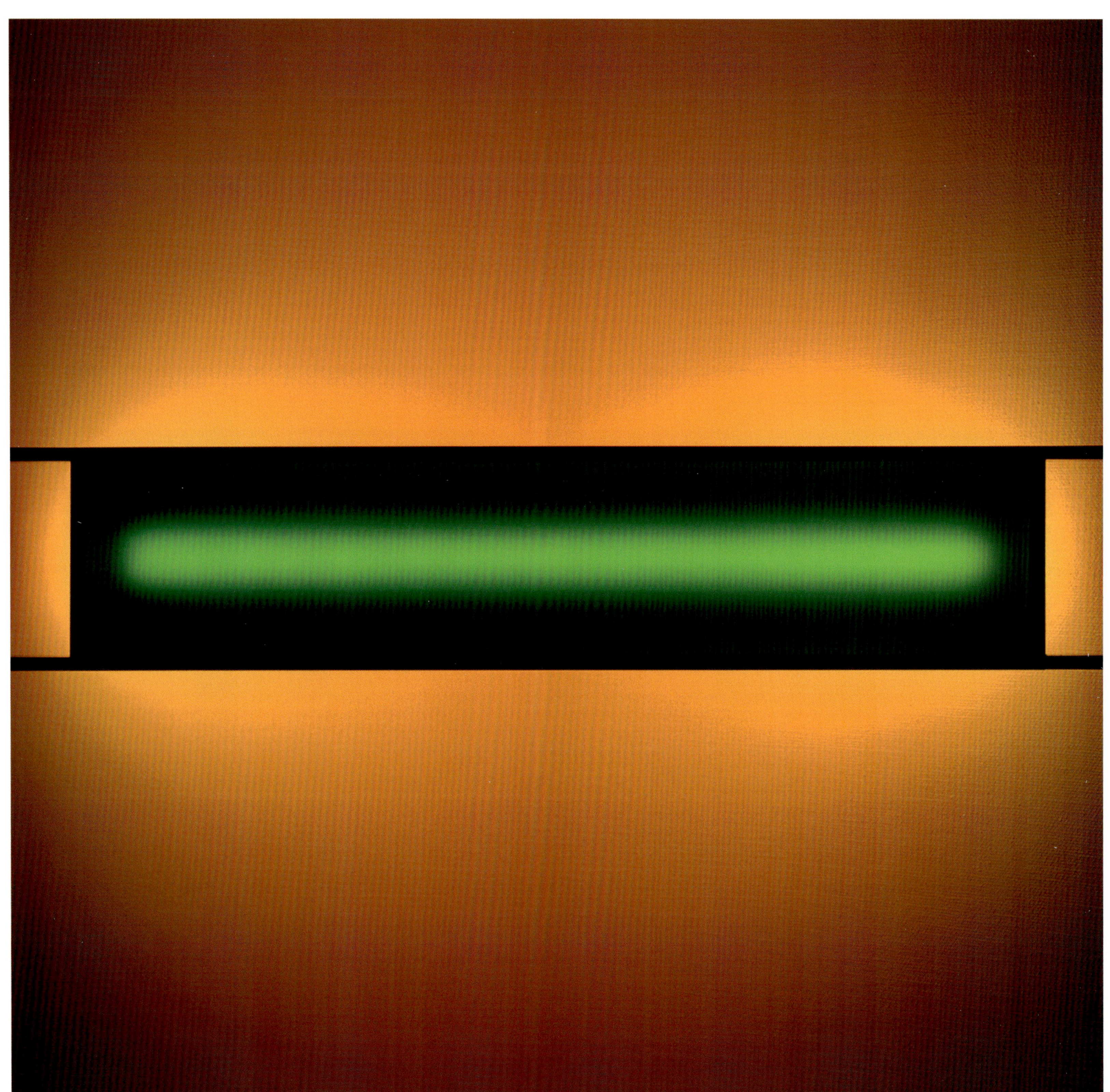

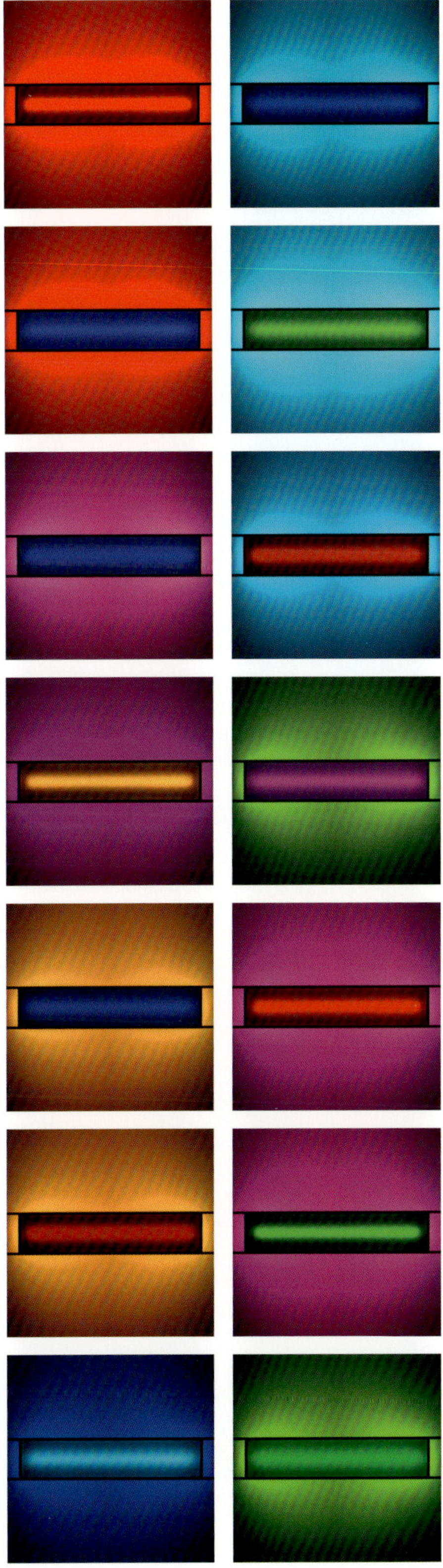

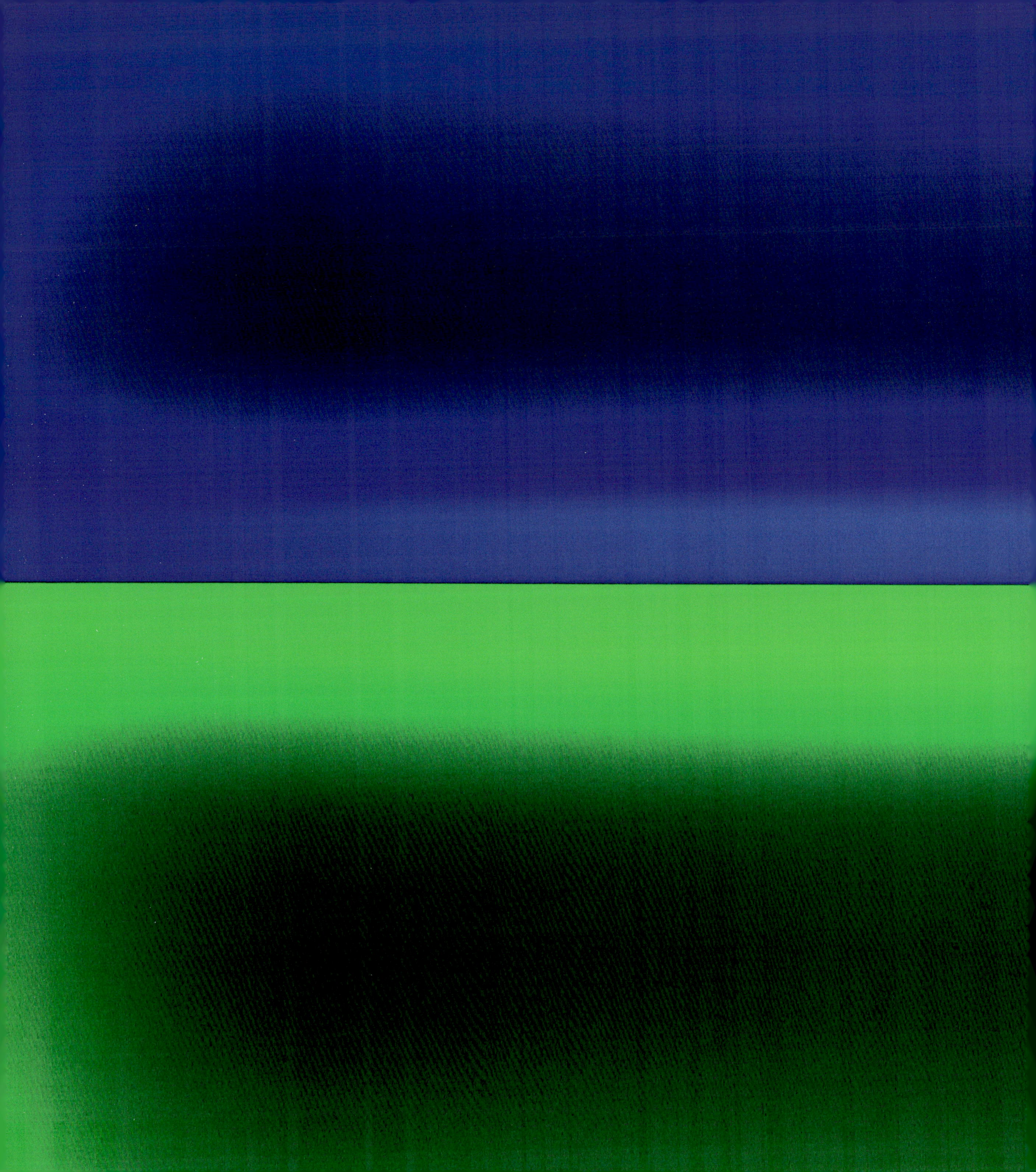

## LUMINOUS ICONS PART TWO
# ROBERT C. MORGAN
## THE BROWN LIGHT SERIES TO THE PRESENT 2006–2011

**ONE OF THE ISSUES THAT COMES UP WITH REGARD TO THE DOCUMENTATION** of Steven Scott's work is the problem of temporality in relation to the static image. Whereas a painting by Piet Mondrian or Richard Mortensen can be photographed and reproduced on the page of a catalogue or book, and although there are limitations in terms of scale, material, texture and light, one may generally agree that the page reveals an index of the actual work. This is not always true in relation to the light works by Scott. The difference should be obvious.

While the canvases of Mondrian or Mortensen do not significantly change, unless the colours fade over time or the picture dulls because of grime that adheres to the surface, the image remains the same. In a photographic still reproduction of *Black Light One* (2005), for example, only a fragment of information will appear. The format of the box will be consistent and the shape of the colours will translate, but the transitions between the colours will not. This is because a still photograph can never really capture the movement of transition between one colour and another. In that the visual process of colour transition is the essential component in Scott's work, this becomes problematic. One solution that the artist has employed for print publications is to use sequential stills of the process, so that instead of perceiving a single still image – although these, too, can be breathtaking – one is given a serial view of the colours in constant flux. Even so, a literal translation of these chromatic variations is unable to connect with the actual experience. In this sense, I would argue that to actually stand in front of *Black Light Two* is like none other. It is phenomenological to the extent that time and space cohere, as do colour and light. In doing so, a synchronic event emerges in the foreground, a momentary consciousness capable of sustaining itself over a period of time. It is this kind of real-time experience whereby the perception of time within colour constitutes the actual existence as a work of art. If time cannot be felt in relation to Steven Scott's work, then the project has no validity.

The value of this experience is based in phenomenology, even more than aesthetics or politics, although each of these combine to proffer an event that carries a transcendent aspect beyond the ordinary. It is this transcendent aspect that carries the alleviation of weight in relation to experience and thereby provides the viewer with a sense of lightness, or absence of weight.

Whereas the black light offers a hard edge in the act of perceiving colour, brown light may offer a mixed penumbra, somewhat more transitional, less definitive, with colour less defined and that gradually mutates from one state of being into another. This implies both the virtue of the frame and the impossibility of the frame as related to the openness and confinement of the colour spectrum. Colour cannot easily be confined as pure colour. The mixing of colour pigment does not behave the same way as the mixing of light colours. This is one of the important principles in Scott's work and the basis for his shifting our static idea of colour towards a transitory phenomenon. In a posthumously compiled treatise, titled *Remarks on Colours* (Sect. 60), the philosopher Ludwig Wittgenstein analyzes the optical function of the colour brown:

> **"Brown is, above all, a surface colour, that is to say, there is no such thing as a *clear* brown, but only a muddy one. Also: brown contains black – (?) – How would a person have to behave for us to say, of him that he knows a *pure, primary* brown?"**

Wittgenstein's argument, of course, precedes the invention of electronic colour generated through light. According to the De Stijl group in the Netherlands (1917–31), the primaries were red, yellow and blue. When mixed they became brown – muddy brown.

## LUMINOUS ICONS PART TWO

## THE BROWN LIGHT SERIES TO THE PRESENT 2006–2011

Electronic light replaces yellow with green as colour is generated differently through light. In contrast, the three primary light colours, red, green and blue, form white when mixed in equal proportions. Brown may facilitate the appearance of another colour without ever becoming a pure colour unto itself. Scott has worked with many applications of this idea, which began to appear in late 2005. In *Flood* and *Brown Light* (2007), installed at the Galerie König in Hanau and Galleri Weinberger in Copenhagen, he uses the floor and wall – in other words, the origins of placement for sculpture and painting respectively – to identify the manner in which light is perceived within the confines of a specific form. This formal aspect of Scott's work is truly original and something as yet to be investigated. In fact, it is the clarity between hard-edge geometry and the softness of these colour formats within the frame that defines the subtle and often acute differences between the effects of black and brown light. In both cases, the wedge-like floor sculpture, *Flood*, and the *Brown Light* wall piece, one senses a slow reading, an application of brown that may contain black, yet operates contextually in relation to other colours of the spectrum.

Recent works from 2011 are largely what constitute the exhibition at Galleri Weinberger at the outset of the same year. They include the horizontal *Nominal Eight*, in which the stark lines of light are seen unconcealed within the space of the black frame, and *Nominal Twenty One*, in which a sequence of shorter optical lines is placed vertically and equidistantly across a horizontal field within a frame (measuring 300 x 100 x 8 cm) of the same scale as *Nominal Eight*. The rhythmic differences are striking in terms of how the colours modulate within each of these works. In contrast to *Nominal Eight*, where the light bleeds up and down the lateral striations, the sense of time within *Nominal Twenty One* is more punctuated as the light moves in and out and sideways. While the latter may refer to counterpoint rhythms found in jazz, the former sustains the kind of smooth flow one might associate with Debussy's *Afternoon of the Faun*. In either case, the musical metaphor is difficult to avoid. In his book *The Art of Time* (1969), drama theorist Michael Kirby discusses the transensory properties of certain works of visual art in which one sees the temporal evolution of colour, yet feels music, or vice versa, where one hears music and envisions rhythmic structures commensurate to optical sensations.

In two smaller square works, titled *Icon 2.0* and *Icon 2.1*, abstract signs and symbols emerge that are atypical of earlier works by Scott. Mounted side by side on the gallery wall upstairs, *Icon 2.0* emits a sequence of signs using white dots against a black field, while *Icon 2.1* appears to move a separate lexicon of blurred colour shapes at a much slower pace. After several minutes of observation of these two exquisite works, I felt there was a conversation happening between the two, as if they were talking to one another, yet coming from two very different places. The unlikely combinations suggested irrational juxtapositions found in the work of postmodern painters, such as the late Sigmar Polke. In *Ecstasy One* and *Ecstasy Two*, the format is again horizontal and the colour is blurred. Here in each case, the colours move between horizontal lines and blocks of colour, virtual smudges that appear over, under and side by side. In either case, the work carries its own intensity, its own virtual nascence of something about to occur or in the process of occurring or reaching a simulation or a resolution that is deferred until replaced by something unexpected and elegant, vibrating with light.

# THE BROWN LIGHT SERIES TO THE PRESENT 2006–2011

**FLOOD** | 200 x 100 x 90 cm | **BROWN LIGHT** | 93 x 151 x 15 cm
BROWN LIGHT EDITION OF FOUR
GALLERI WEINBERGER   COPENHAGEN   DENMARK
FLOOD COLLECTION OF ARTIST | BROWN LIGHT PRIVATE AND PUBLIC COLLECTIONS | DENMARK & SWEDEN

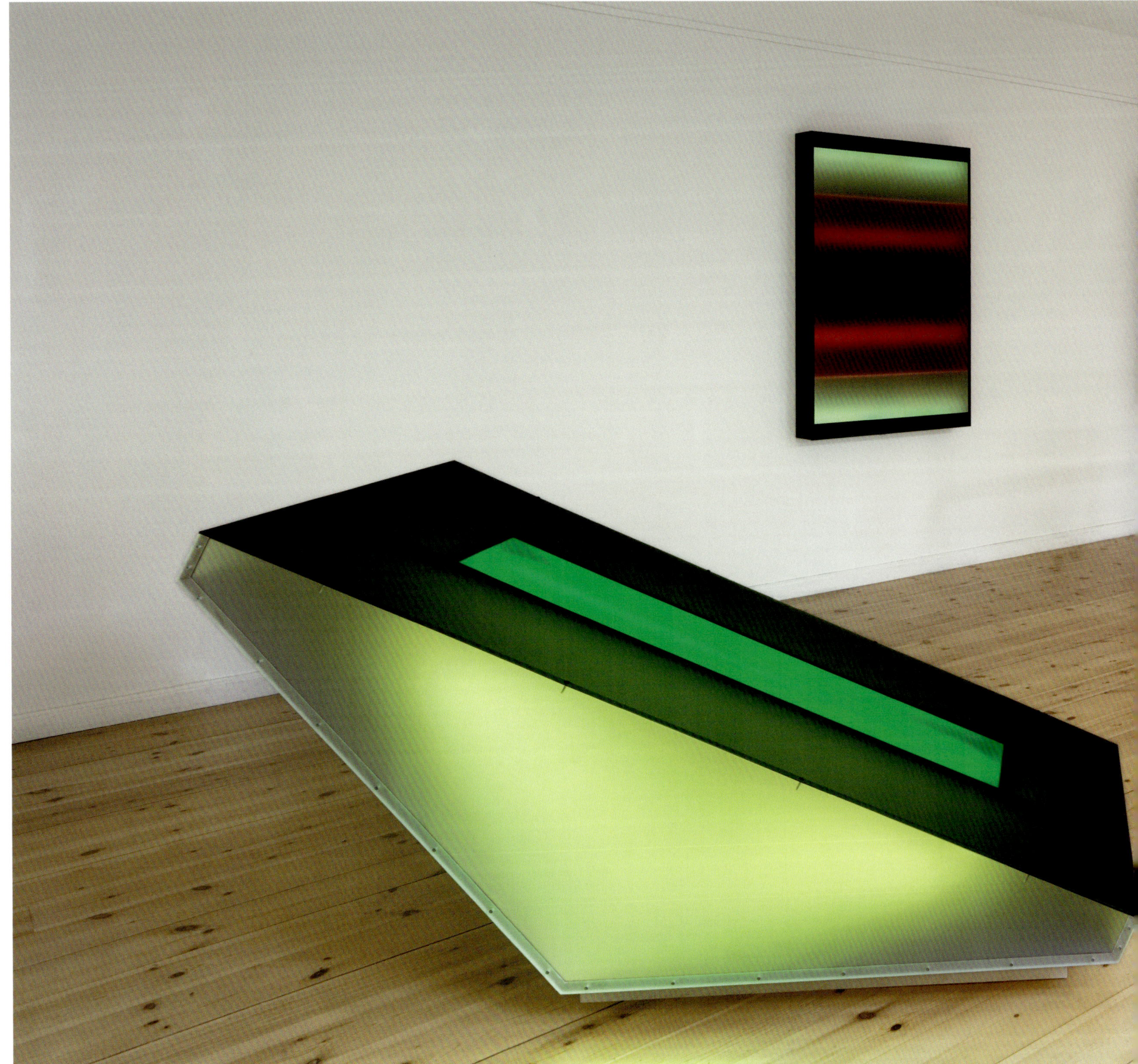

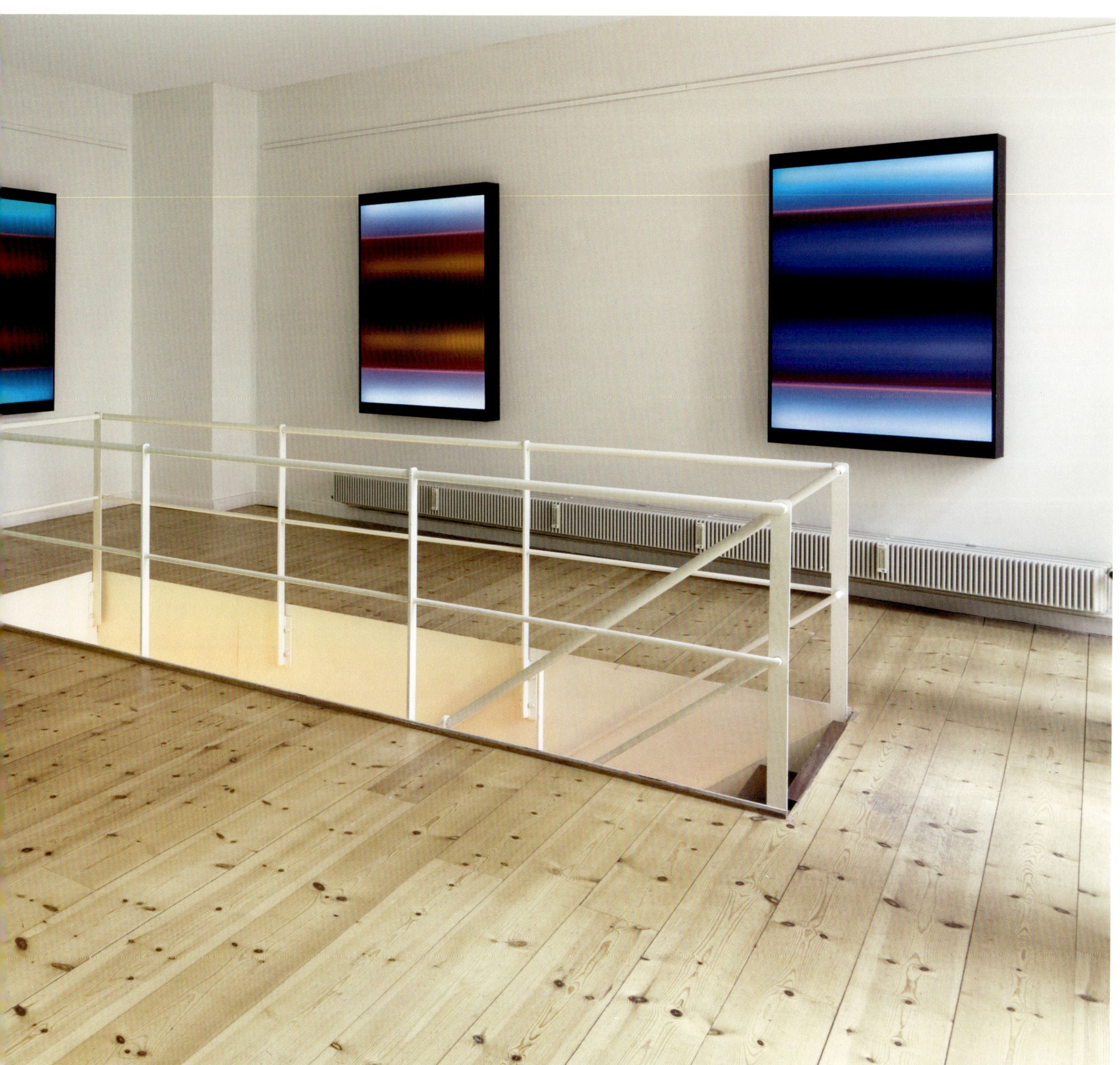

 **LUMINOUS ICONS** 1999–2011  |  SOLO EXHIBITION  |  SHARED SPACE THREE  |  2007
**FLOOD**  |  200 x 100 x 90 cm  |  **BLACK LIGHT ONE**  |  140 x 34 x 8 cm
BLACK LIGHT ONE EDITION OF FIVE
GALERIE KÖNIG   HANAU   FRANKFURT   GERMANY
FLOOD COLLECTION OF ARTIST  |  BLACK LIGHT PRIVATE COLLECTIONS  |  UNITED KINGDOM, GERMANY & DENMARK

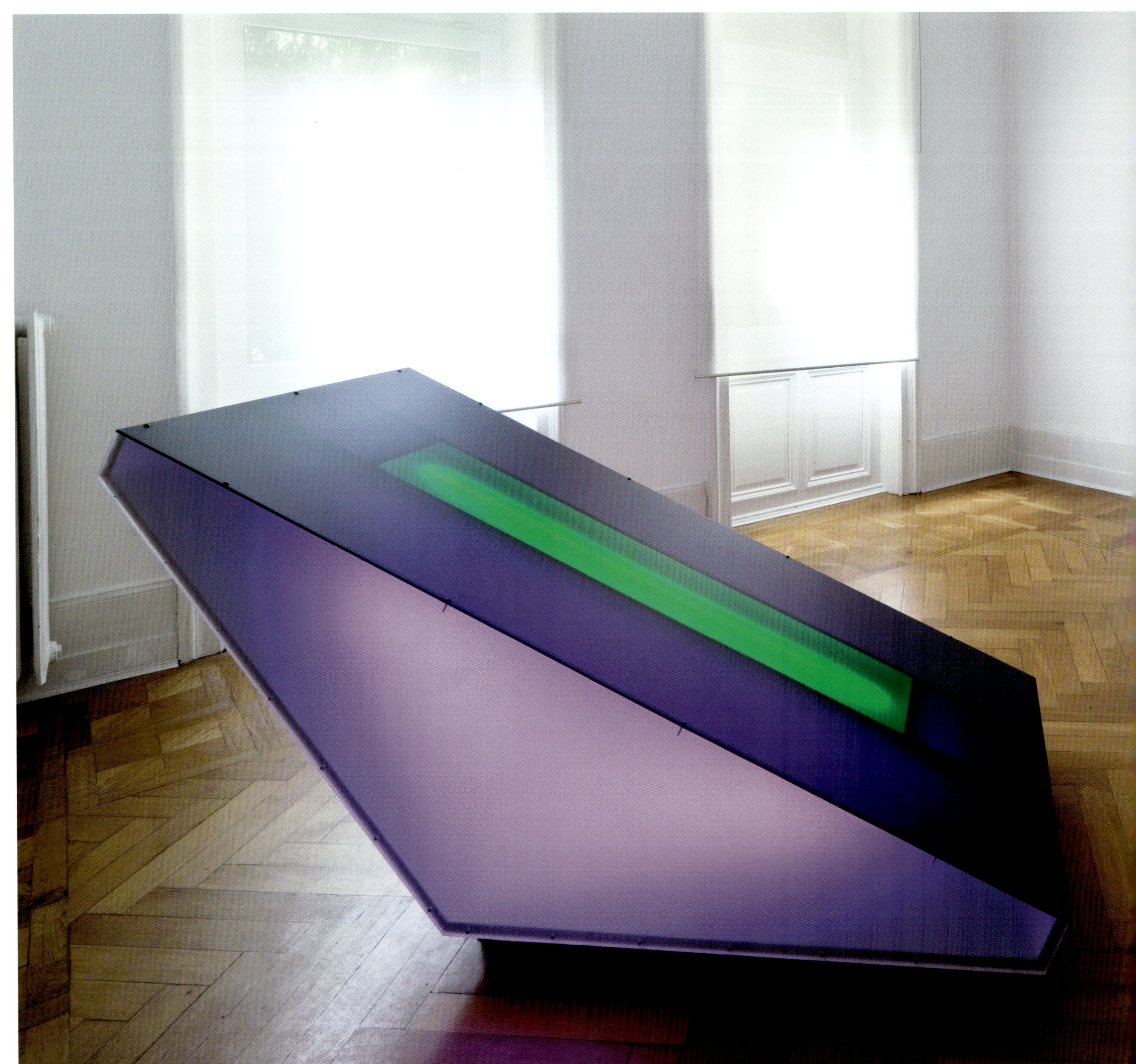

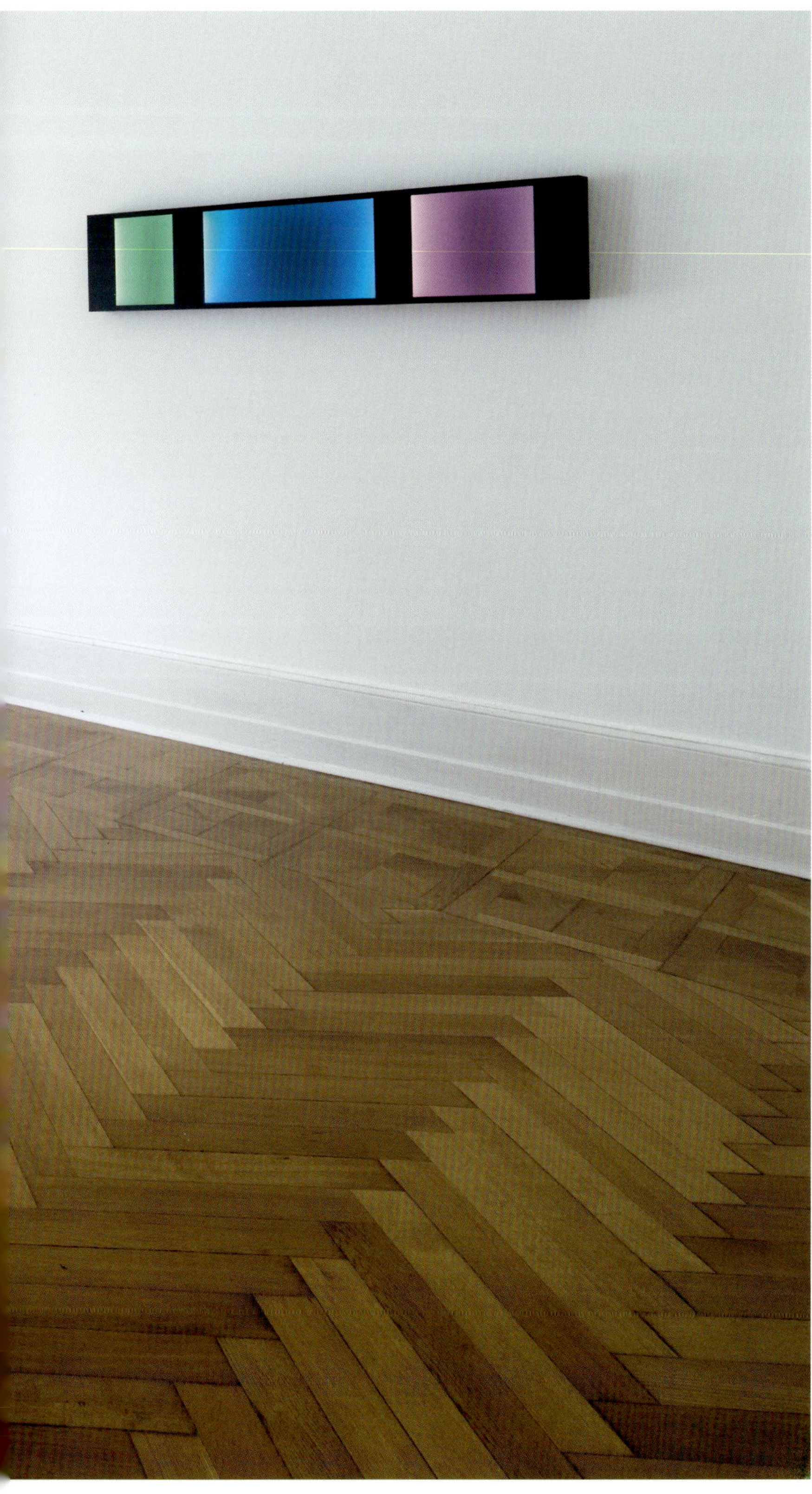

**BROWN LIGHT** | 93 x 151 x 15 cm
BROWN LIGHT EDITION OF FOUR
GALERIE KÖNIG HANAU FRANKFURT GERMANY
BROWN LIGHT PRIVATE AND PUBLIC COLLECTIONS | DENMARK & SWEDEN

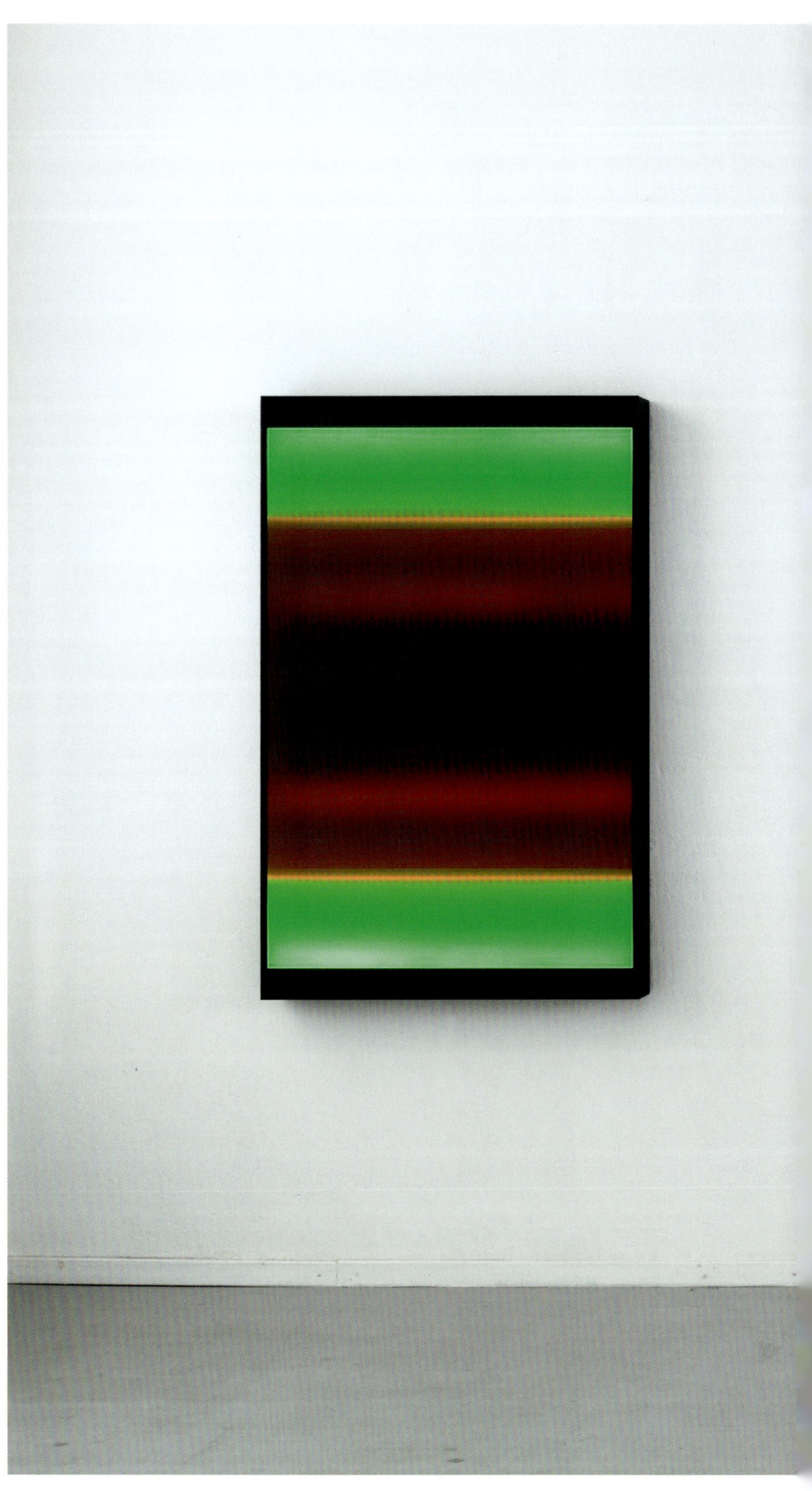

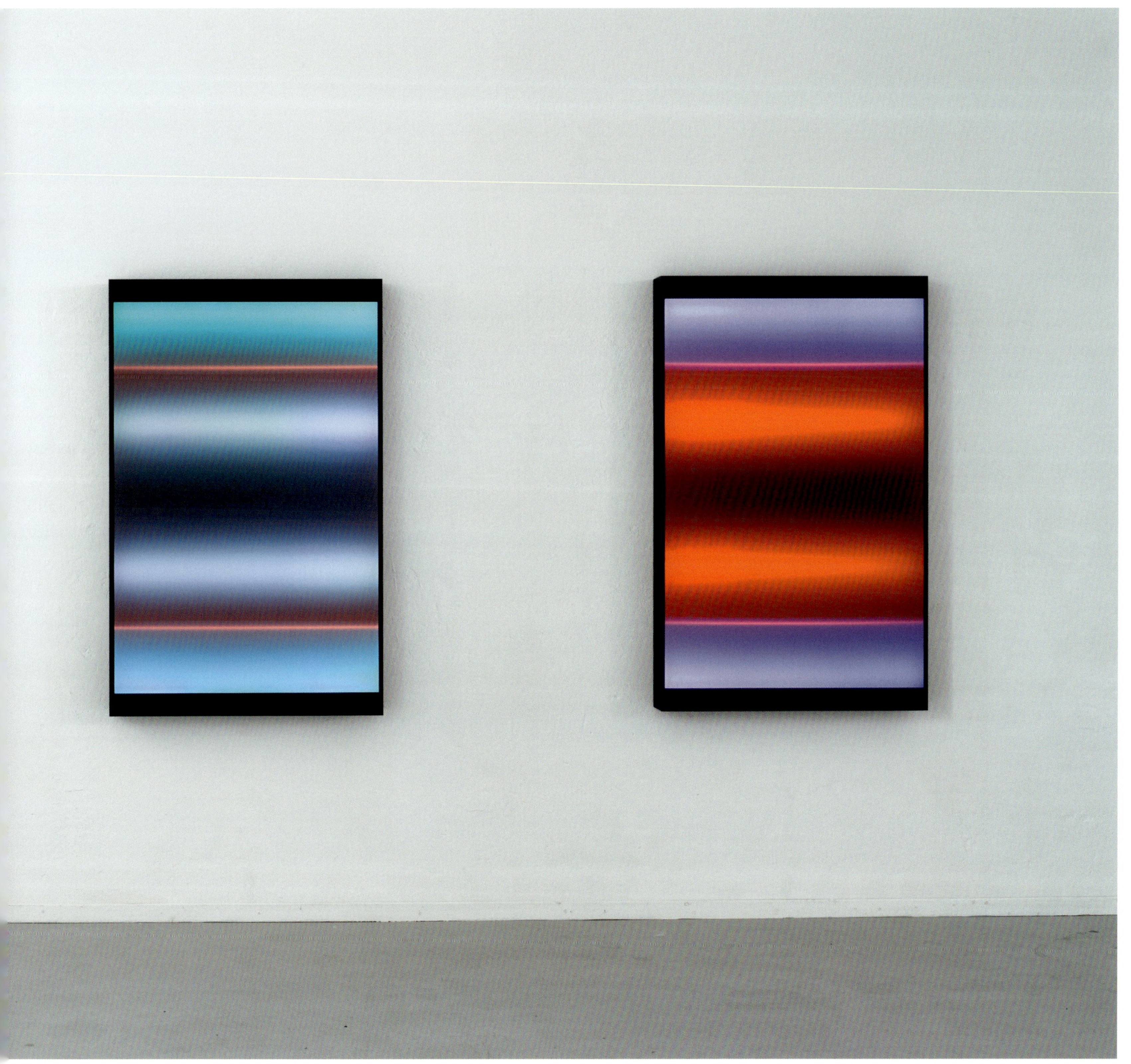

**BROWN LIGHT** | 93 x 151 x 15 cm
BROWN LIGHT EDITION OF FOUR
GALLERI WEINBERGER   COPENHAGEN   DENMARK
BROWN LIGHT PRIVATE AND PUBLIC COLLECTIONS | DENMARK & SWEDEN

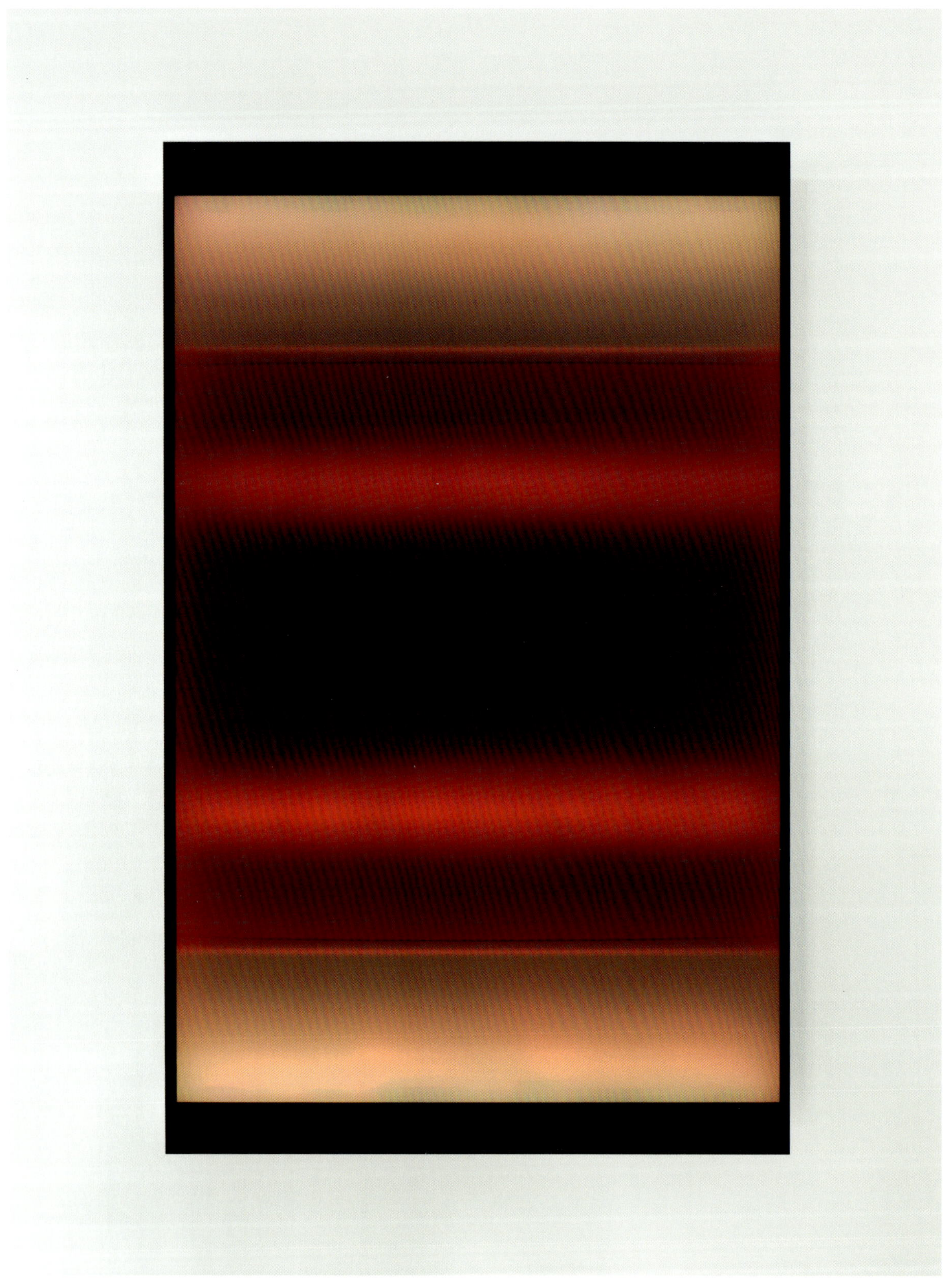

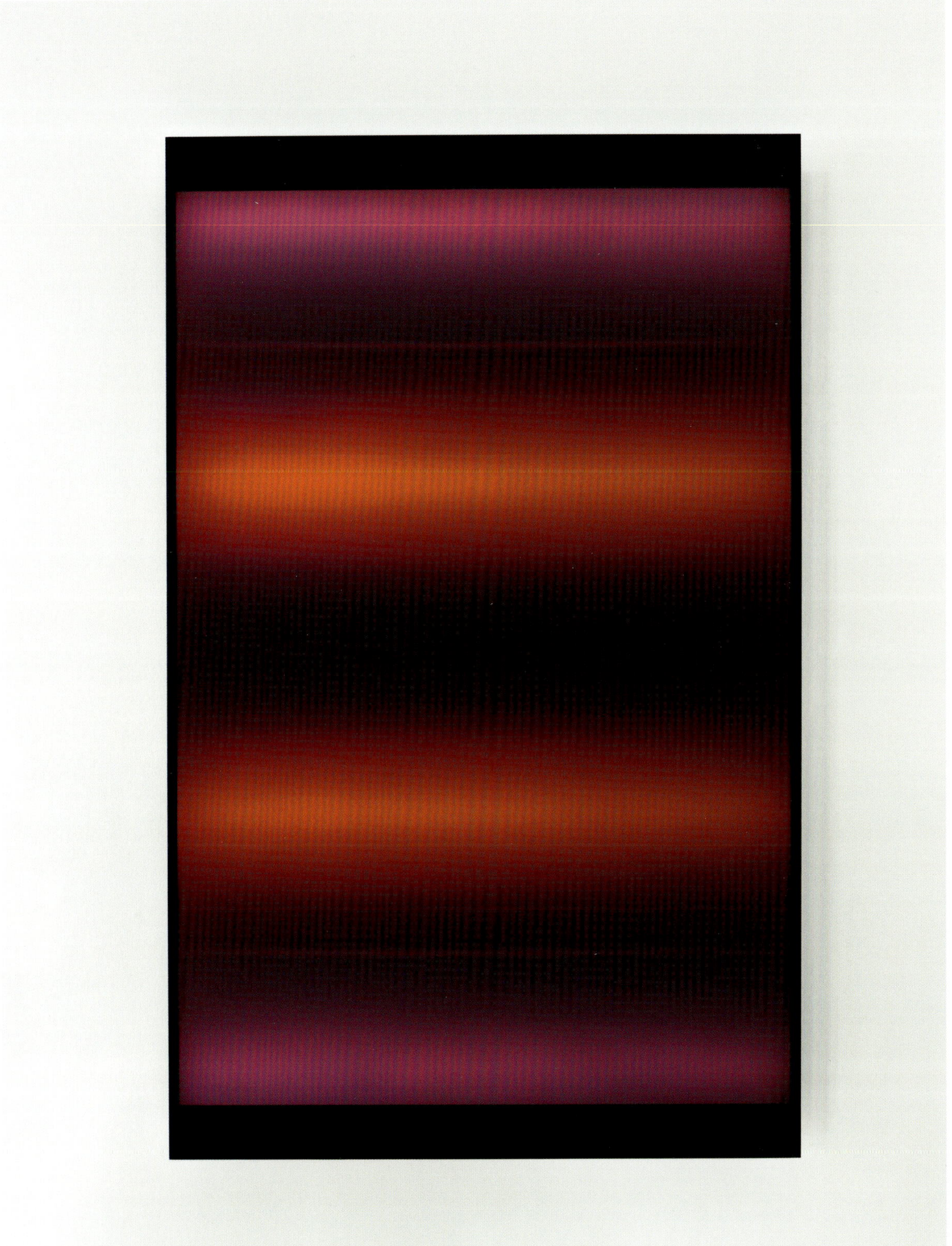

**BROWN LIGHT** | 93 x 151 x 15 cm
BROWN LIGHT EDITION OF FOUR
GALLERI WEINBERGER COPENHAGEN DENMARK
BROWN LIGHT PRIVATE AND PUBLIC COLLECTIONS | DENMARK & SWEDEN

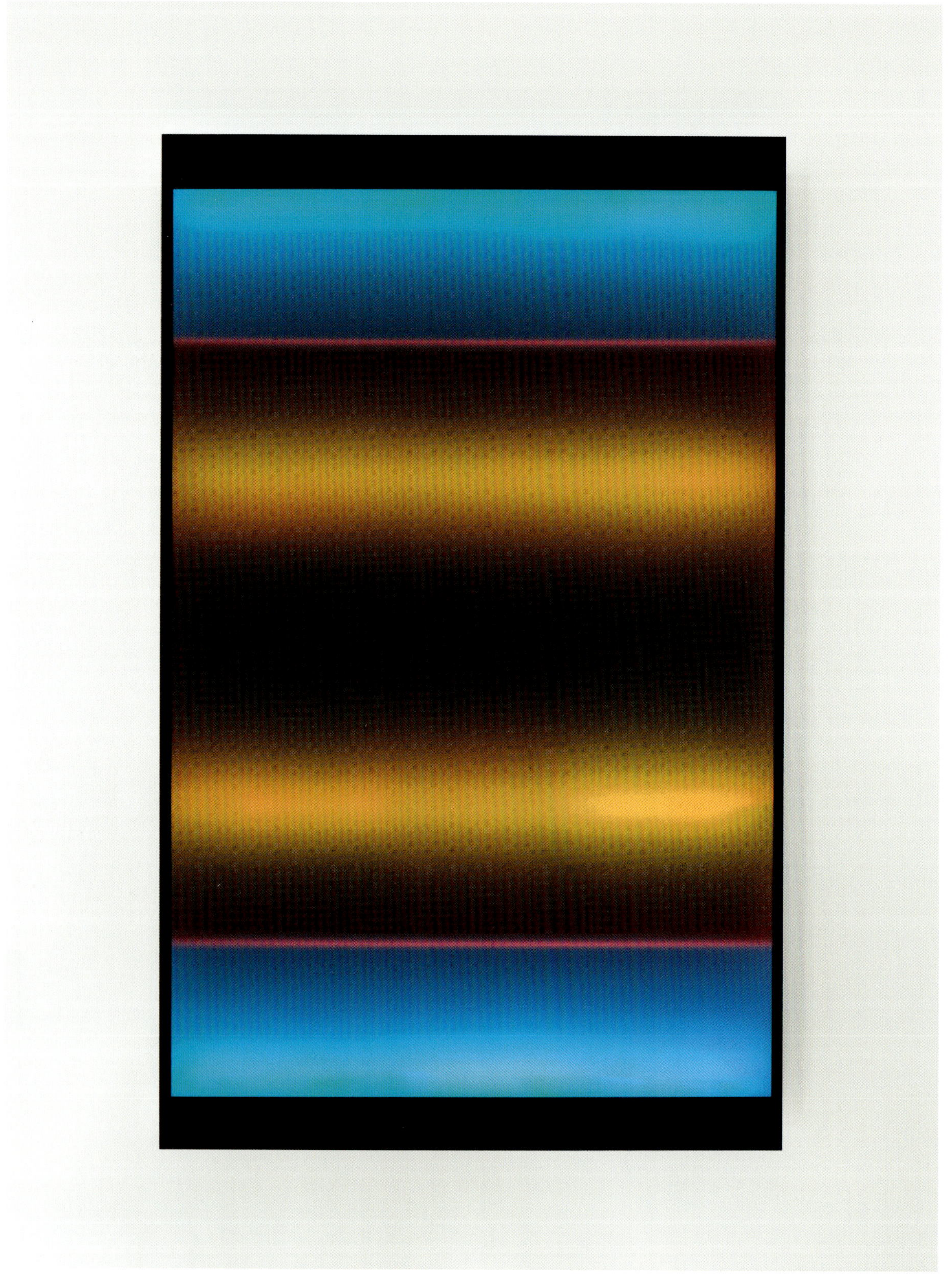

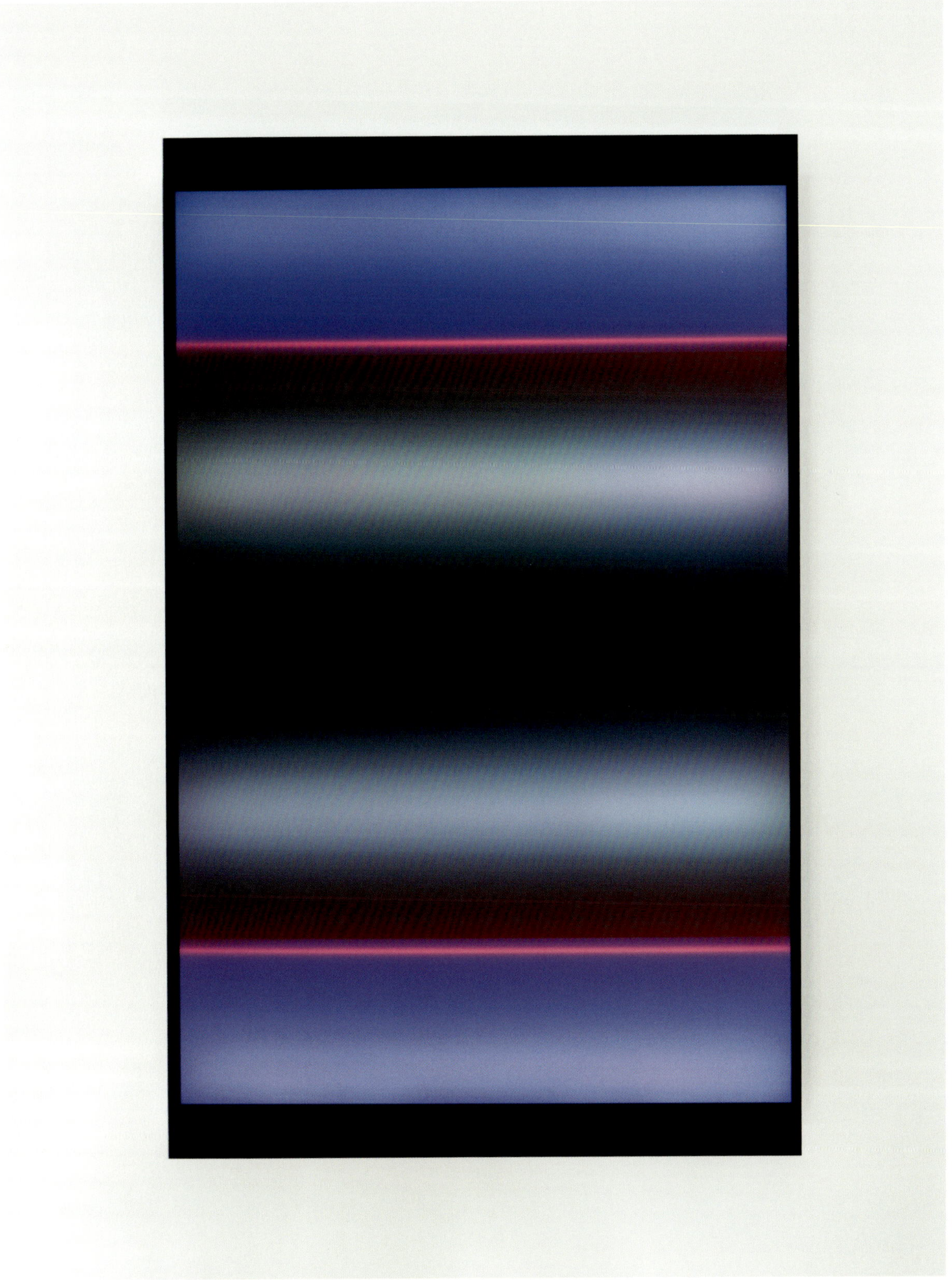

 | **LUMINOUS ICONS** 1999–2011 | SOLO EXHIBITION | LIGHT WORKS | 2011
**NOMINAL EIGHT** | 300 x 100 x 8 cm | **NOMINAL TWENTY ONE** | 300 x 100 x 8 cm
GALLERI WEINBERGER   COPENHAGEN   DENMARK
NOMINAL TWENTY ONE PRIVATE COLLECTION DENMARK

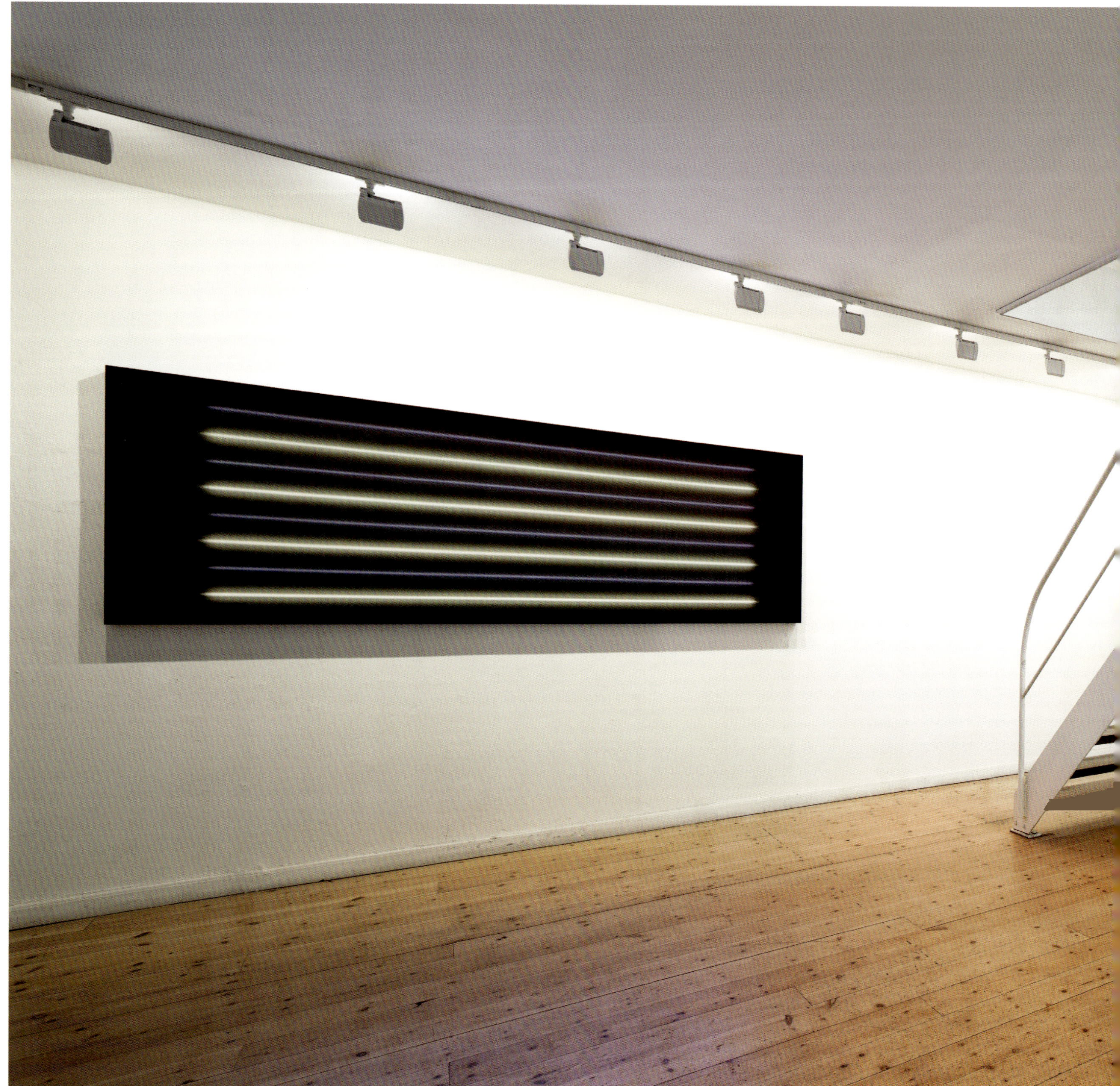

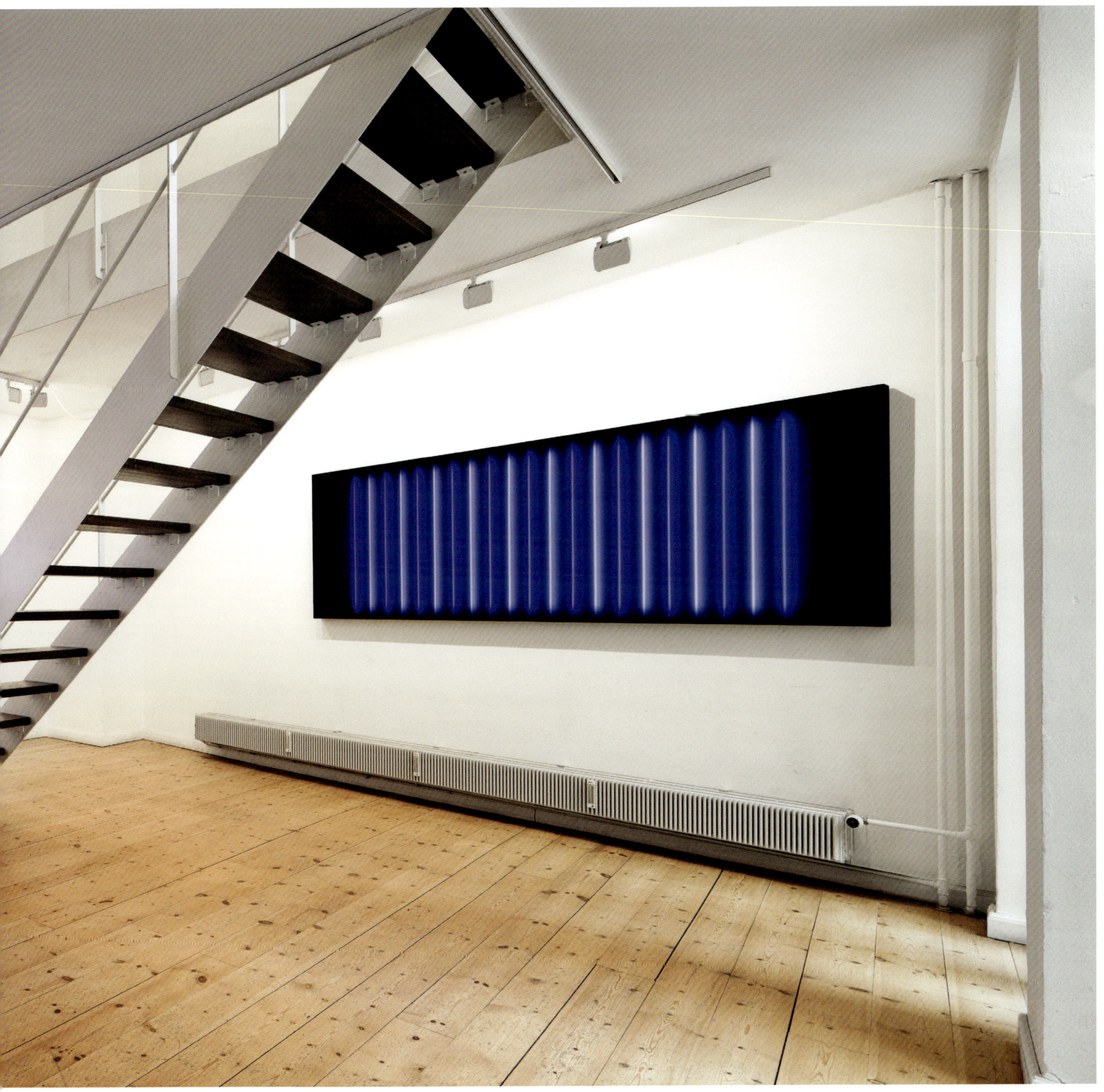

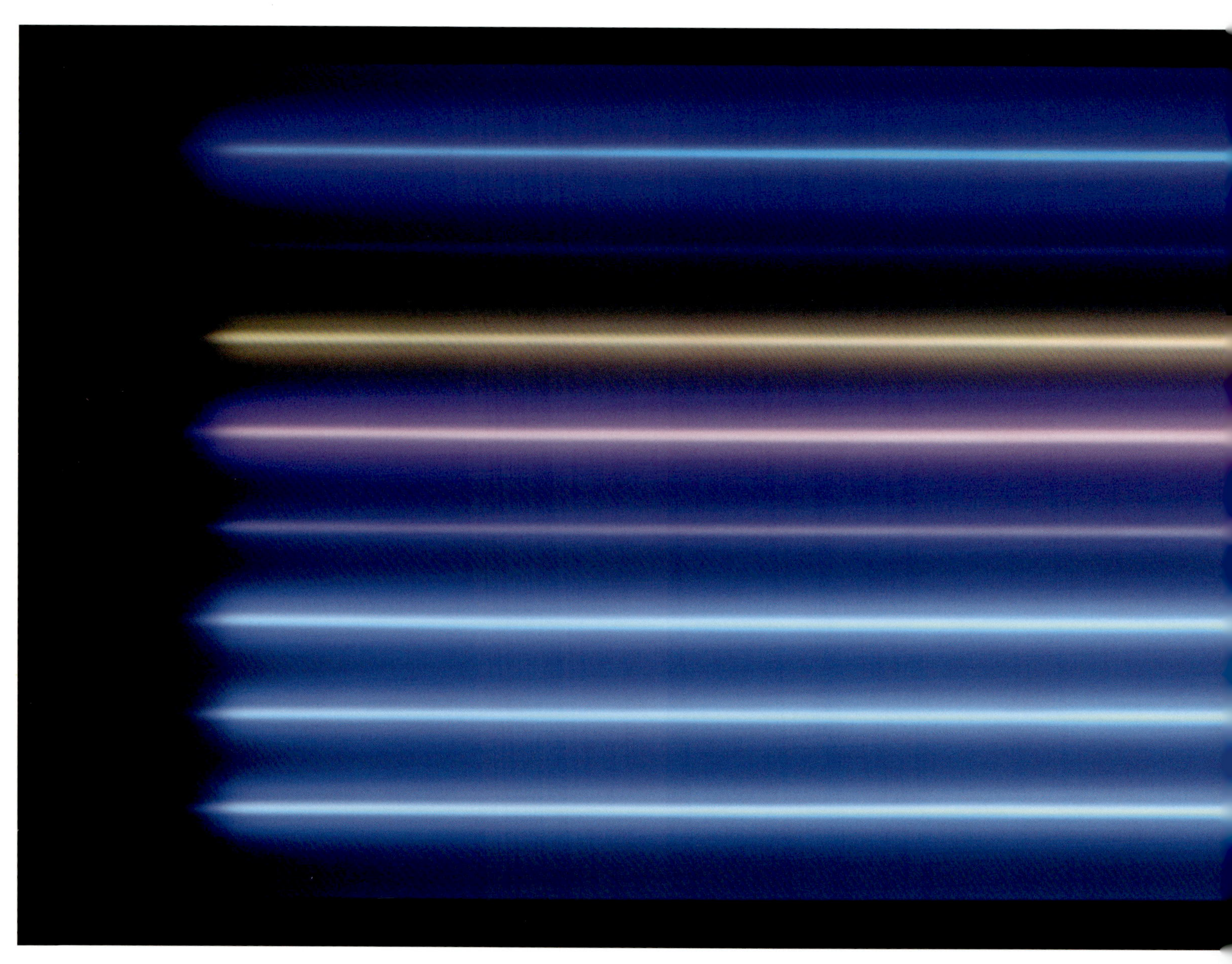

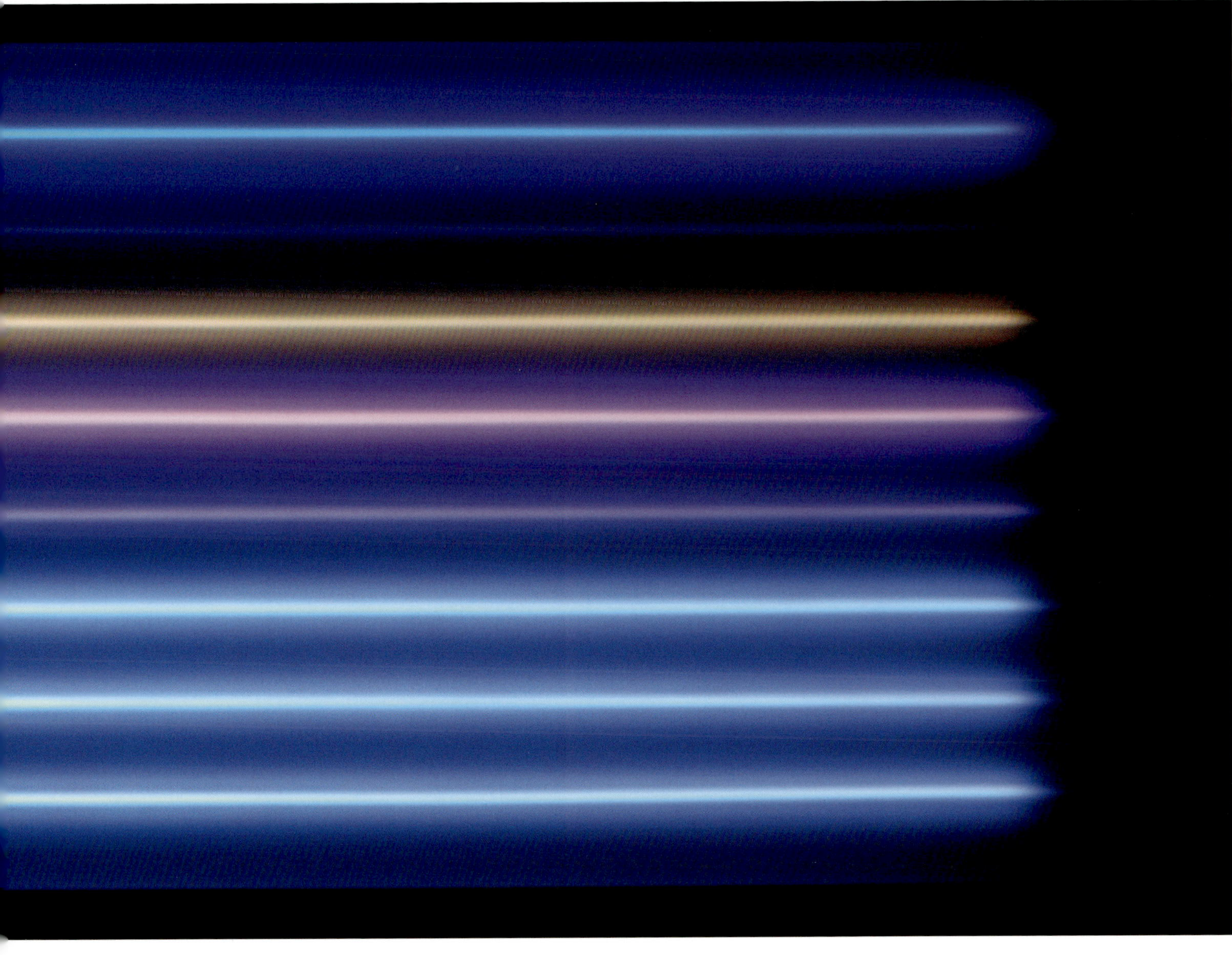

**NOMINAL EIGHT** | 300 x 100 x 8 cm
GALLERI WEINBERGER   COPENHAGEN   DENMARK

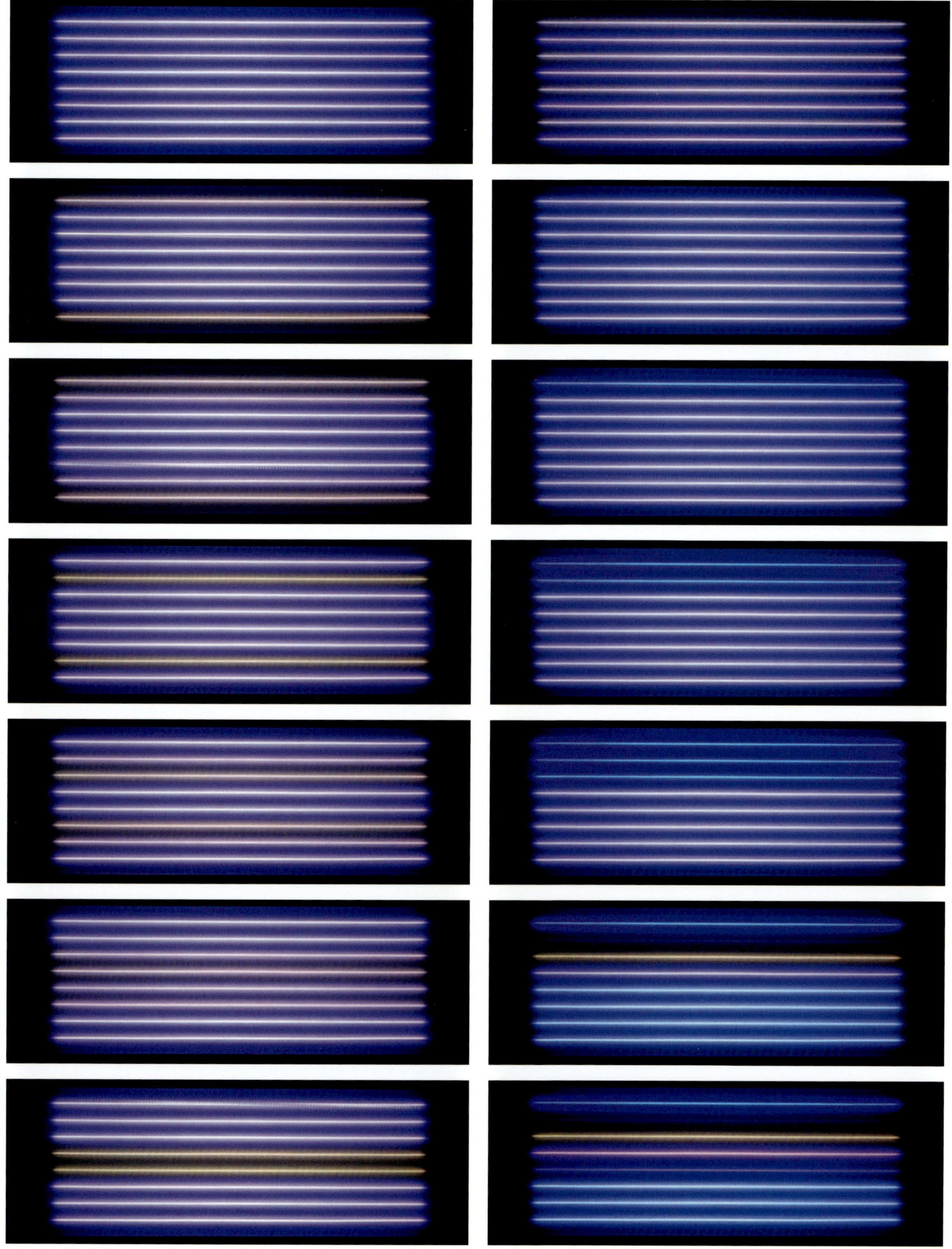

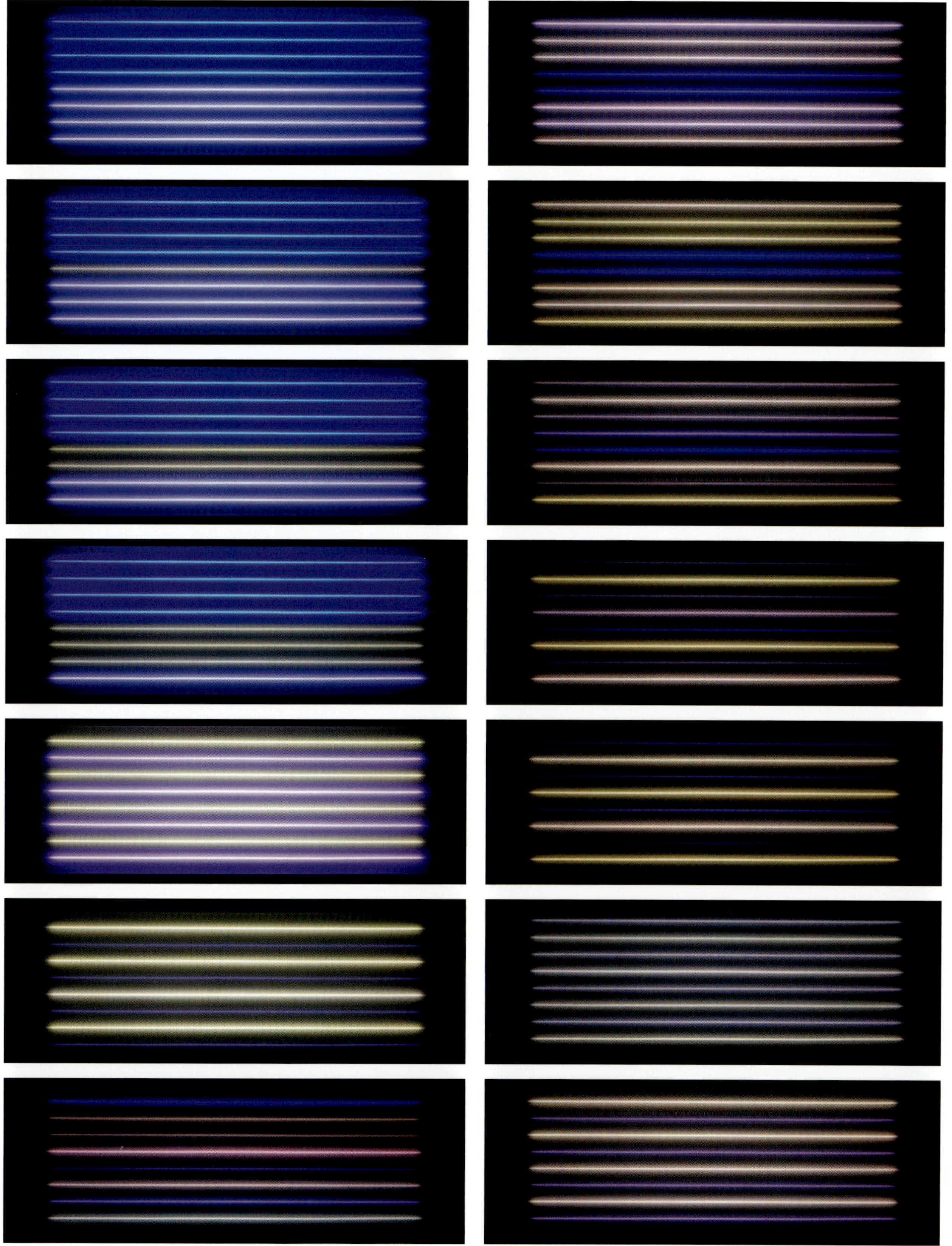

 | **LUMINOUS ICONS** 1999–2011 | SOLO EXHIBITION | LIGHT WORKS | 2011
**NOMINAL TWENTY ONE** | 300 x 100 x 8 cm
GALLERI WEINBERGER COPENHAGEN DENMARK
PRIVATE COLLECTION | DENMARK

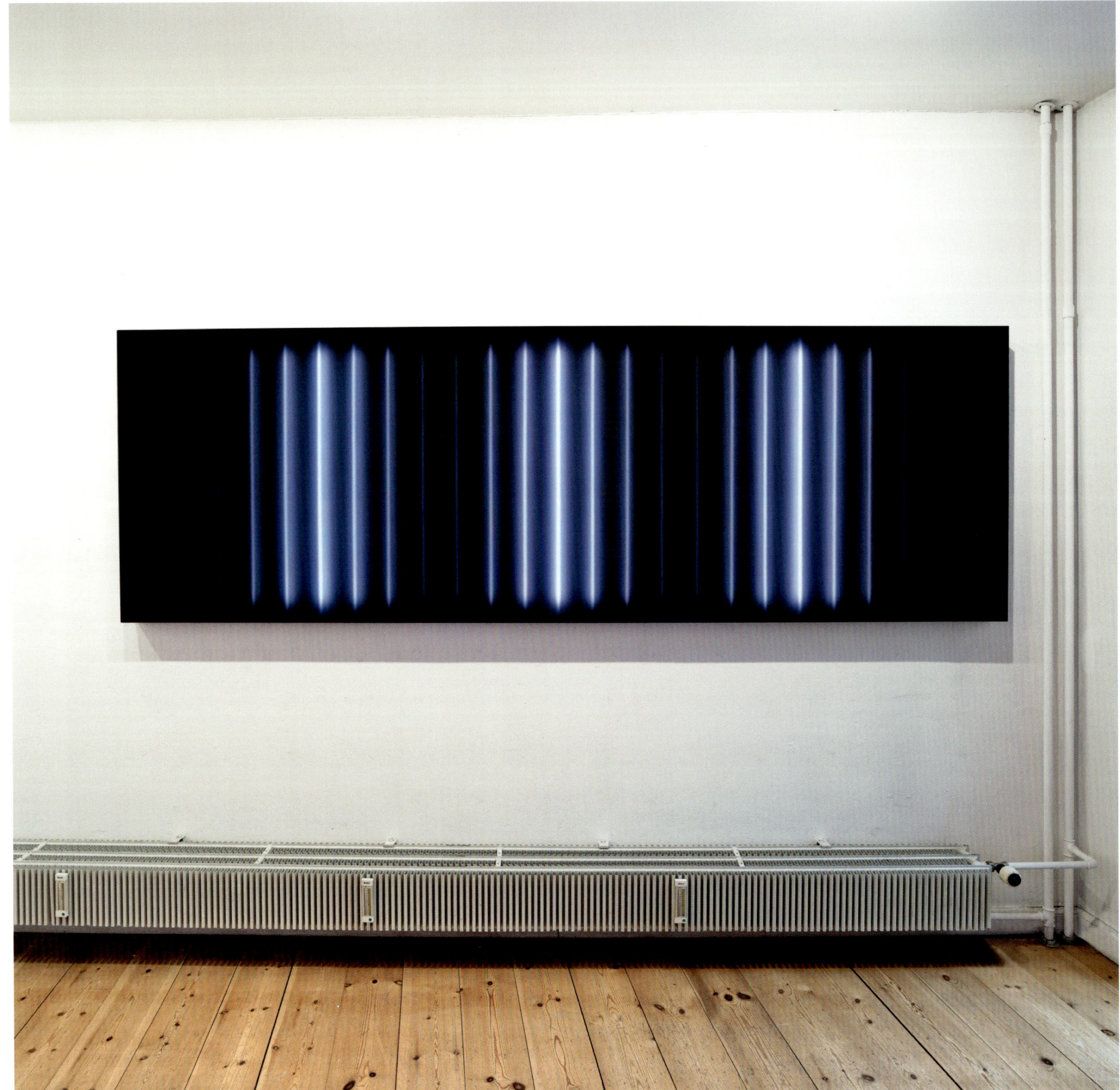

**NOMINAL TWENTY ONE** | 300 x 100 x 8 cm
GALLERI WEINBERGER COPENHAGEN DENMARK
PRIVATE COLLECTION | DENMARK

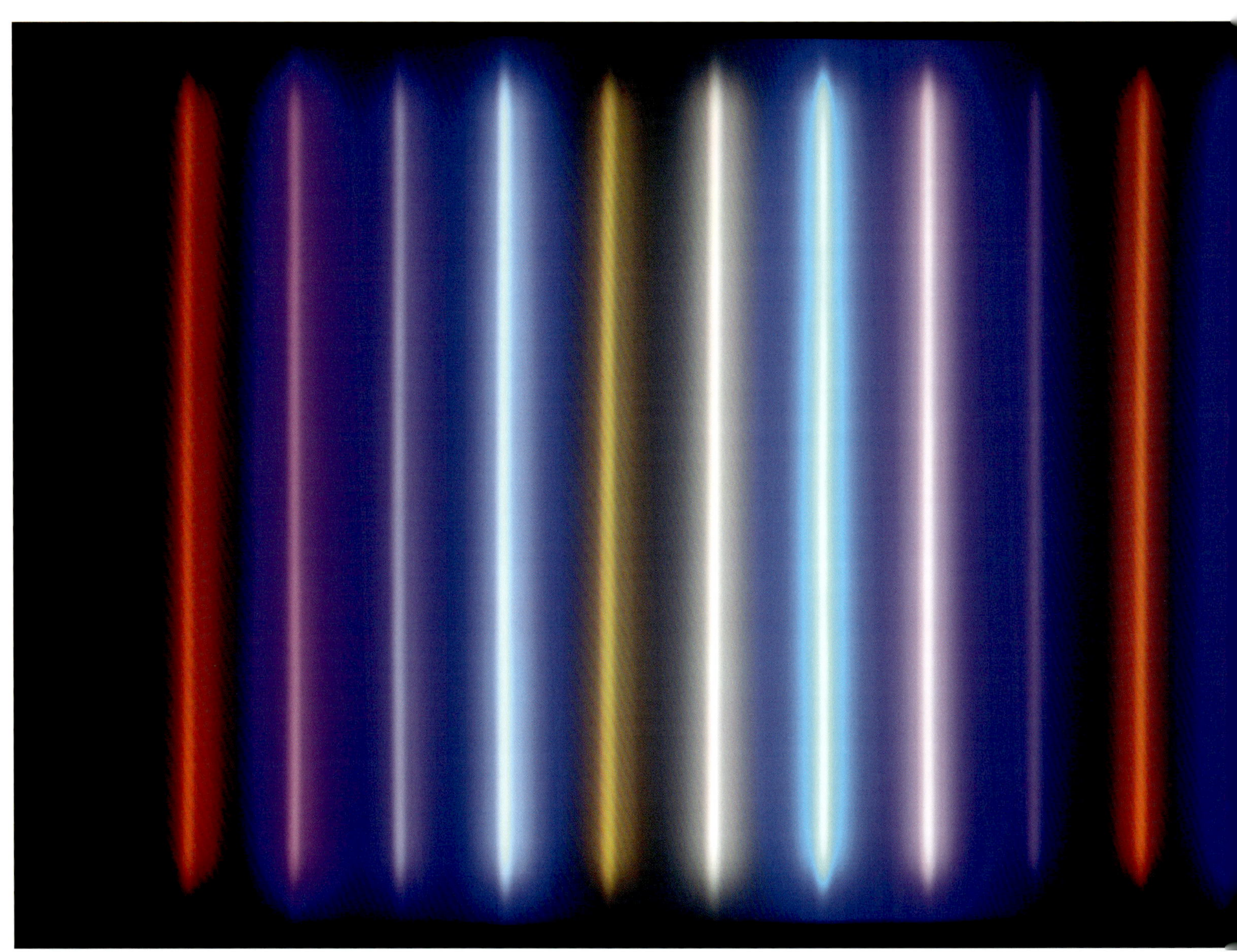

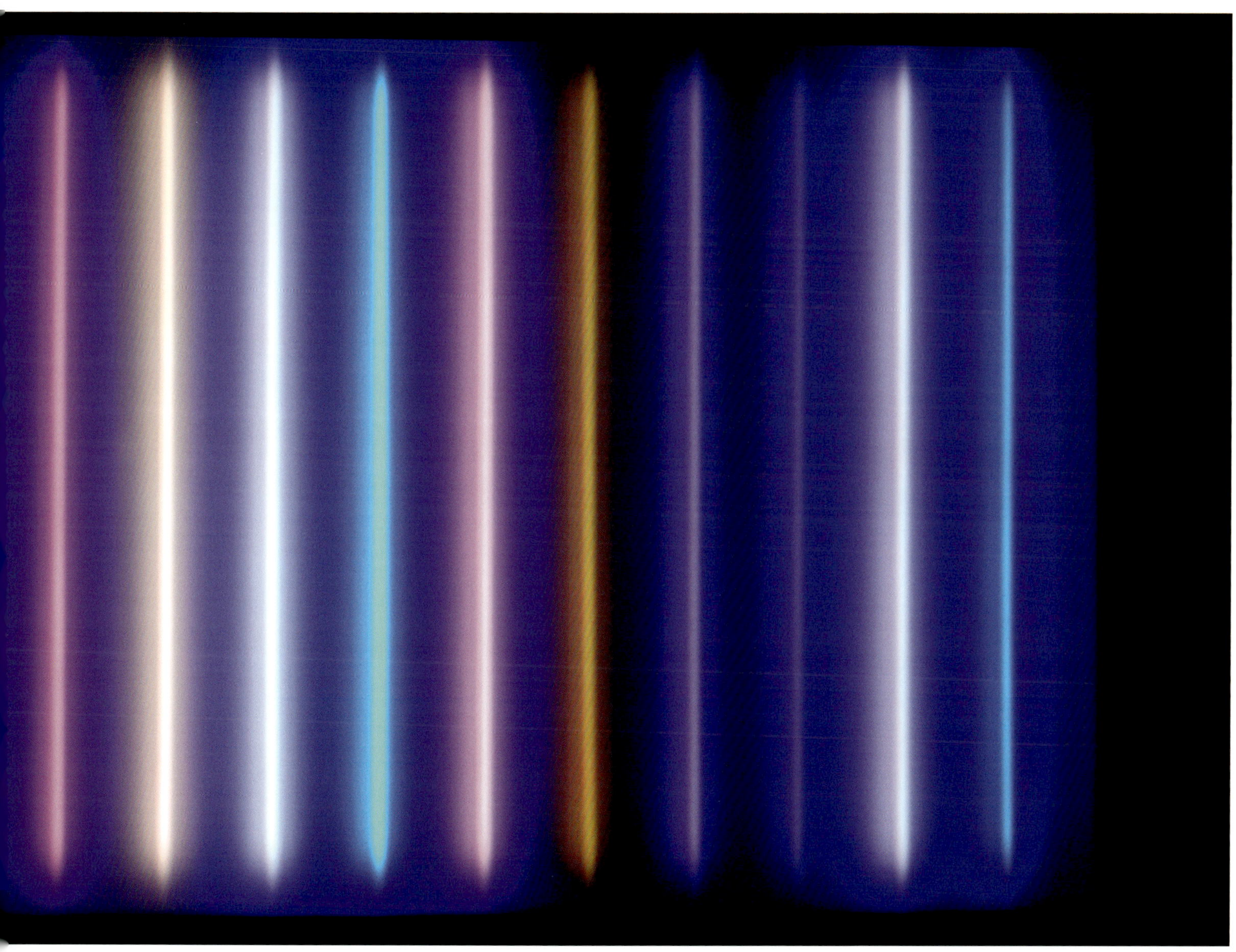

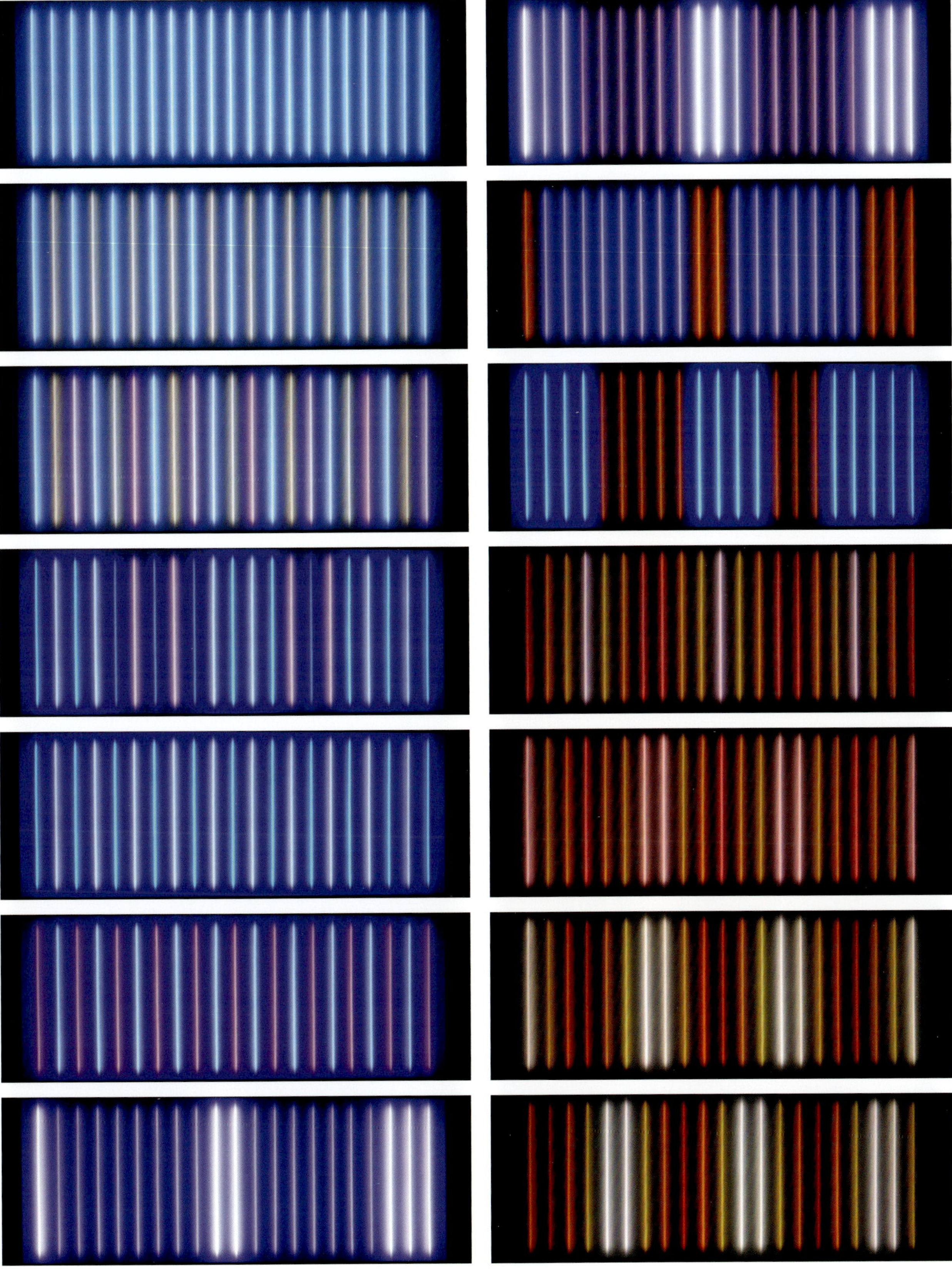

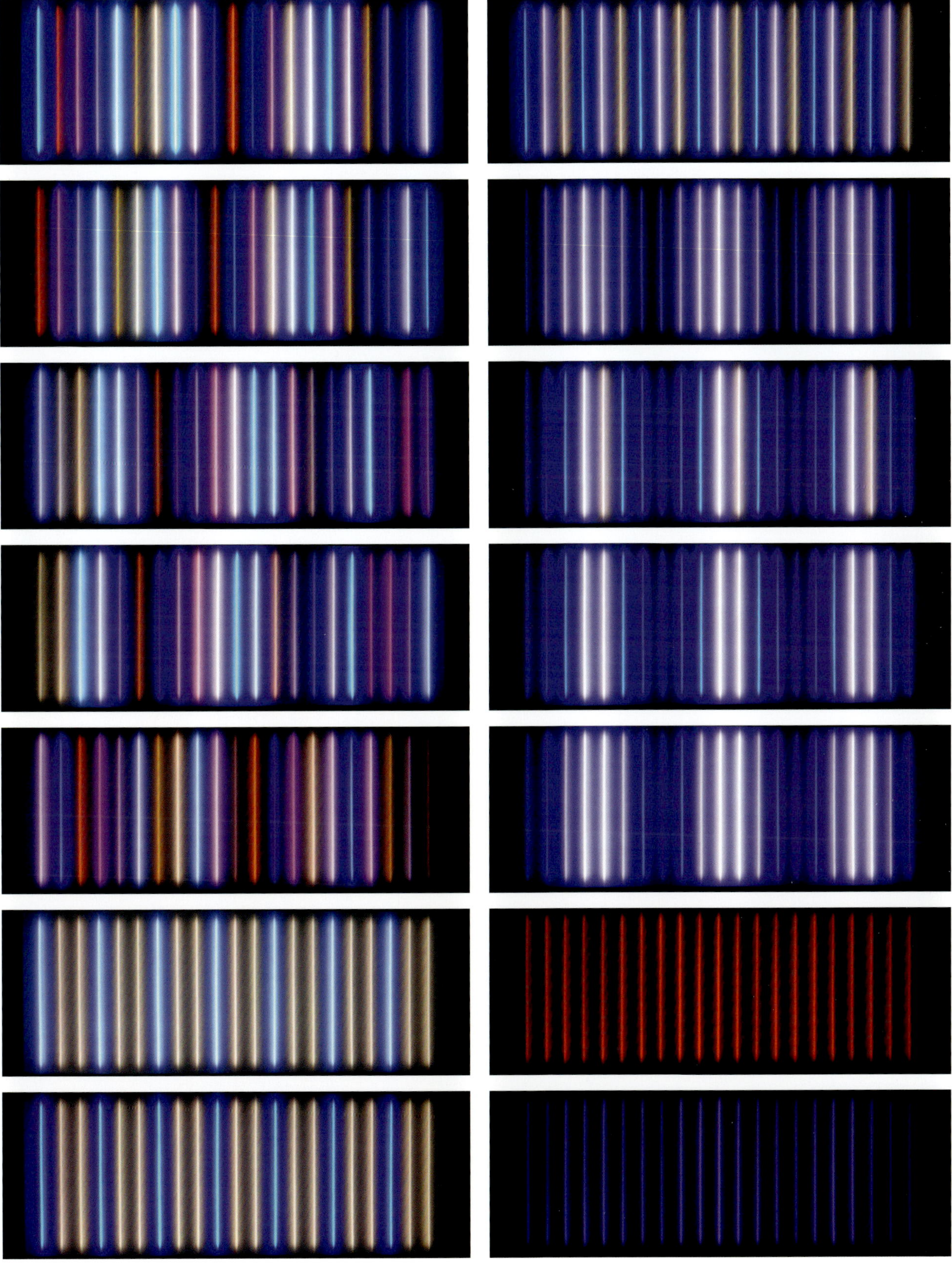

**ECSTASY ONE** | 123 x 38 x 12 cm | **ECSTASY TWO** | 123 x 38 x 12 cm
**ICON 2.1** | 49 x 37 x 8 cm | **ICON 2.0** | 49 x 37 x 8 cm
GALLERI WEINBERGER   COPENHAGEN   DENMARK
PRIVATE AND PUBLIC COLLECTIONS IN DENMARK AND SWEDEN

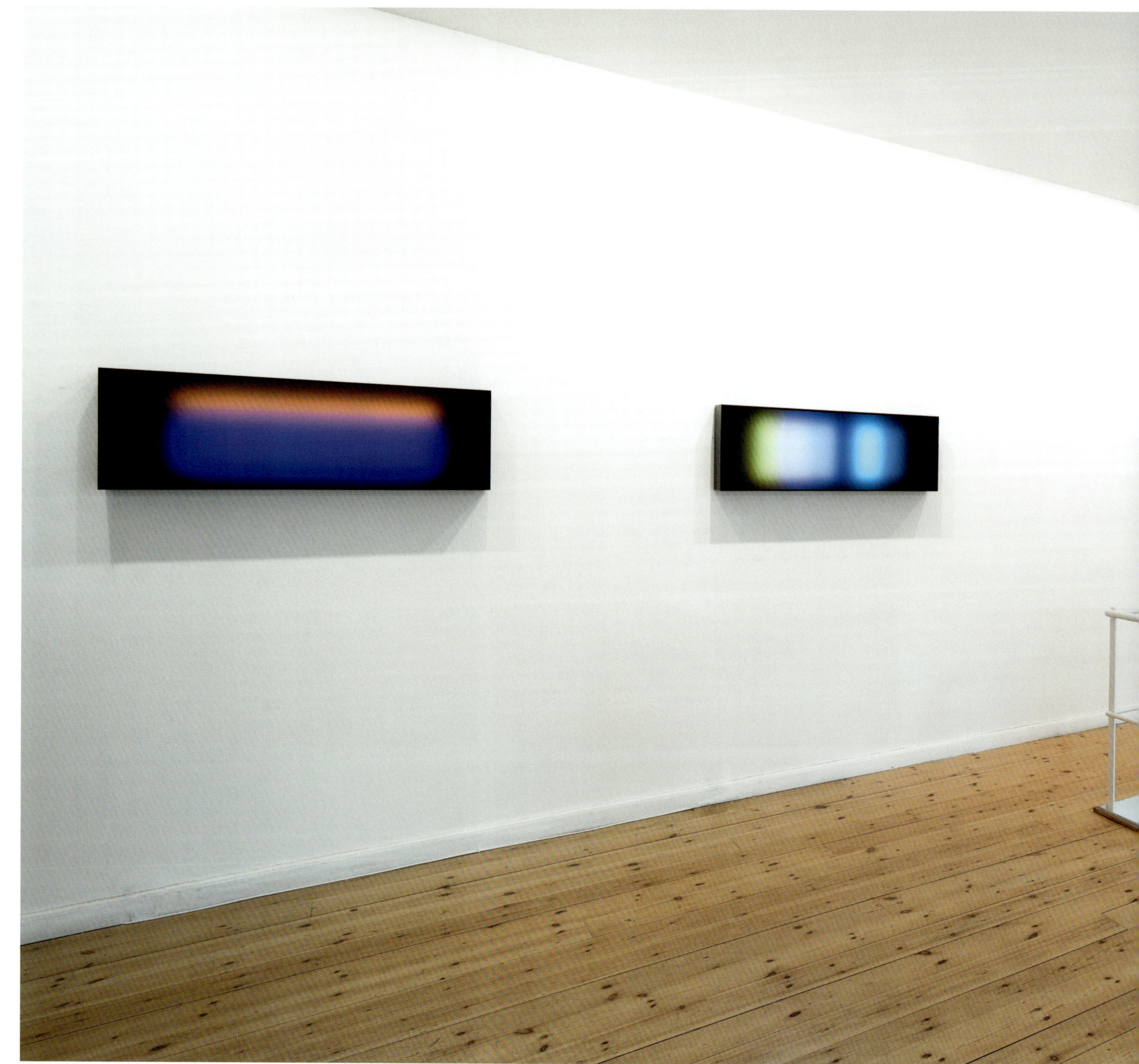

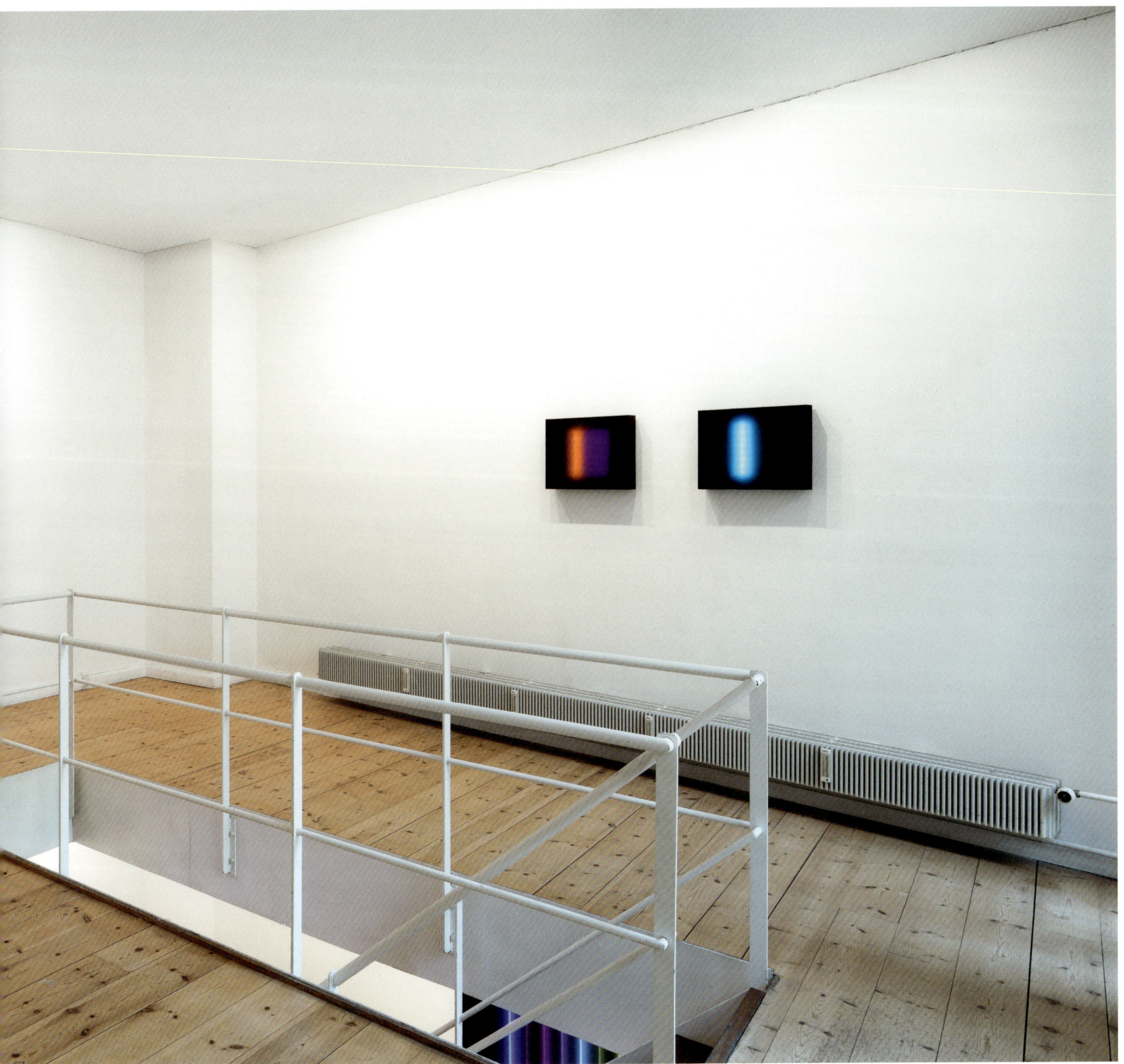

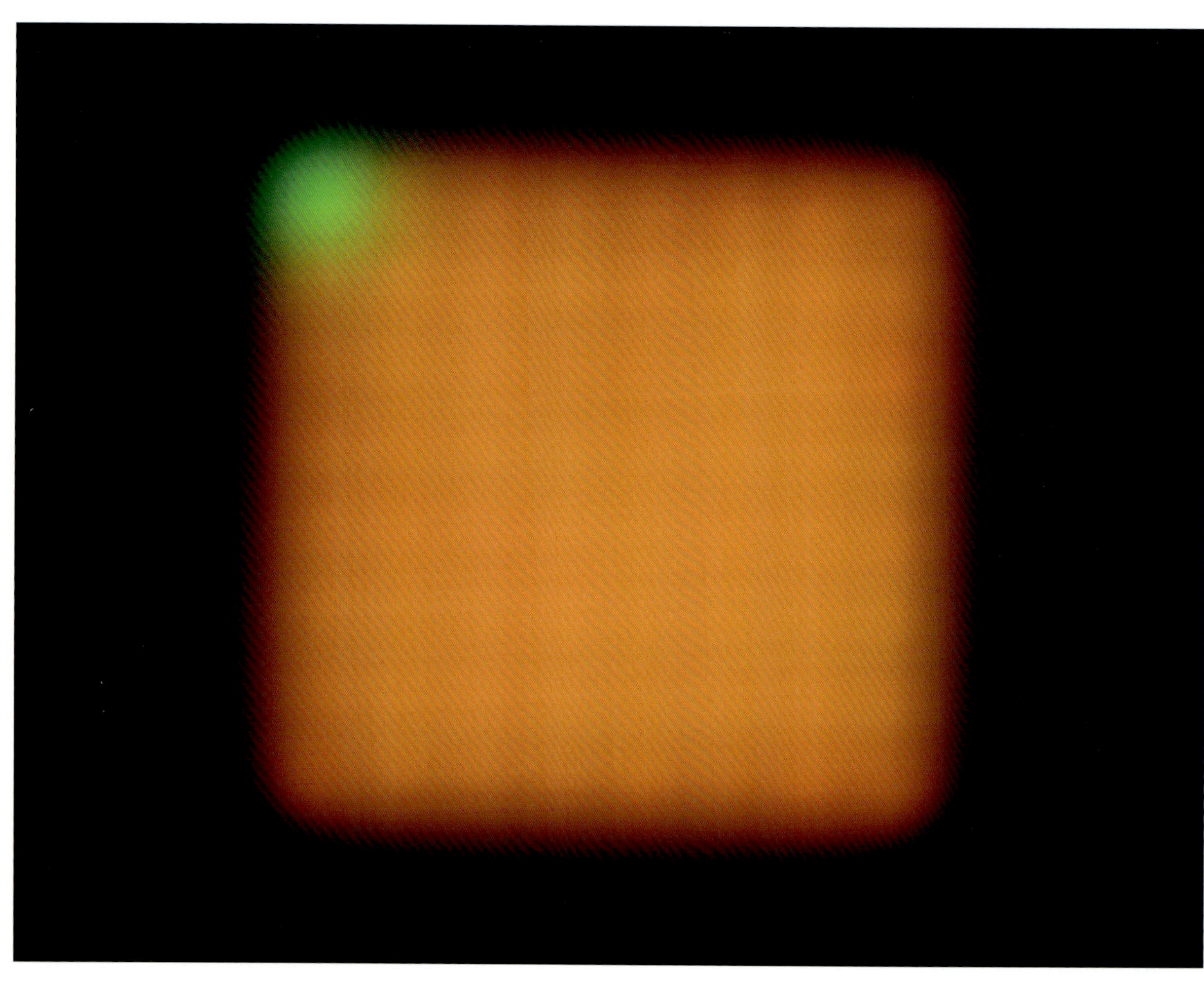

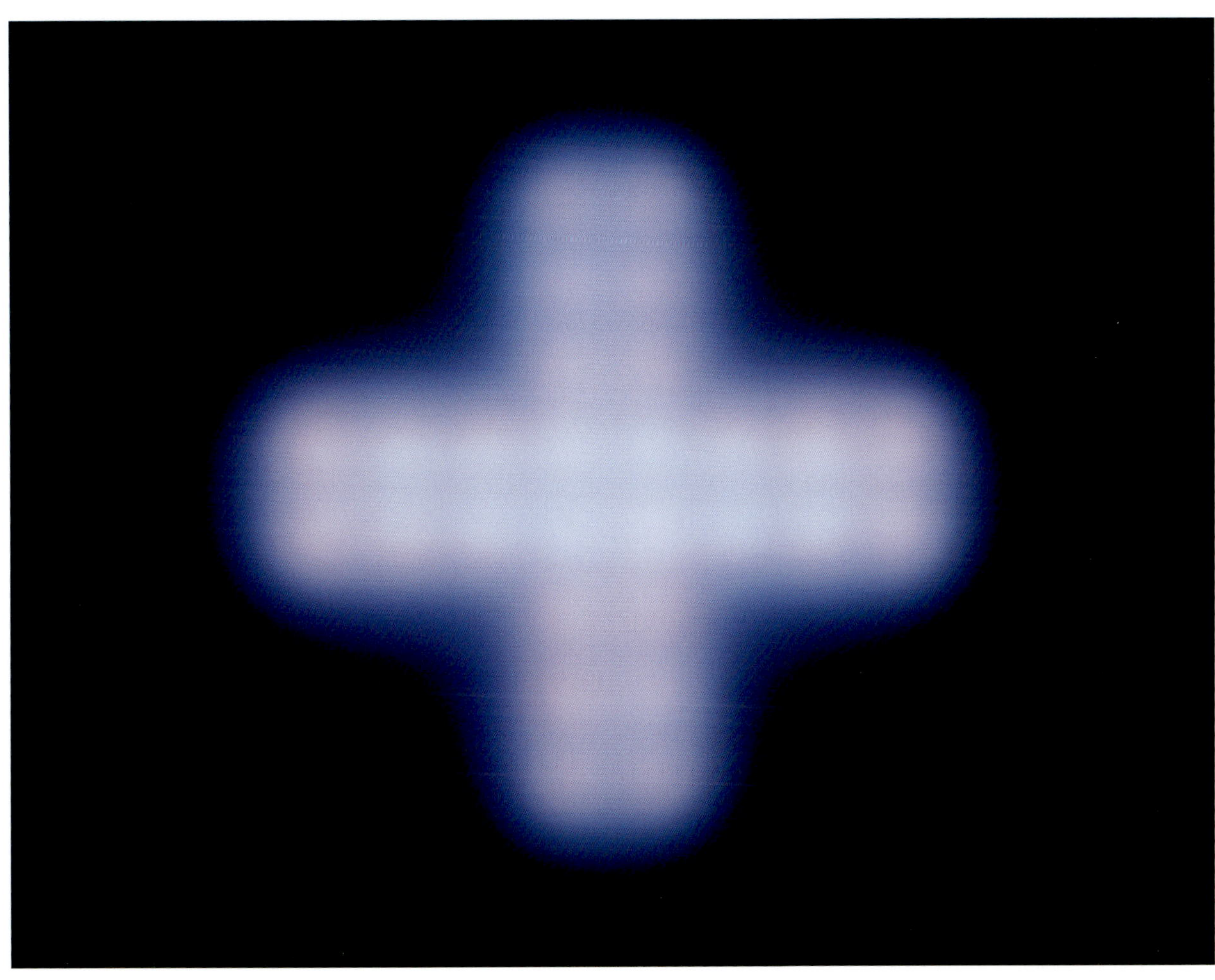

**ICON 2.0** | 49 x 37 x 8 cm
GALLERI WEINBERGER  COPENHAGEN  DENMARK

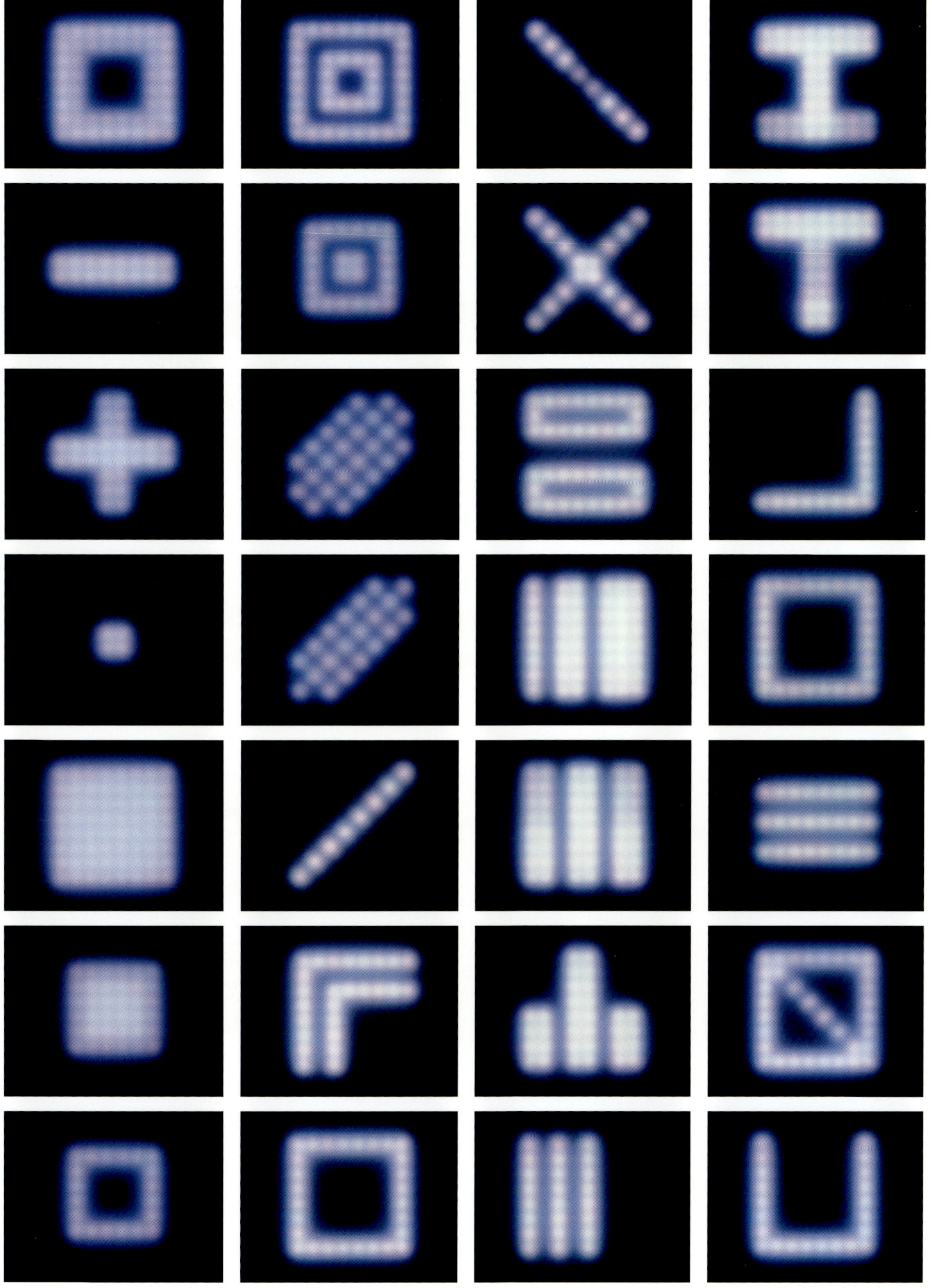

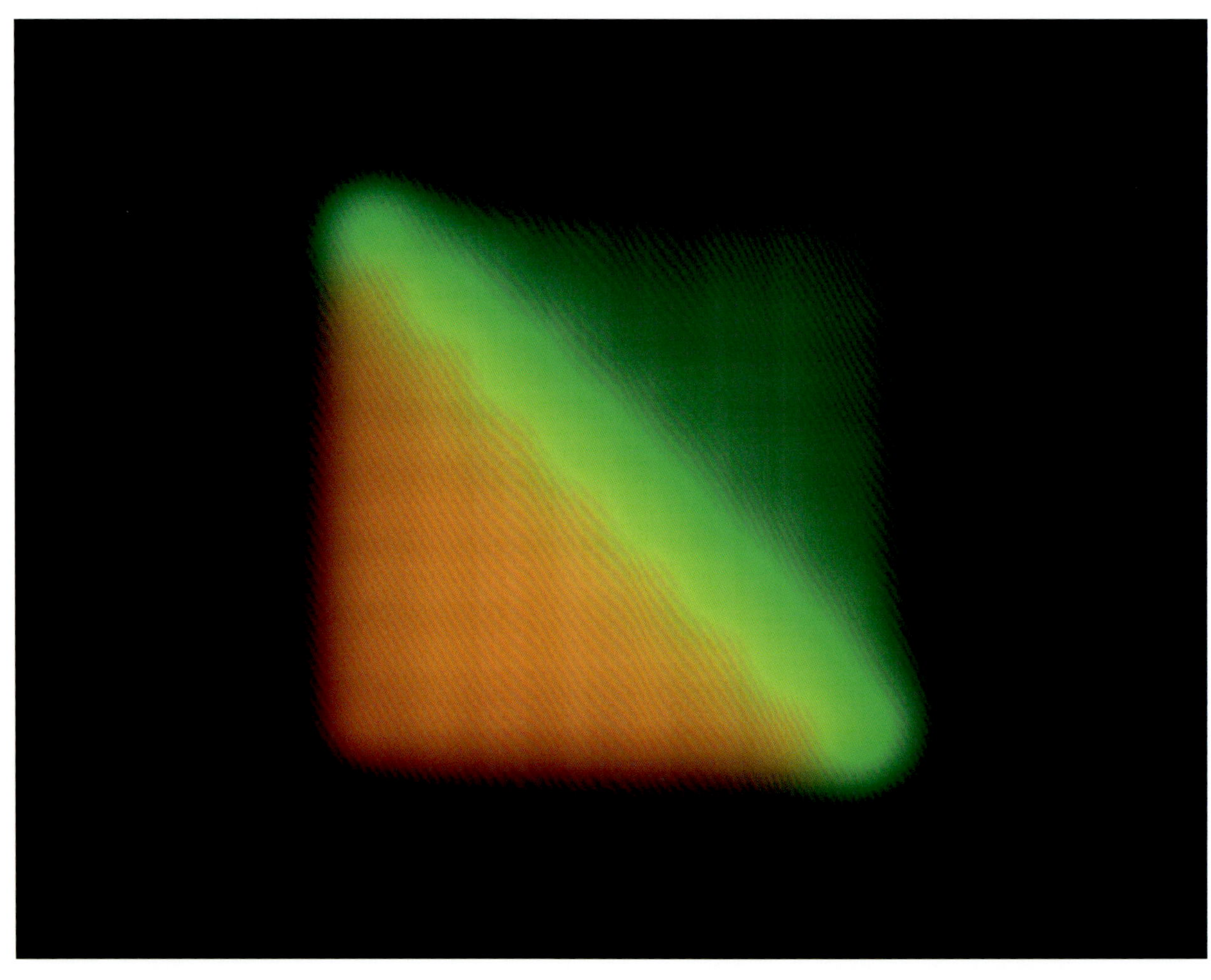

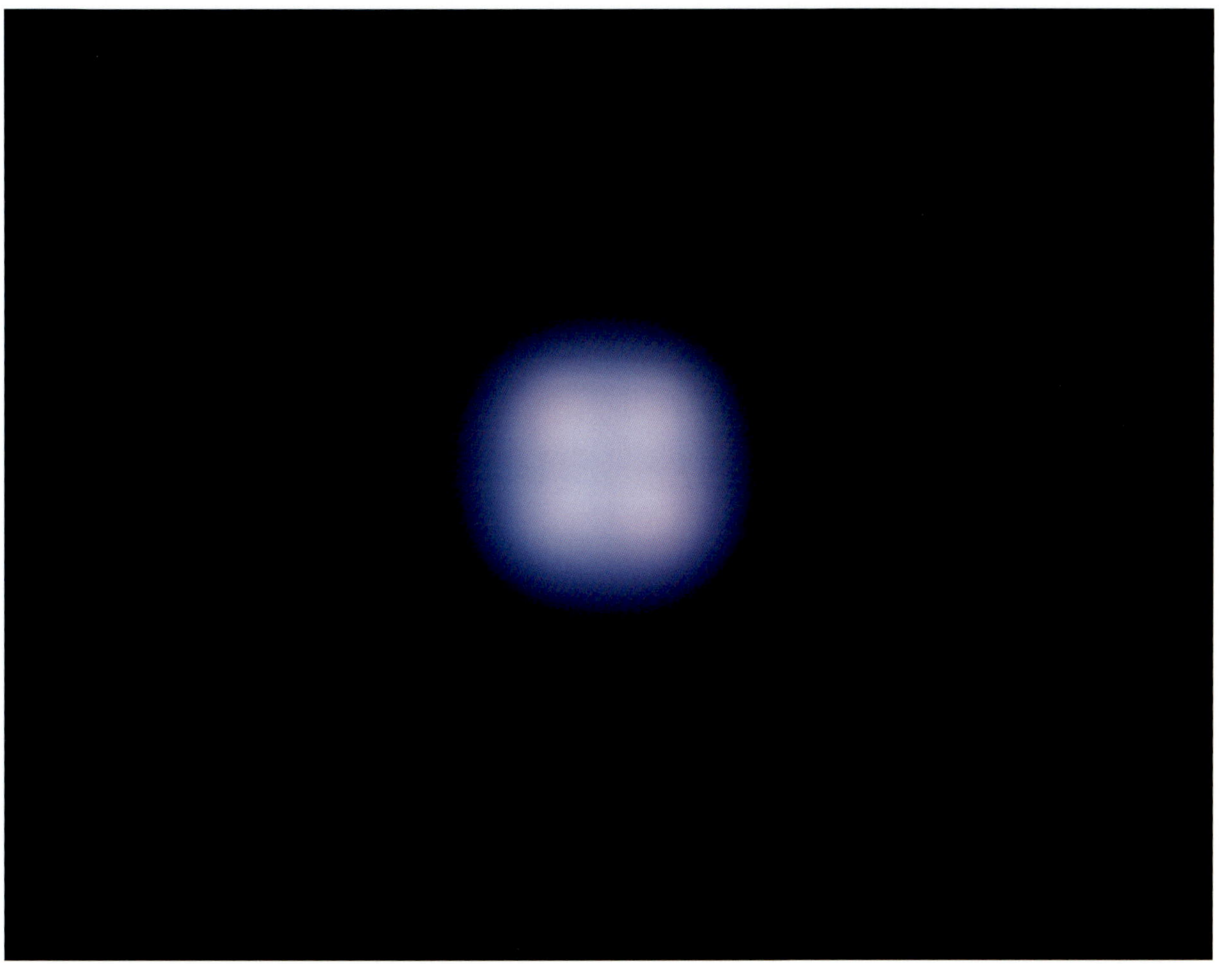

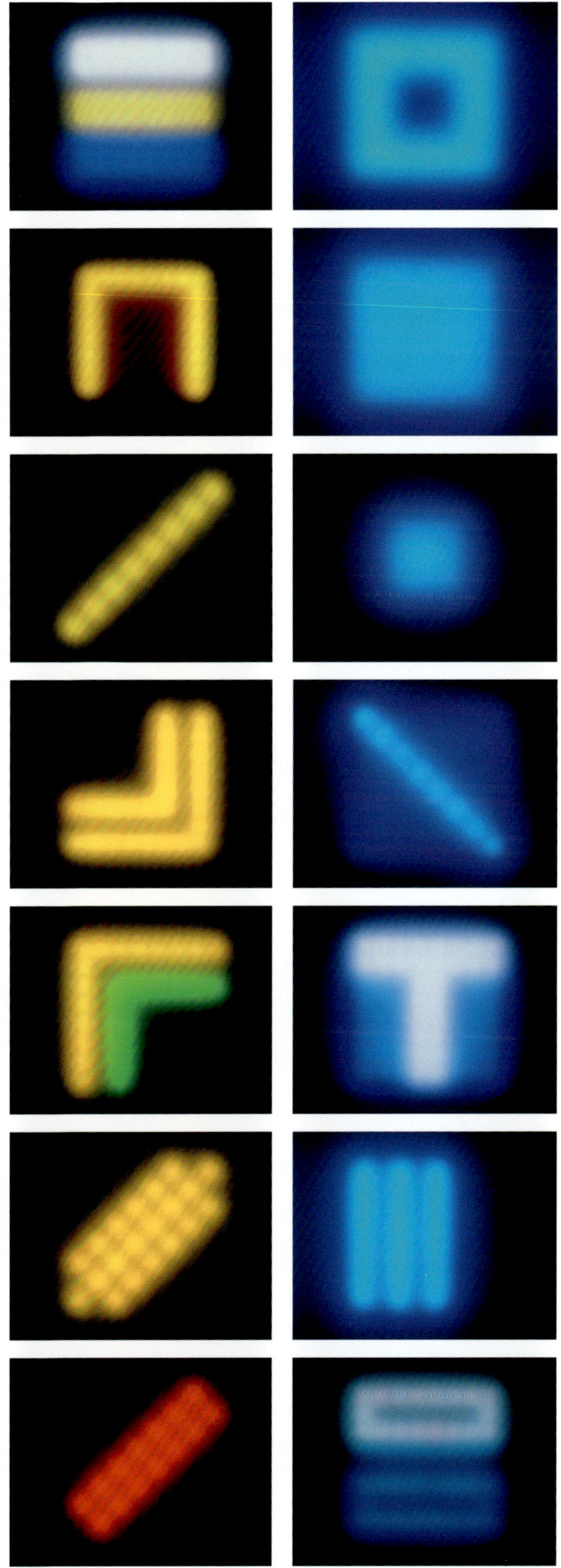

**ECSTASY ONE** | 123 x 38 x 12 cm | **ECSTASY TWO** | 123 x 38 x 12 cm
GALLERI WEINBERGER   COPENHAGEN   DENMARK
ECSTASY TWO PUBLIC COLLECTION SWEDEN

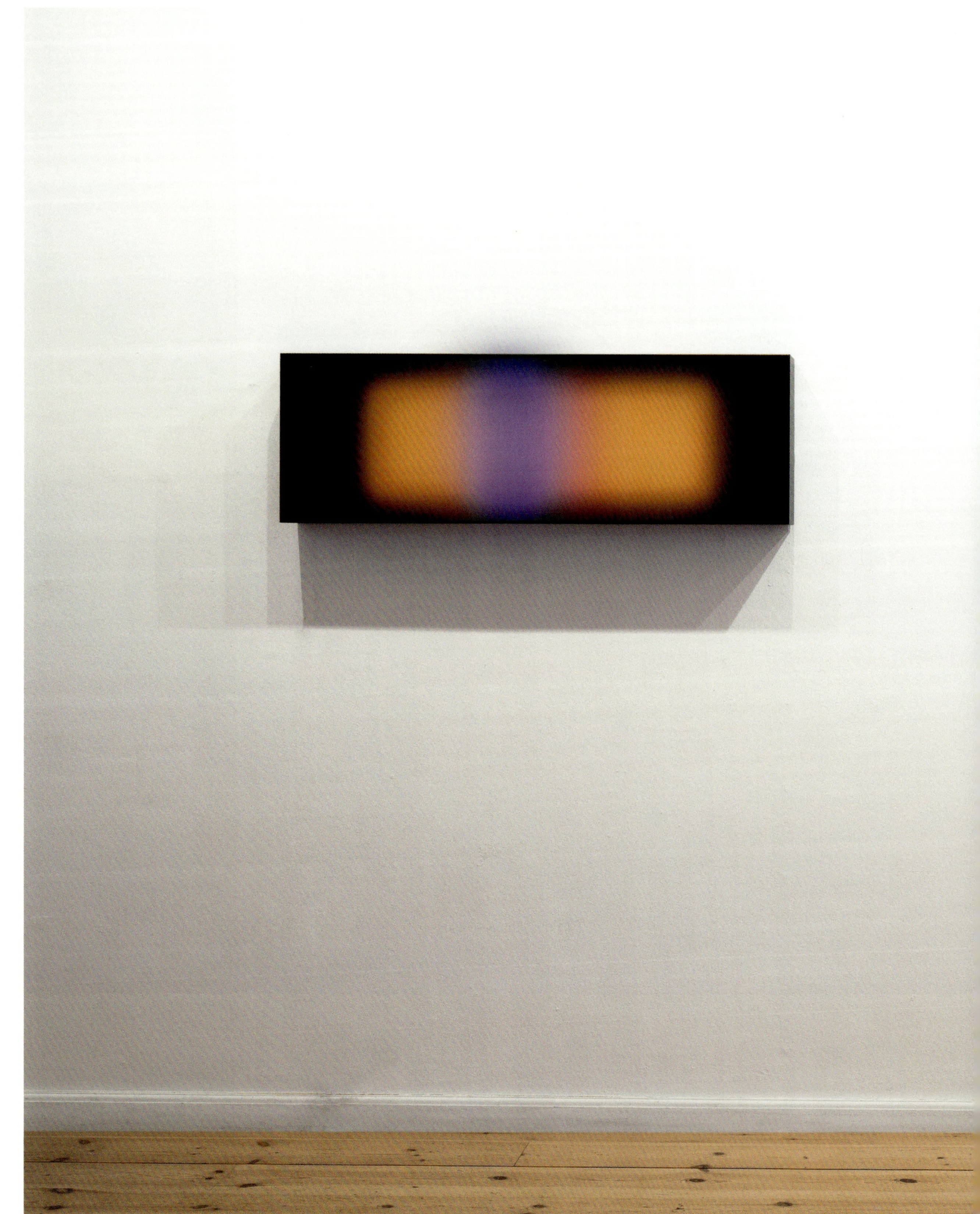

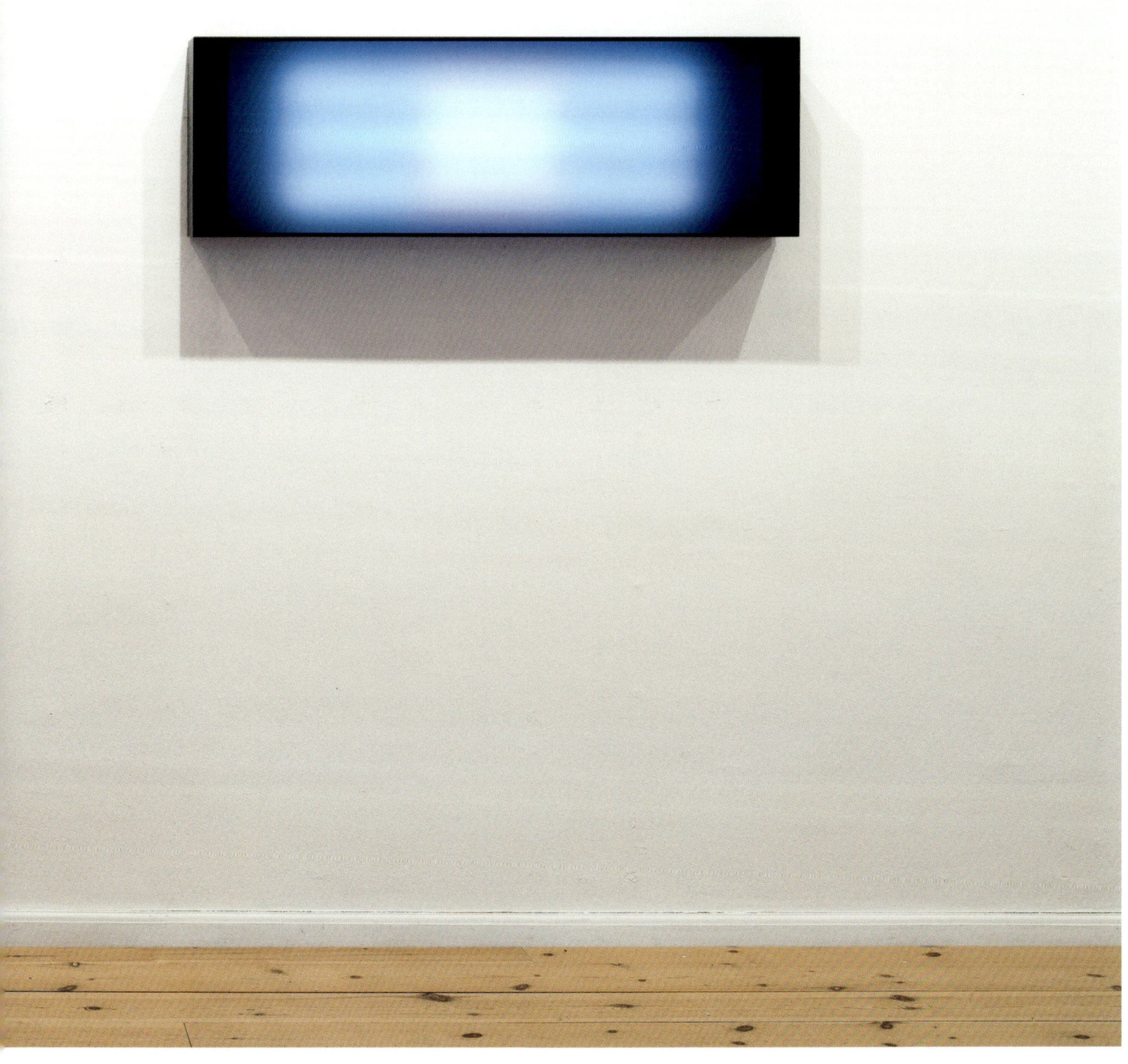

**ECSTASY ONE** | 123 x 38 x 12 cm
GALLERI WEINBERGER   COPENHAGEN   DENMARK

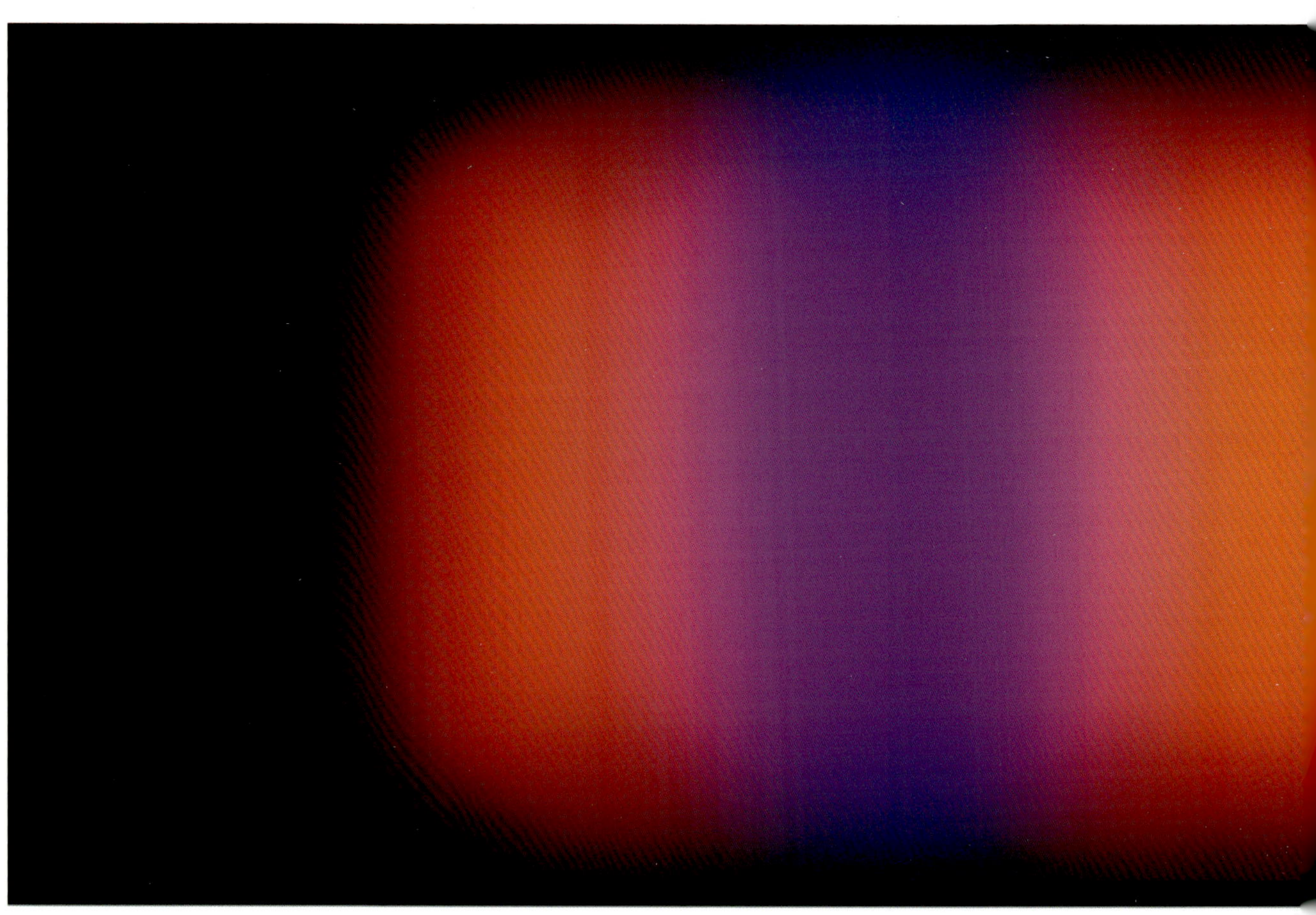

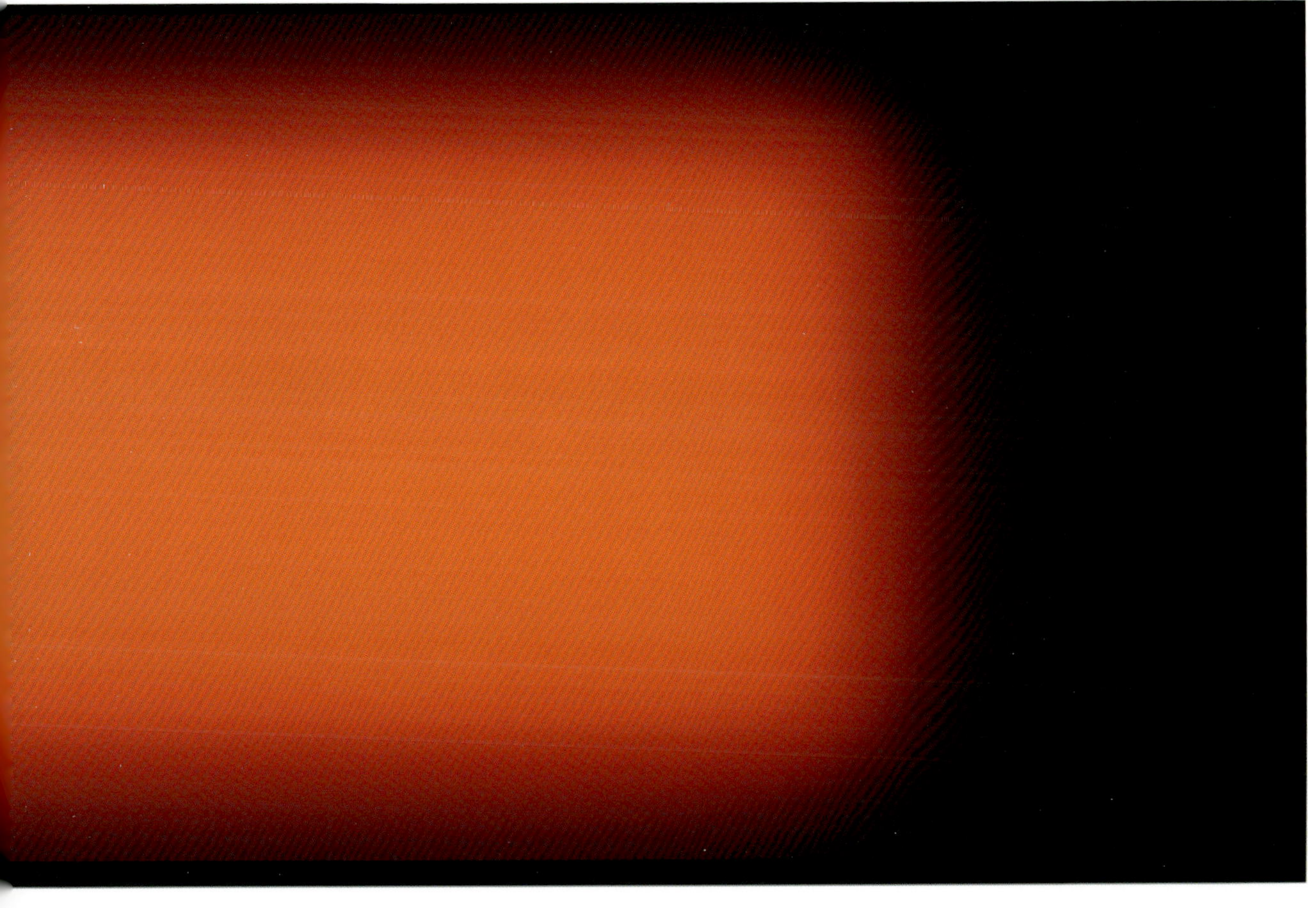

**ECSTASY ONE** | 123 x 38 x 12 cm

GALLERI WEINBERGER   COPENHAGEN   DENMARK

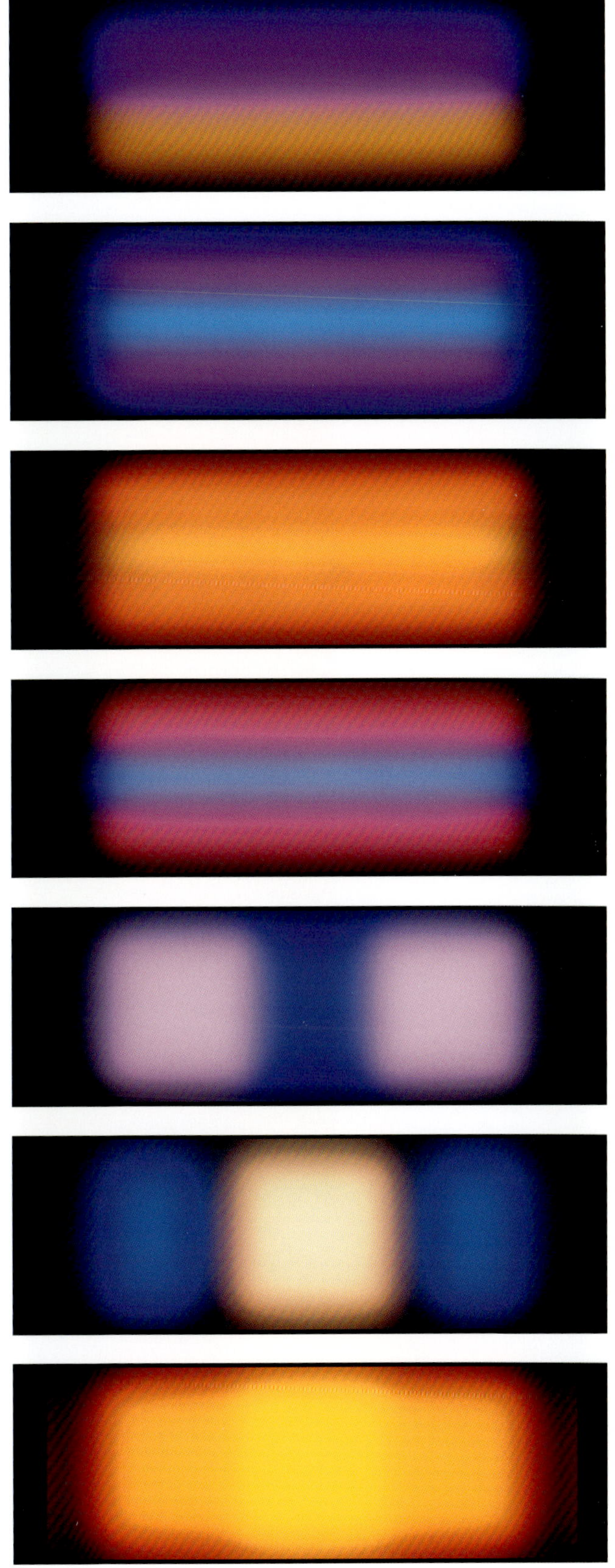

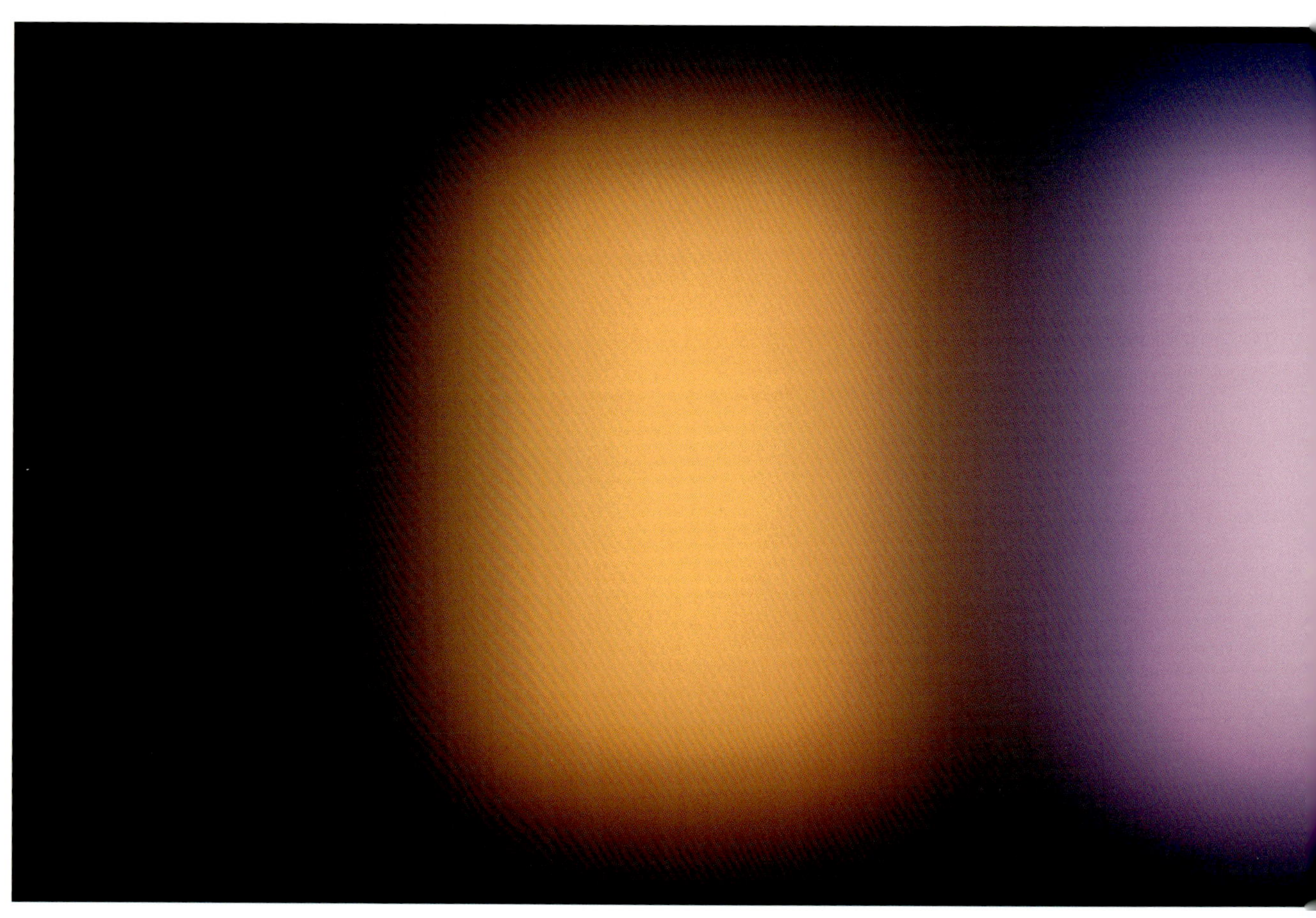

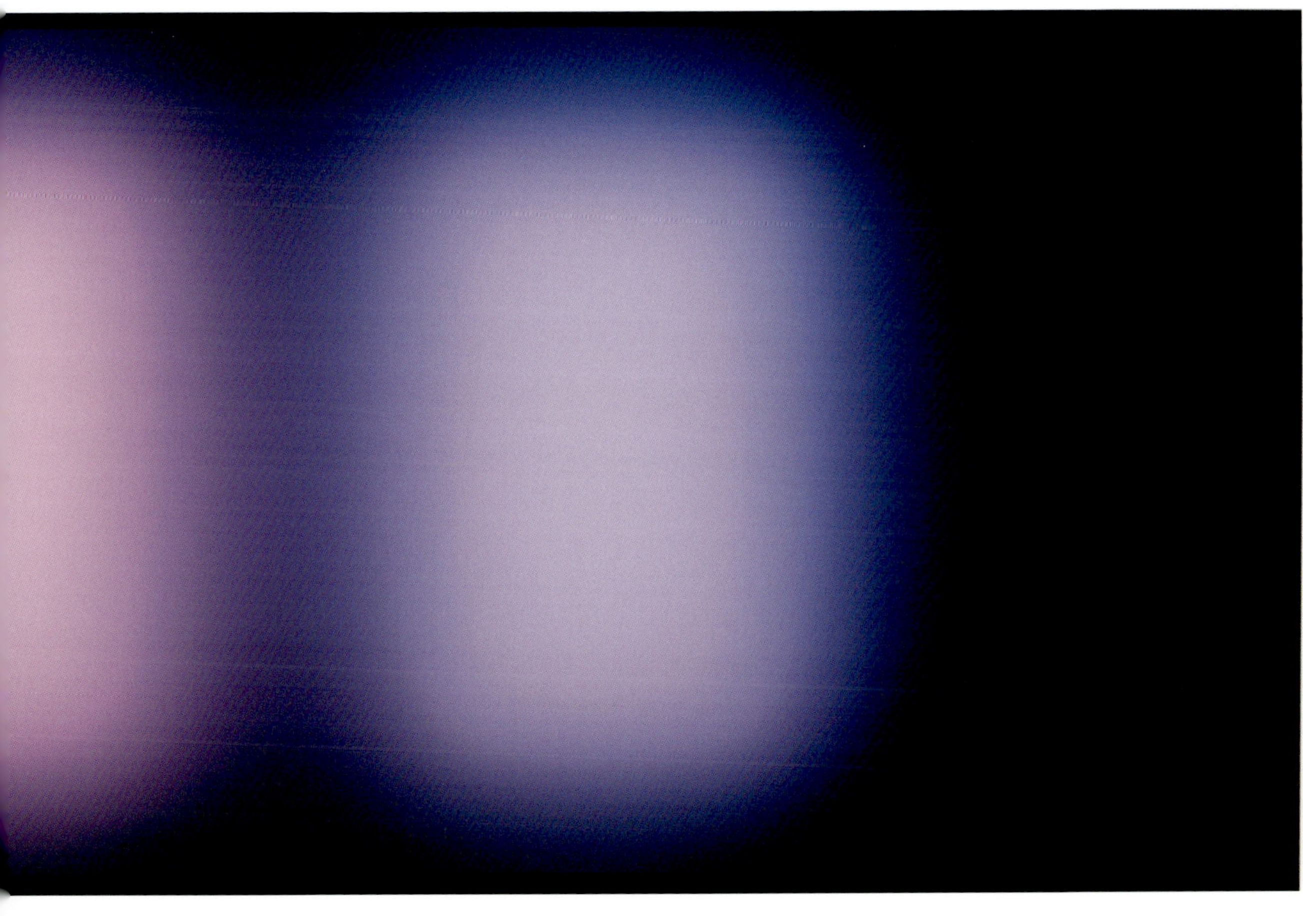

**ECSTASY TWO** | 123 x 38 x 12 cm
GALLERI WEINBERGER    COPENHAGEN    DENMARK
ECSTASY TWO PUBLIC COLLECTION SWEDEN

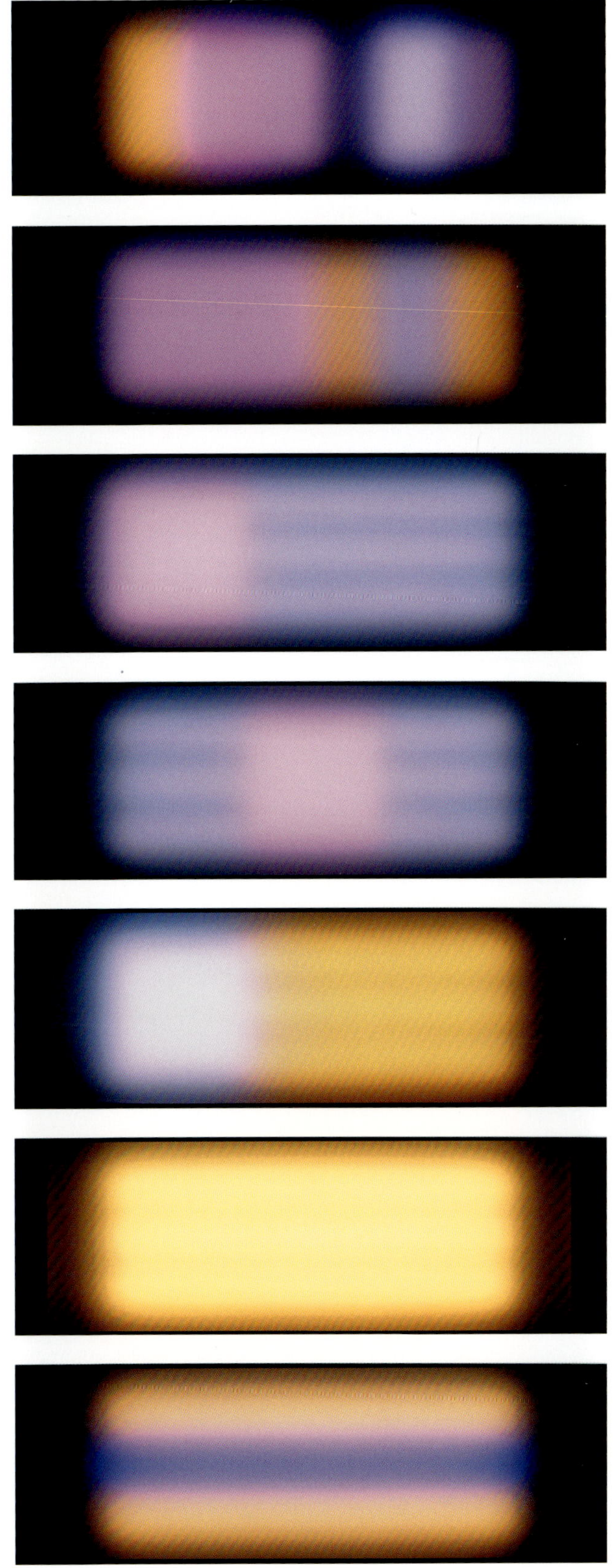

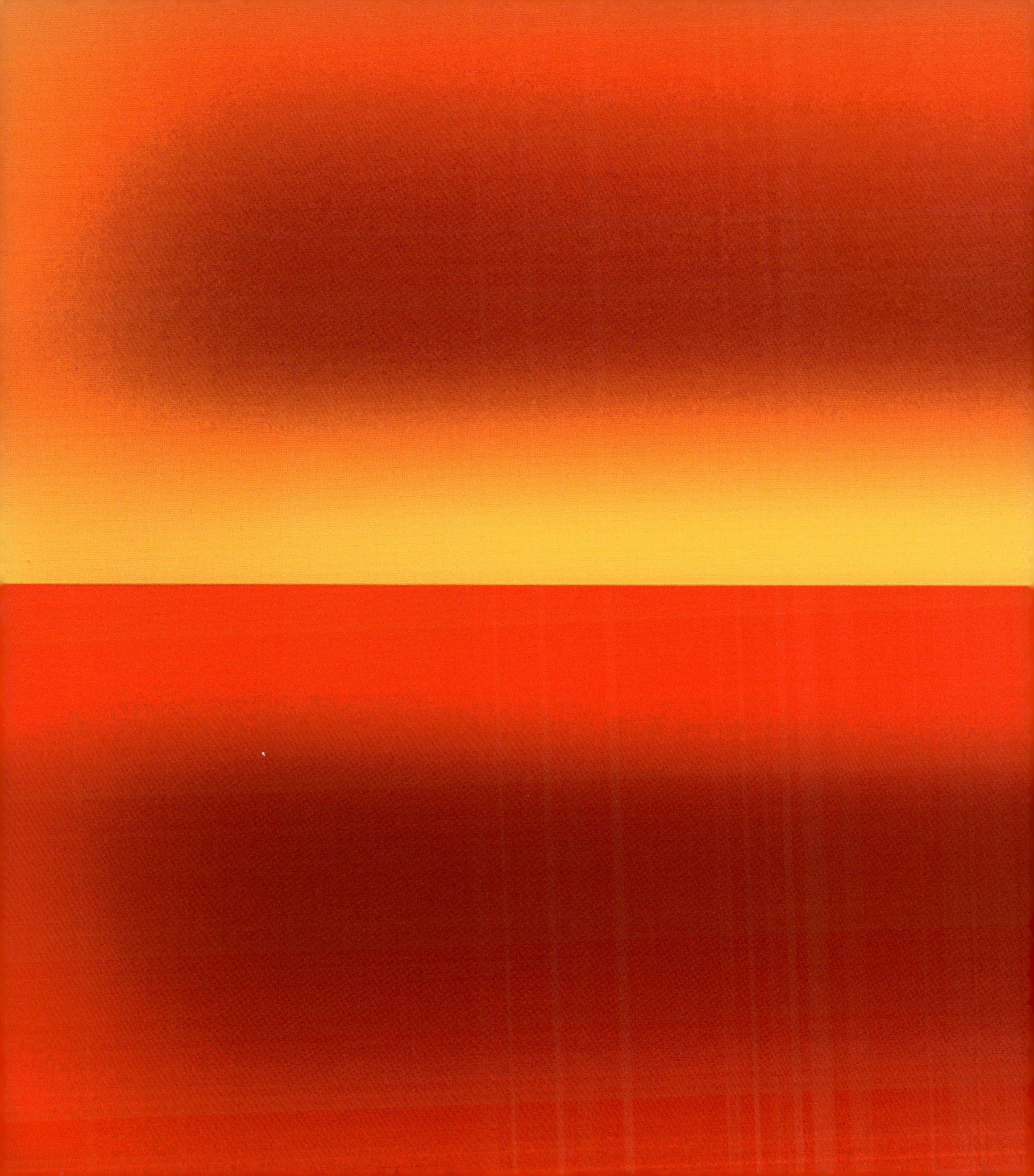

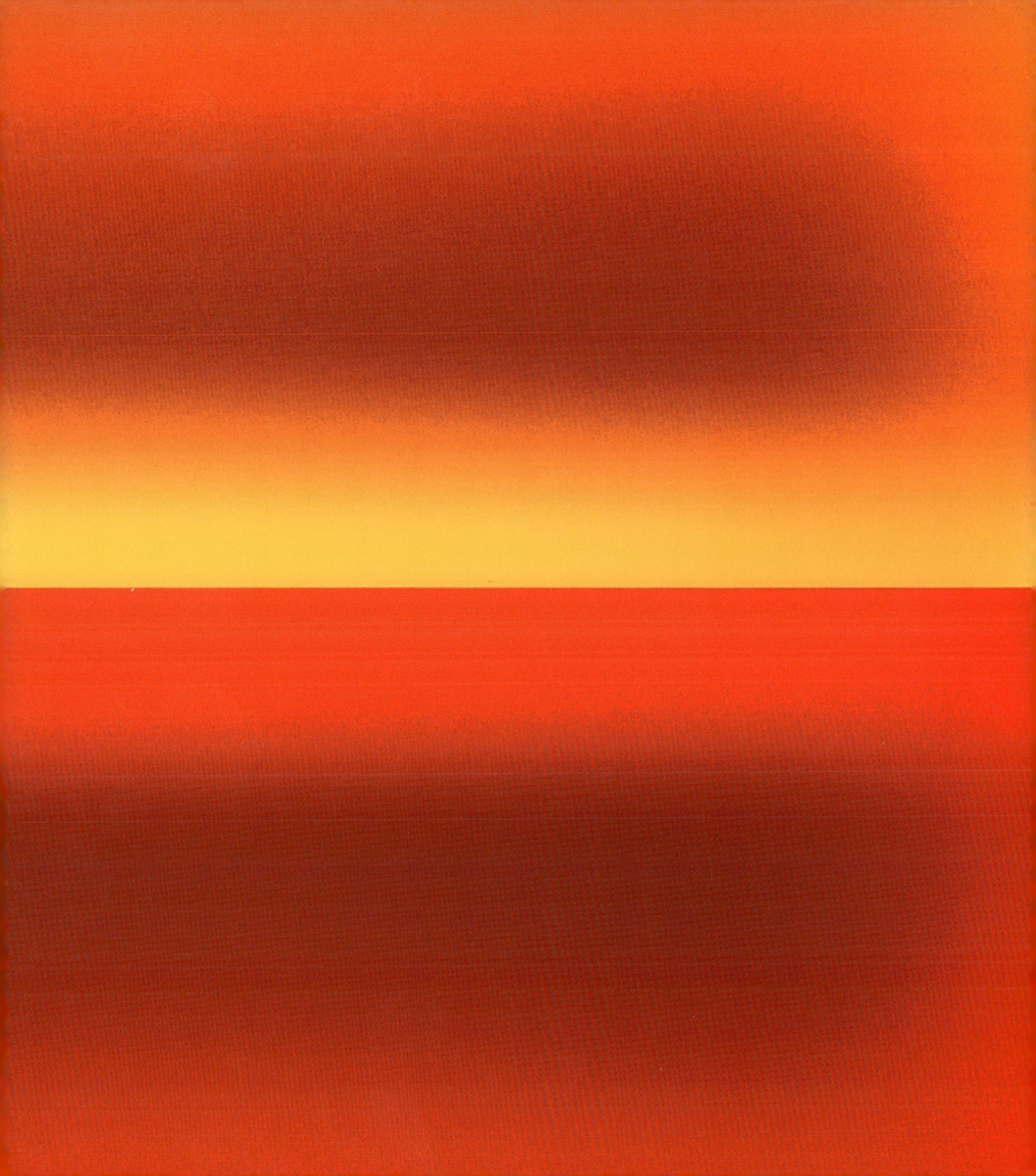

LUMINOUS ICONS PART THREE
# ROBERT C. MORGAN
LIGHT WORKS IN PUBLIC SPACES

**LIGHT ARTIST, INDUSTRIAL DESIGNER AND ARCHITECTURAL CONSULTANT,** Steven Scott functions on many levels simultaneously. In keeping with new developments in the global frontier that involve all three functions, Scott is an artist interested in enhancing the quality of life in the twenty-first century through applications of advanced technologies that directly affect environmental concerns. Over the past twelve years, he has evolved from working as a painter and former theatre designer towards producing various forms of kinetic light installations for use in both domestic settings and public architecture. In addition to his role as an artist, Scott has designed and developed a system of solar-powered masts that absorb energy in daylight and transform into street lights in the evening, thereby enhancing the appearance and development of urban spaces. In doing so, he has created illumination both carbon-free in terms of atmospheric effects and cost-effective in relying on external electrical power. In addition to Scott's light works that occupy private homes and public spaces, he has further developed ideas for solar-powered land art installations that provide energy for landscape development in exterior settings.

*Digital Sun* – a work commissioned by the Velux Foundation for the Bella Centre in Copenhagen – was created by Steven Scott to mark the occasion of the UN Climate Conference in 2009. In addition to its important environmental and ecological meaning and symbolism, *Digital Sun* – on an abstract formal level – foregrounds the idea of colour not merely as a static entity, but as a phenomenon in transition. In this work, Scott continues to emphasise the fact that we know colour by observing it in time, a concept derived from nature. According to the work's programme, a large spherical form in the center of this wall of light is surrounded by a hard line with a soft glowing penumbra on the outside. The variations in the programme move in relation to how the light is captured within the circular glass form, as if to suggest the weight of the colour that seems to radiate and float discretely above the surface. As stated earlier, the size and scale of a work should not detract from the ability of the work to communicate on an intimate level.

In the case of *Digital Sun,* I would suggest that the emphasis on light within the colour spectrum as a consequence of temporal engagement is what gives this work intimacy.

Here is a public work that moves beyond the abstract limitations of detachment and decorum. Instead it shimmers with significance and grandeur through the allocation of space, time, and colour – catching viewers on their way somewhere, and in their haste, giving them a reason to observe this exemplary phenomenon that has been placed within the realm of their gaze.

Public art, at its best, does precisely this. Ideally, it is a kind of art open to everyone, without restrictions. Here are some paradigmatic models offered by Scott, which also function in the interstices between art, design, science and architecture. This might recall the concept of "total architecture" offered by the Bauhaus architect Walter Gropius or the humanist concept behind Moholy-Nagy's *Light-Space Modulator* (1922–30). The latter was intended to offer a room of solace and relaxation for factory workers to calm the mind during a break from the routine workday. The idea of both Gropius and Moholy-Nagy was that everything within a building should function as a whole. The logic of the workplace should offer a common ground where workers, administrators and other staff members function effectively within their domains yet without feeling confined or prohibited from moving easily from one area to another. Both were interested in the use of natural light in order to give various areas within the space a sense of openness and awareness of time during any given

## LUMINOUS ICONS PART THREE

## LIGHT WORKS IN PUBLIC SPACES

workday. In this context, the Deloitte atrium project in Copenhagen (2003–2006) remains one of Scott's major projects as it amplifies the Bauhaus idea that art serves a primary rather than an ancillary function in relation to the space. It refers back to Kaelin's concept of time in terms of relative motion, rhythm and duration as one observes the modules changing in their colour permutations.

*Walls of Light* at the Contemporary Music Concert Hall in Amsterdam (1999–2005) functions in a similar way, perhaps closer to a large kinetic wall painting than a site-specific sculpture, which would be closer to the activated zigzag construction in the Deloitte atrium. In either case, these installations are conceived in conjunction with the purpose of the space. In Amsterdam, the walls do not compete with the music, but amplify the context of the space in which the music is being heard. In Copenhagen, the modular elements rising up through the seven-storey space create their own visual music without interference from the natural light coming in from the exterior or without competing with functional lights in the offices or corridors surrounding the atrium. In 2000–2001, Scott had designed a project for the merchant bank Finance for Danish Industry, also in Copenhagen, involving an ascending vertical shaft in the atrium of the building with modular light spaces progressing upwards on either side of a series of plate-glass floors with elevators at each level. Resembling Donald Judd's Minimal "stacks", these bipartite horizontal light modules accentuate the up-and-down aspect of the area in which they are equidistantly placed. As people are constantly moving from one floor to another either by stairway or elevator, the space is actively engaged. The fixed positions of the lights contribute to a sense of rhythm (tempi) with their slow evolution of colour change.

While the total architectural concept – art, design and architecture – is clearly the focus of these works, the actual manifestations of these light works are quite distinct from that of the Bauhaus. If anything, they fit more accurately within the globalised postmodernism of the present, where concept and decorum intertwine and proliferate with one another.

Scott's *Blade of Light* (2005) in collaboration with the eminent Danish landscape architect Torben Schonherr, and commissioned by the Foundation of Tech College in Aalborg in celebration of its 200-year anniversary, is a work of sculpture that both intervenes with and nearly escapes the parameters of its architectural placement. A minimal steel cromlech, the vertical steel armatures support a single steel beam that transverses from the central campus out across a forecourt. The dramatic effect of the work is best seen in the evening when the underside of the beam is illuminated by a streak of light that completely transforms the surrounding space. Once lit, it functions as a luminous icon without losing its essential sculptural drift. This acute architectural appendage may appear as a kind of spatial logo, but not in the commercial sense. Rather, its function incites a receptive cognition, which stirs a meditative awareness of the exterior space and a sensory awakening to the cool air. The design of Scott's work suggests the type of structure used by the Abstract Expressionist painter Barnet Newman in *Onement* (1948), where a bright orange "zip" cuts through a vertical, dark red field, symbolising the divine intervention of light. Whether or not this was Scott's intention is another question, but the lingering effect of his *Blade of Light* suggests a formal affinity with Newman as well as a keen formal awareness and sensitivity to a particular space and time.

# LIGHT WORKS IN PUBLIC SPACES

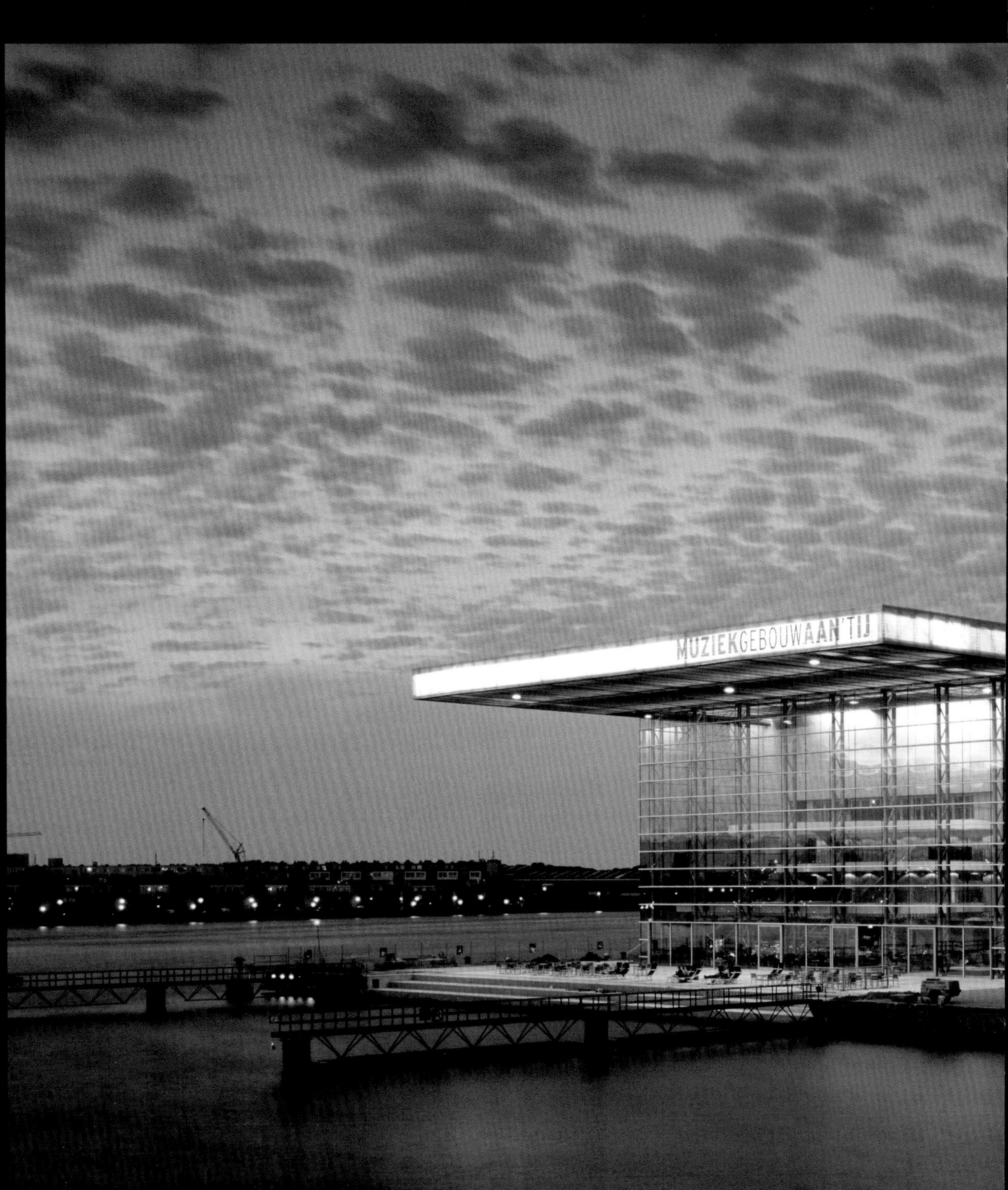
MUZIEKGEBOUWAAN'TIJ

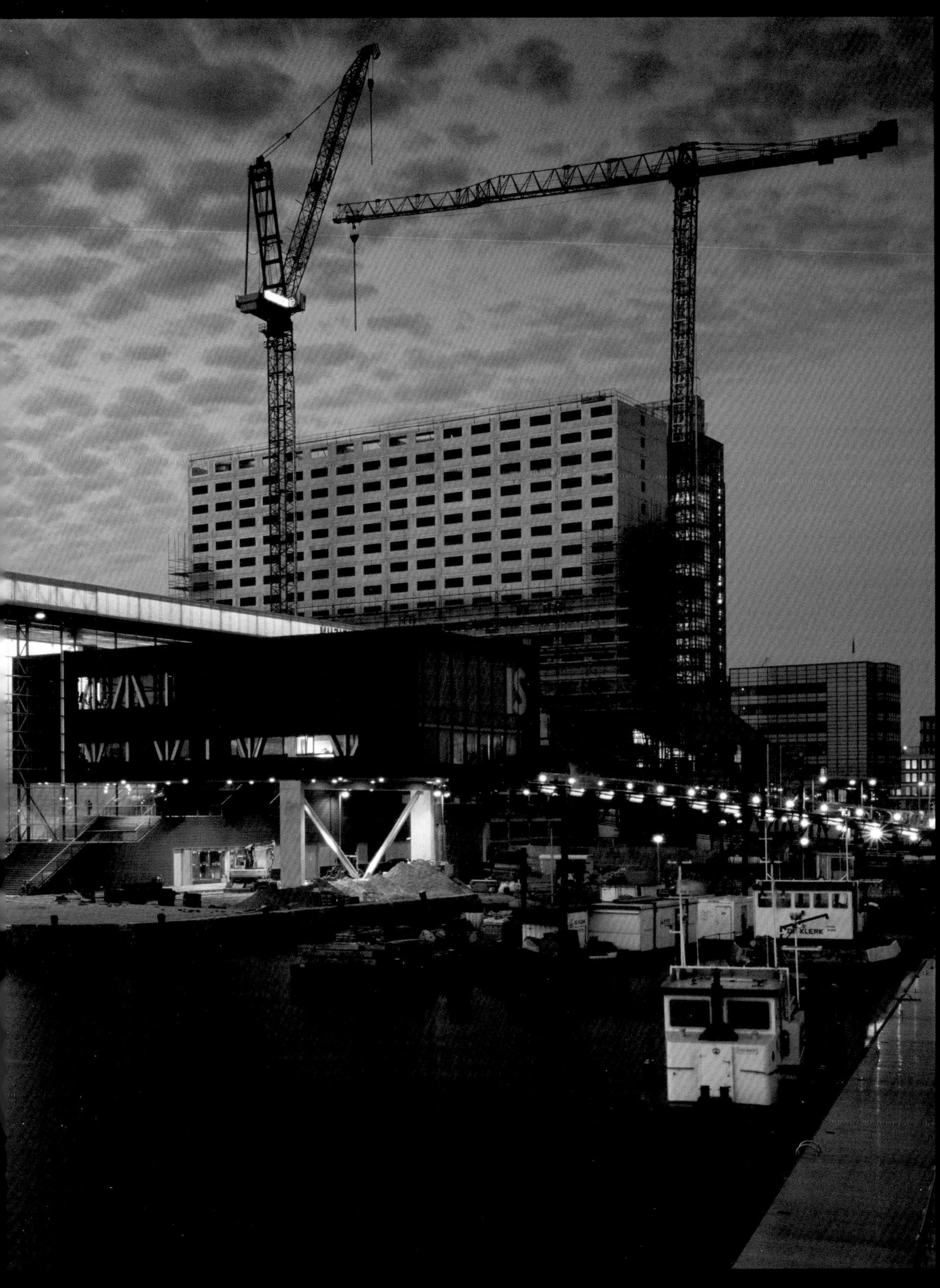

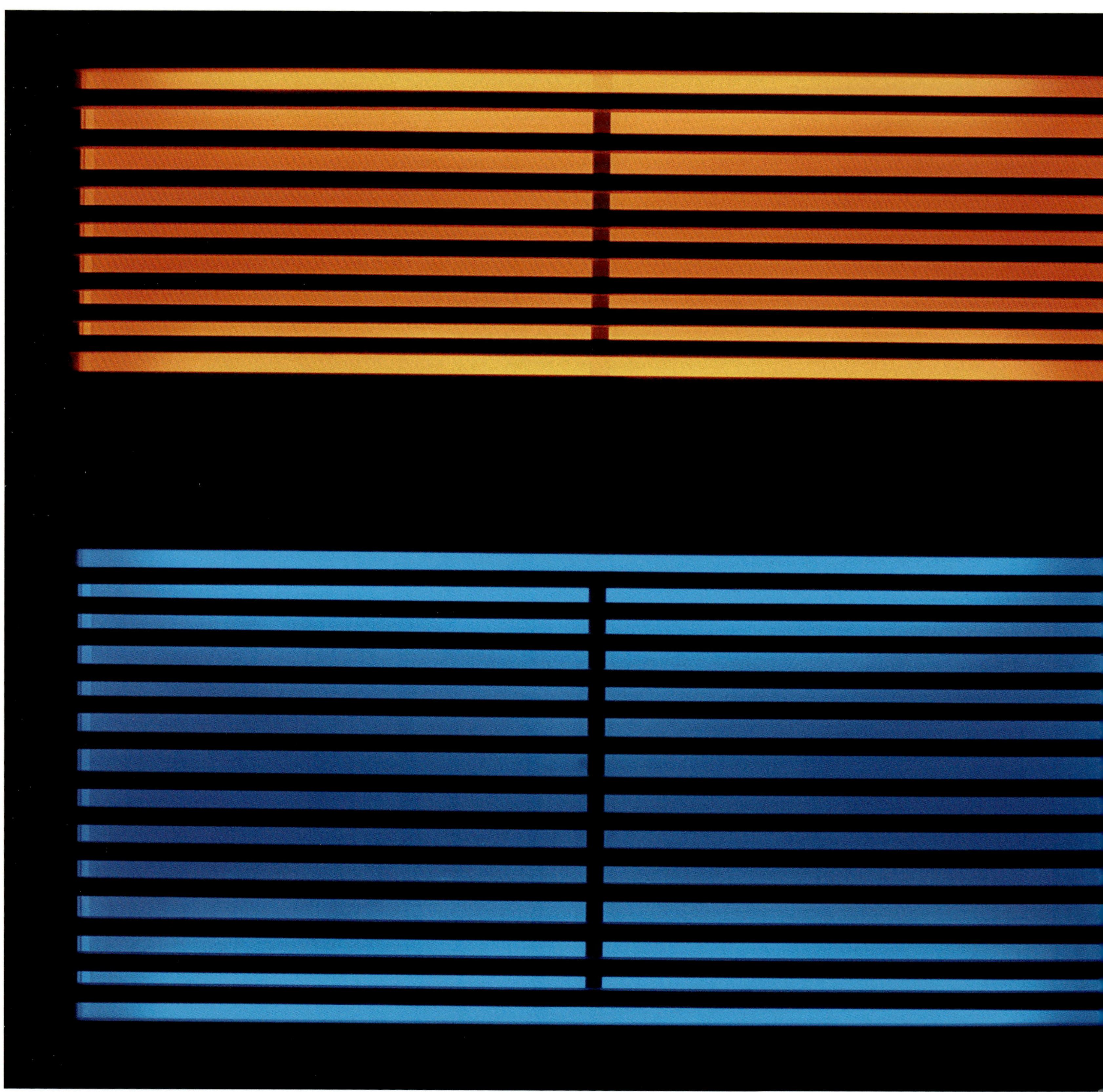

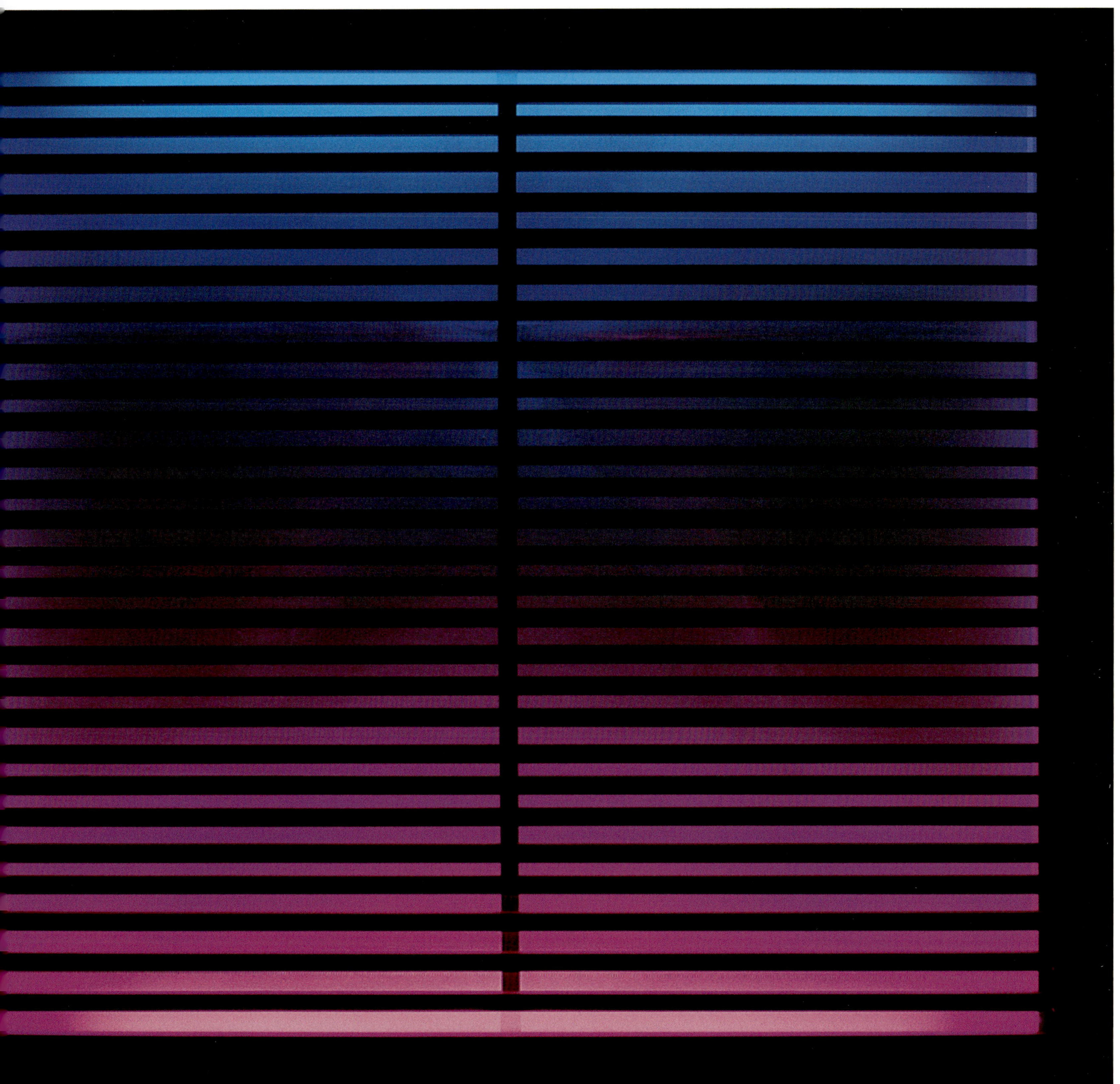

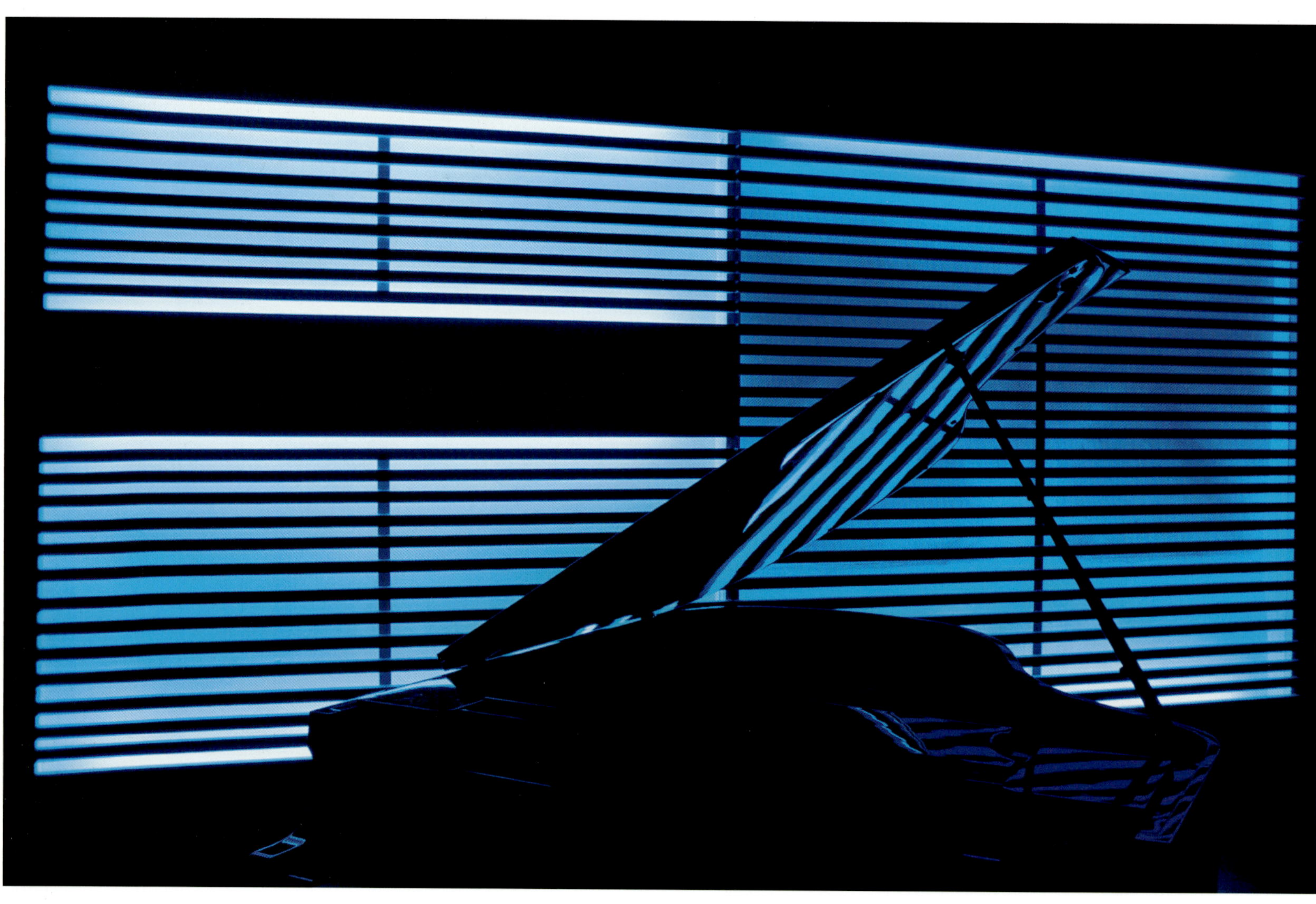

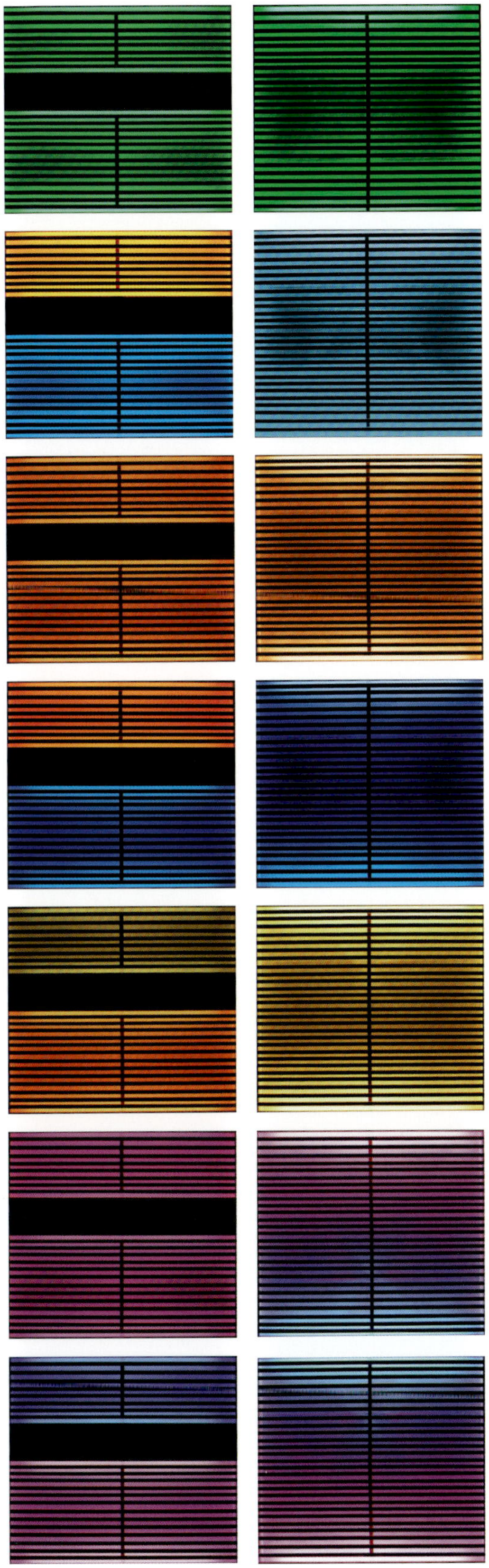

HET MUZIEKGEBOW | ARCHITECTS 3XN
CONTEMPORARY MUSIC CONCERT HALL

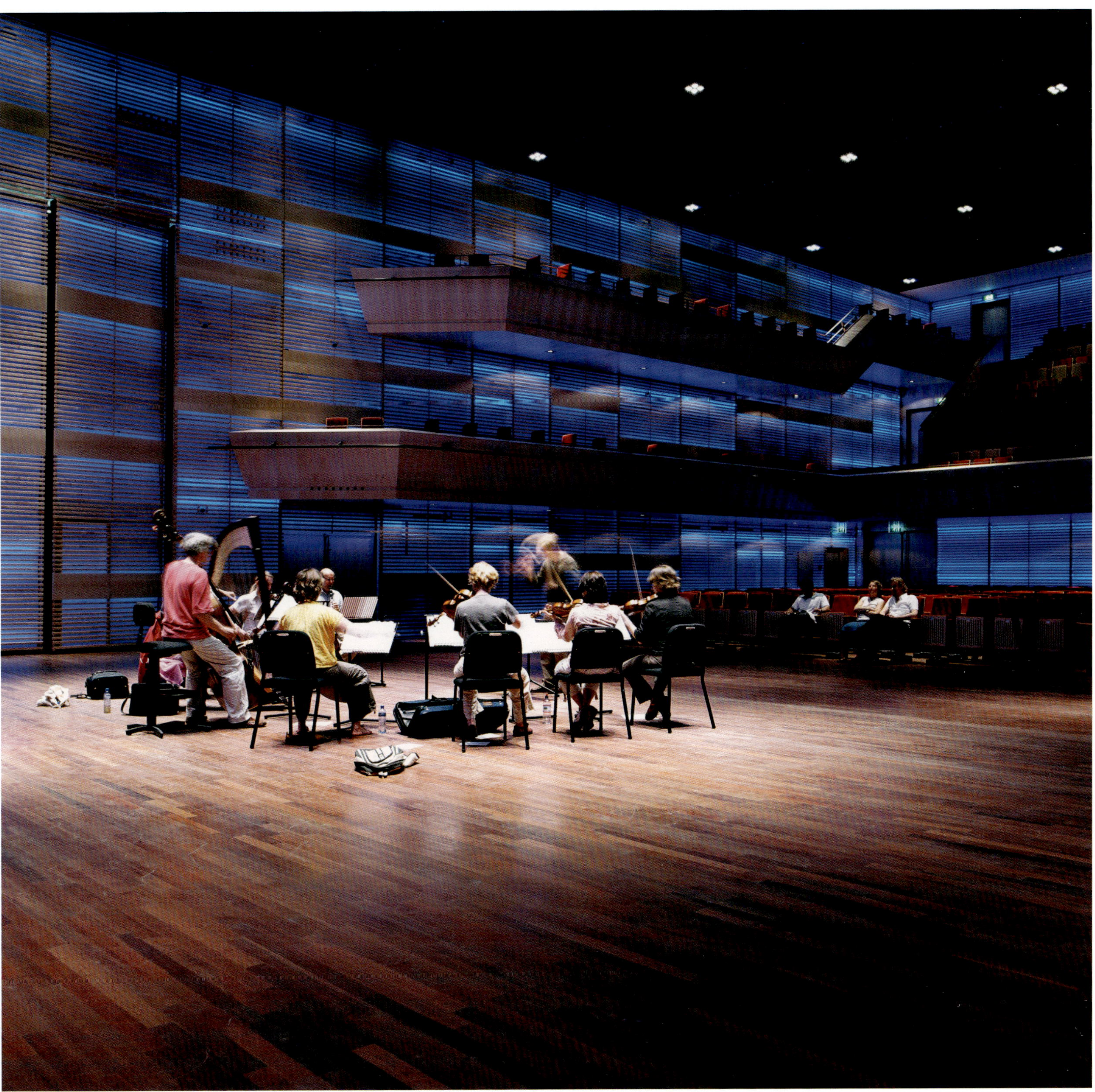

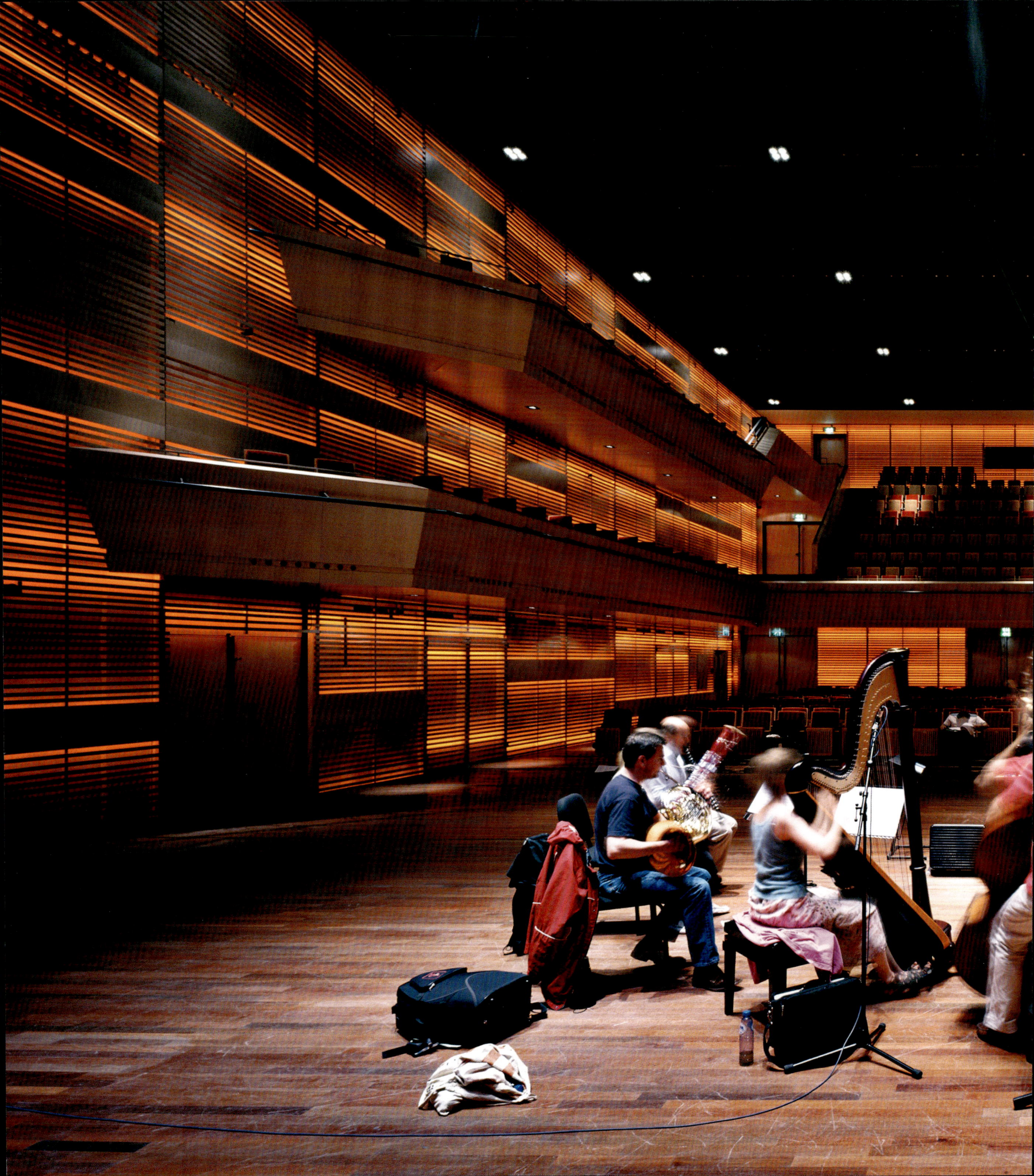

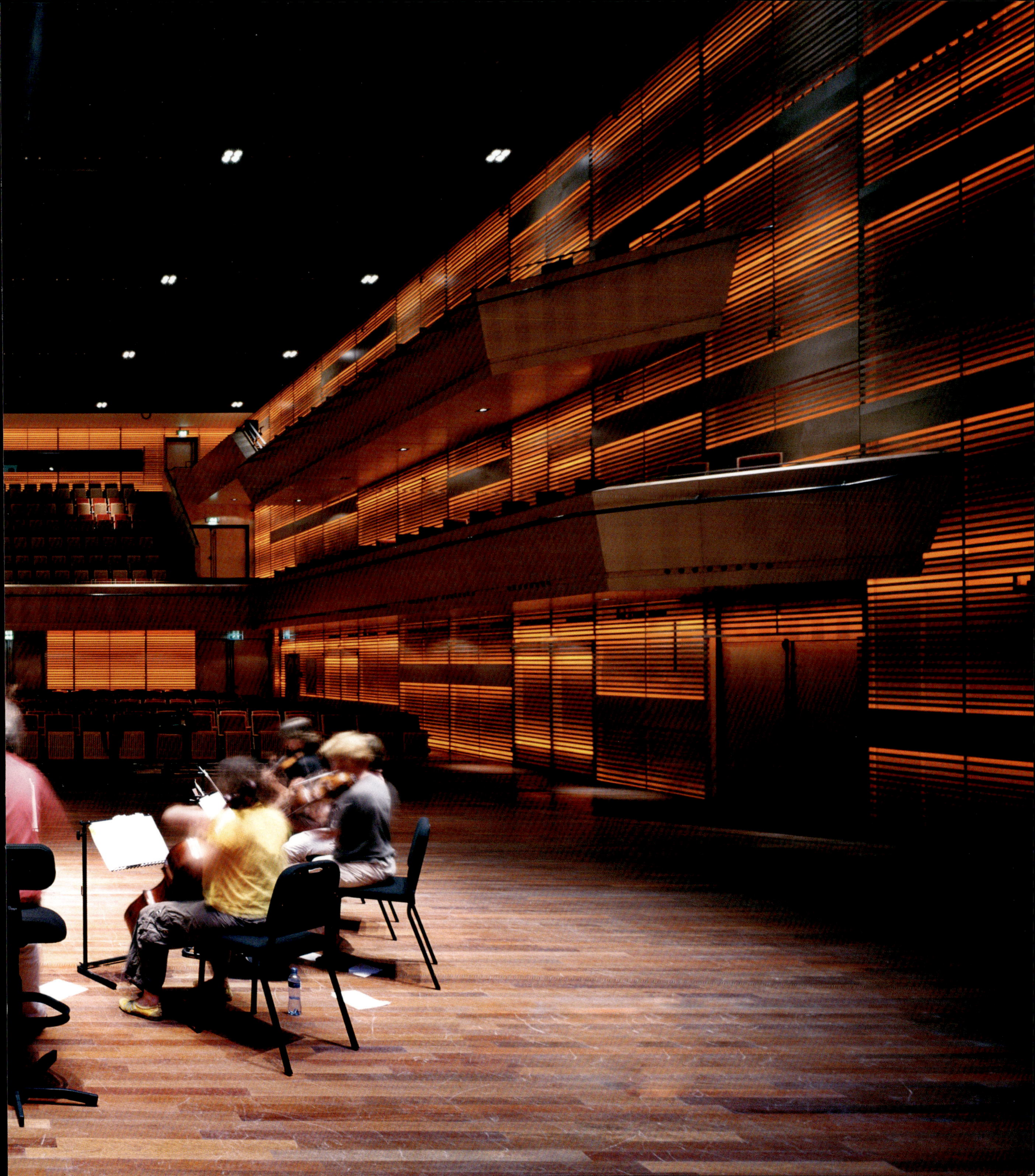

**WALL OF LIGHT**
HET MUZIEKGEBOW | ARCHITECTS 3XN
CONTEMPORARY MUSIC CONCERT HALL

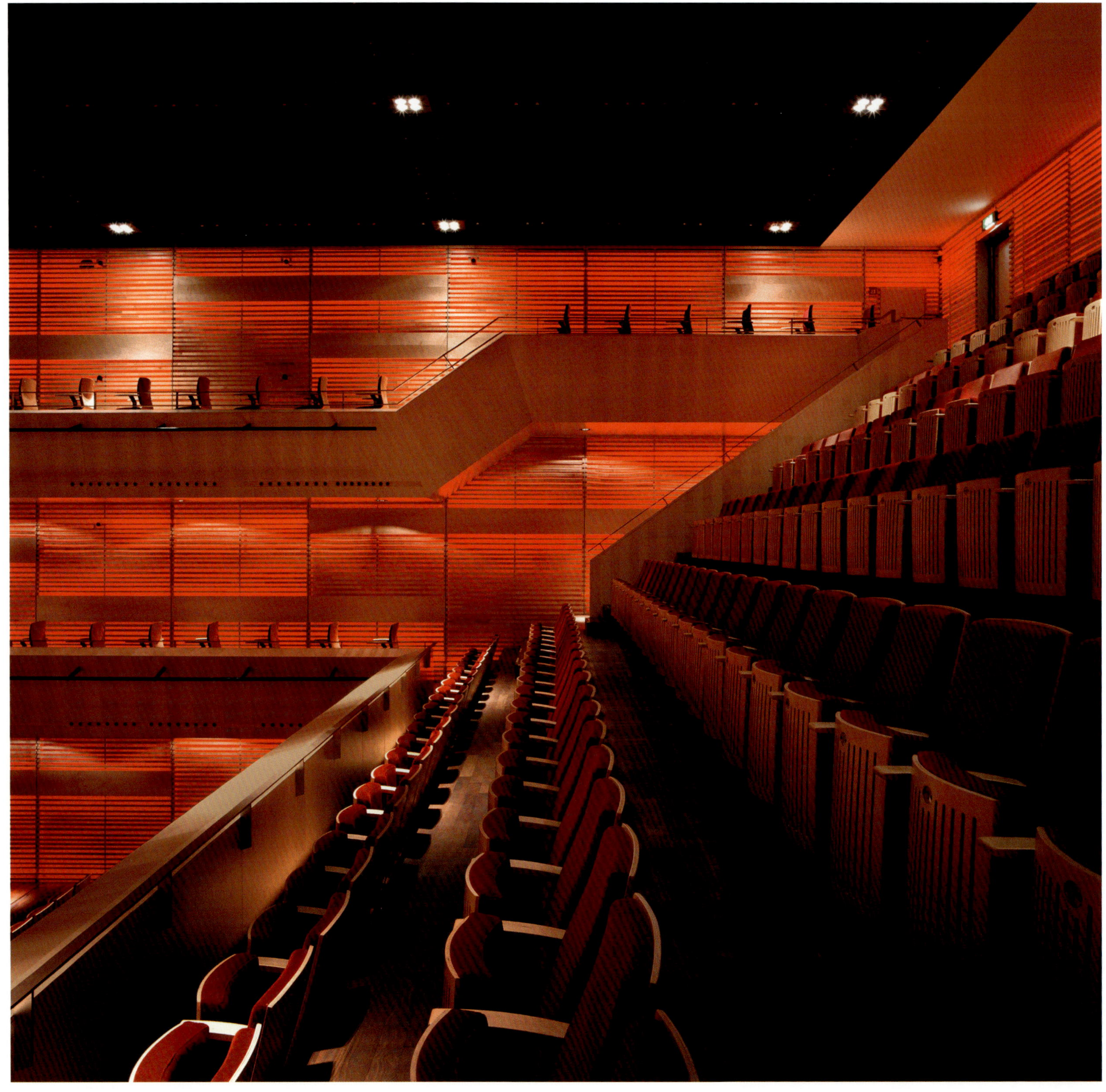

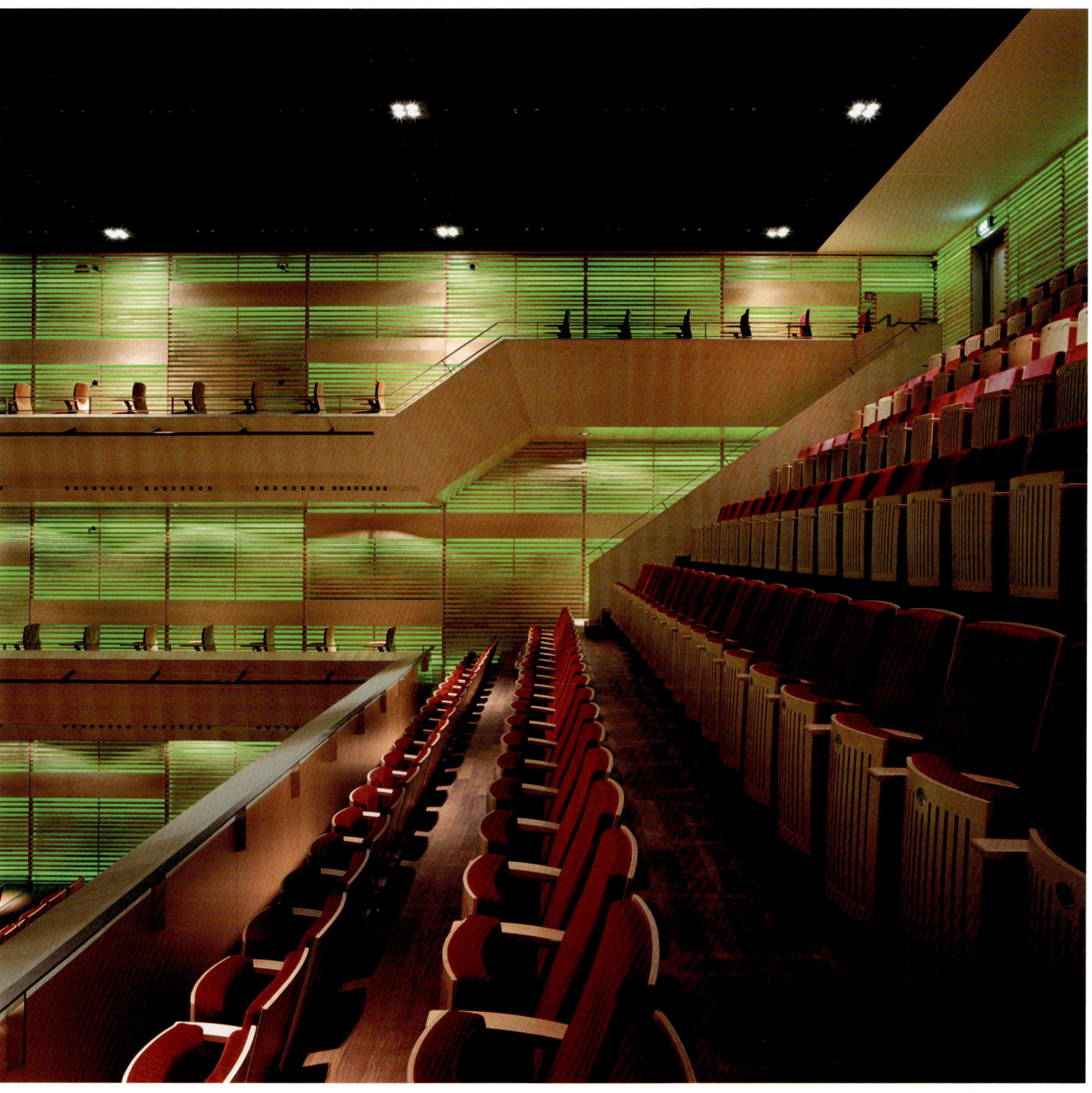

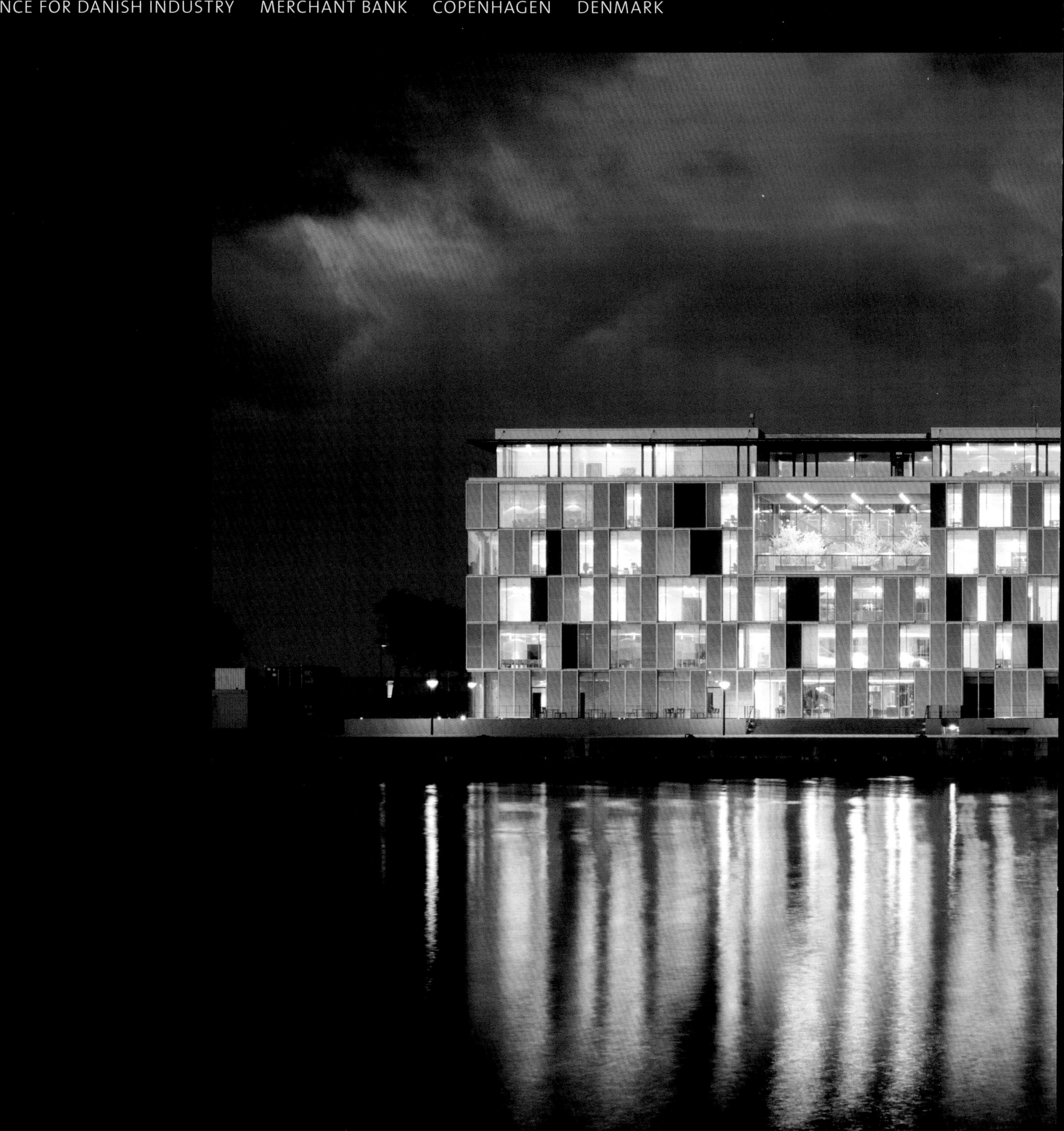

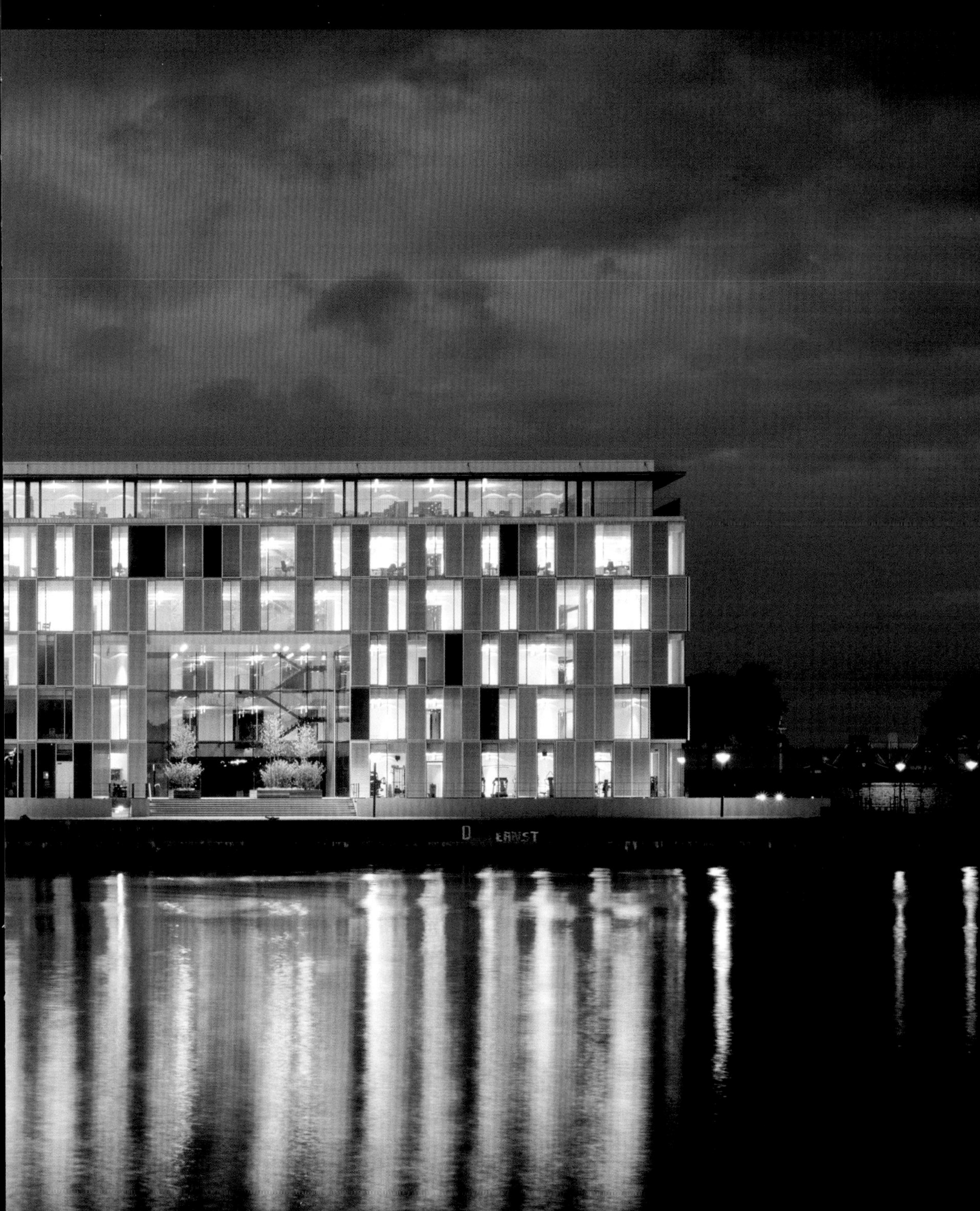

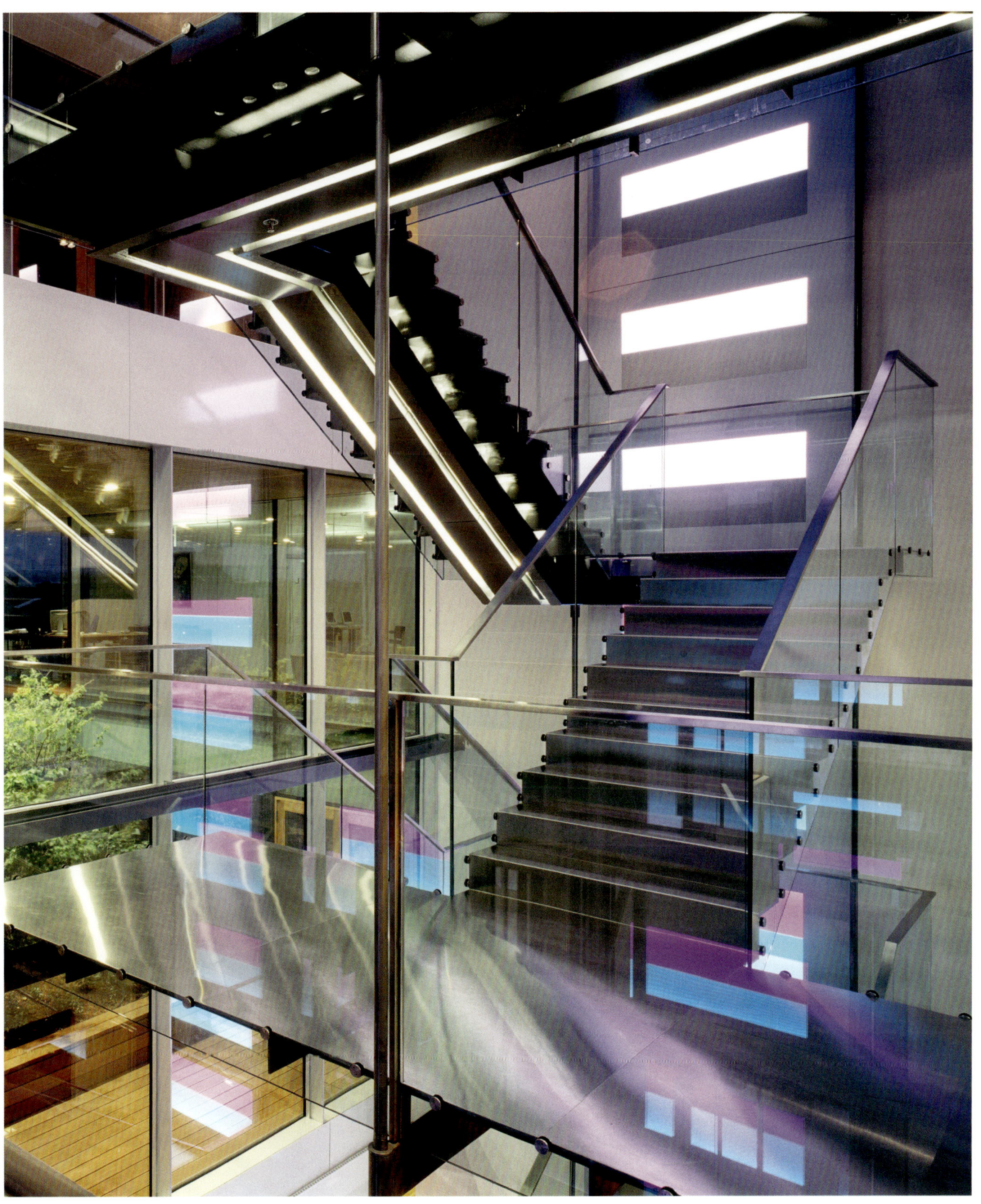

## THIRTY FIVE HORIZONS
FIH | ARCHITECTS 3XN
FINANCE FOR DANISH INDUSTRY | MERCHANT BANK

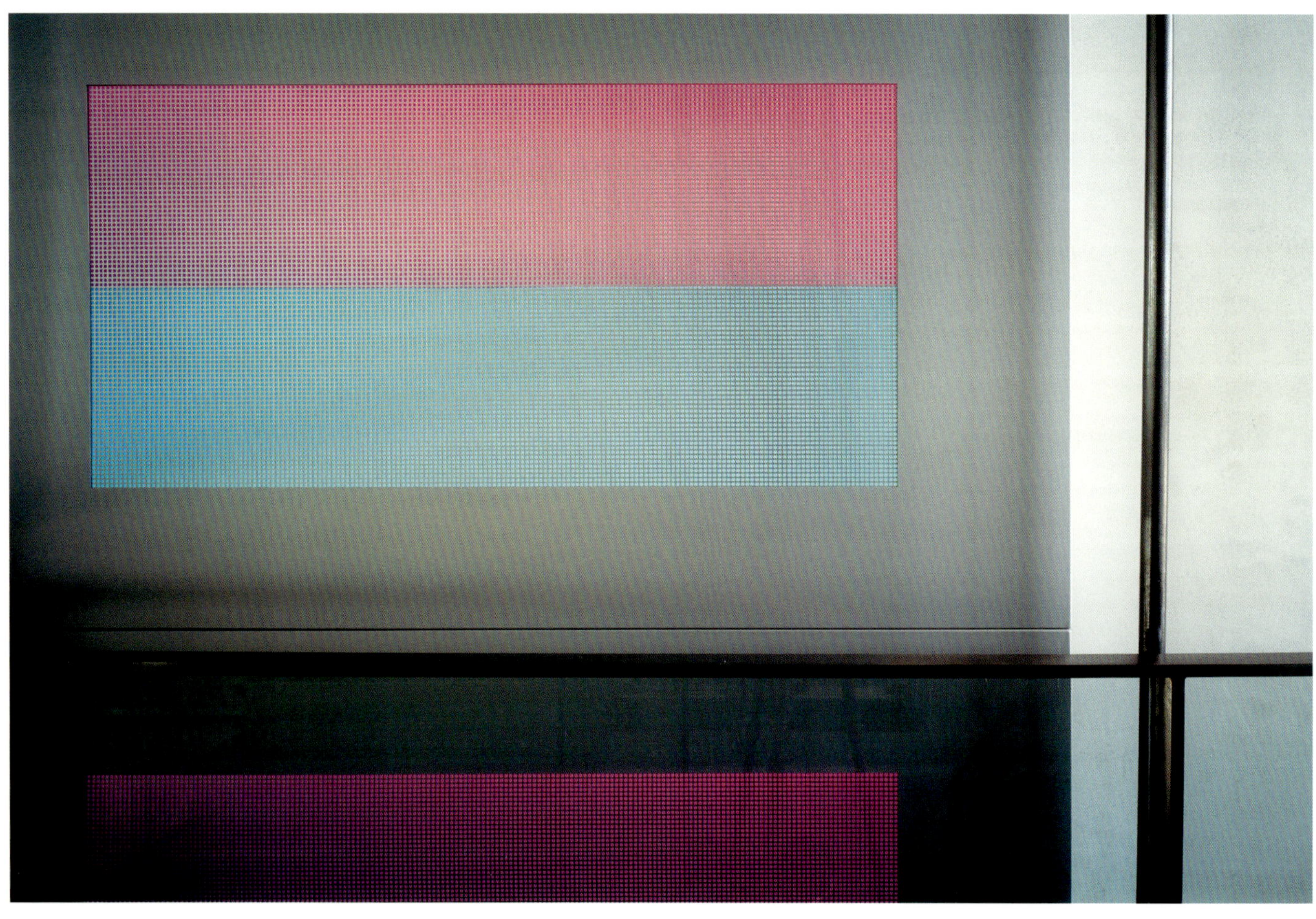

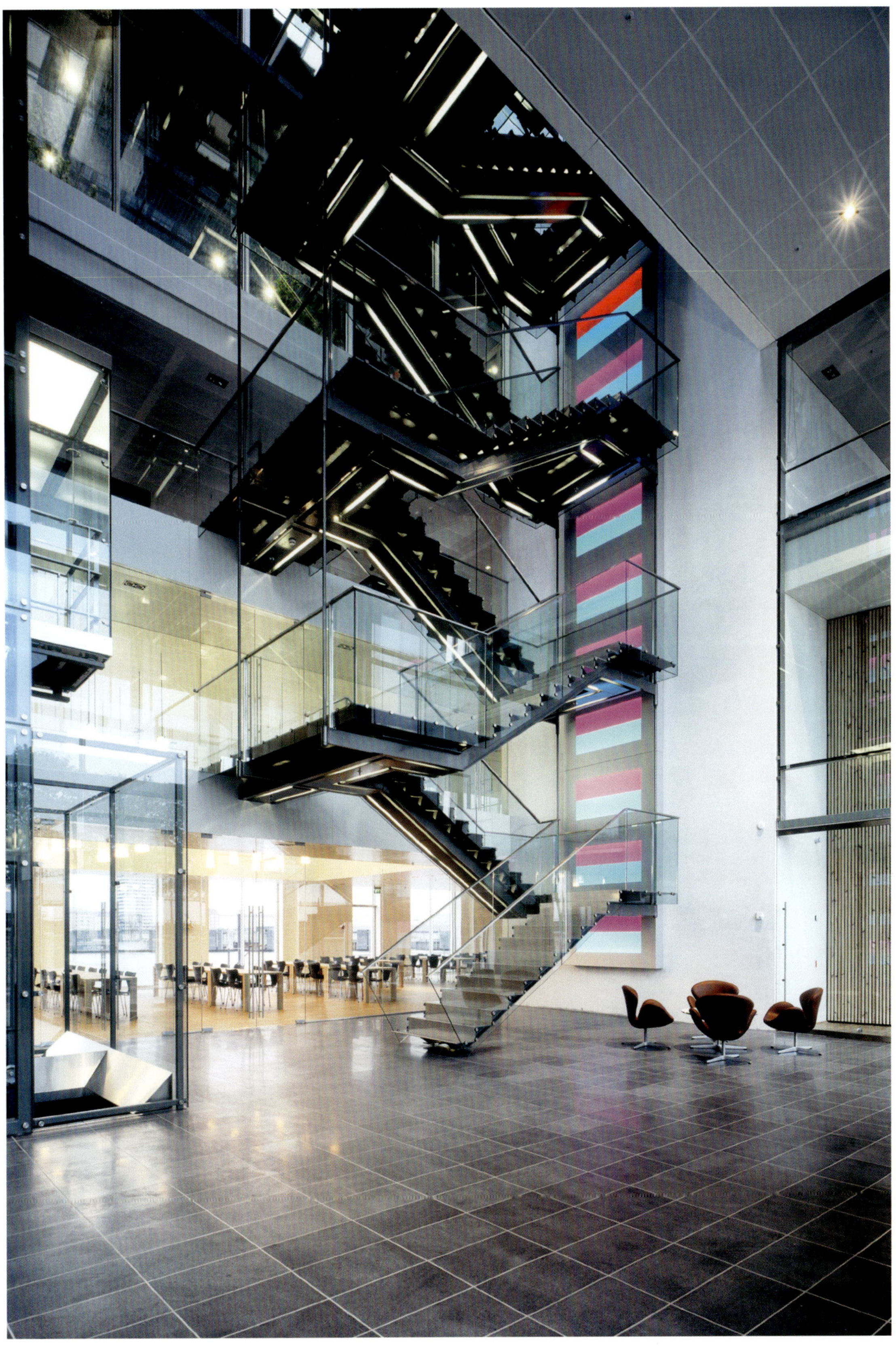

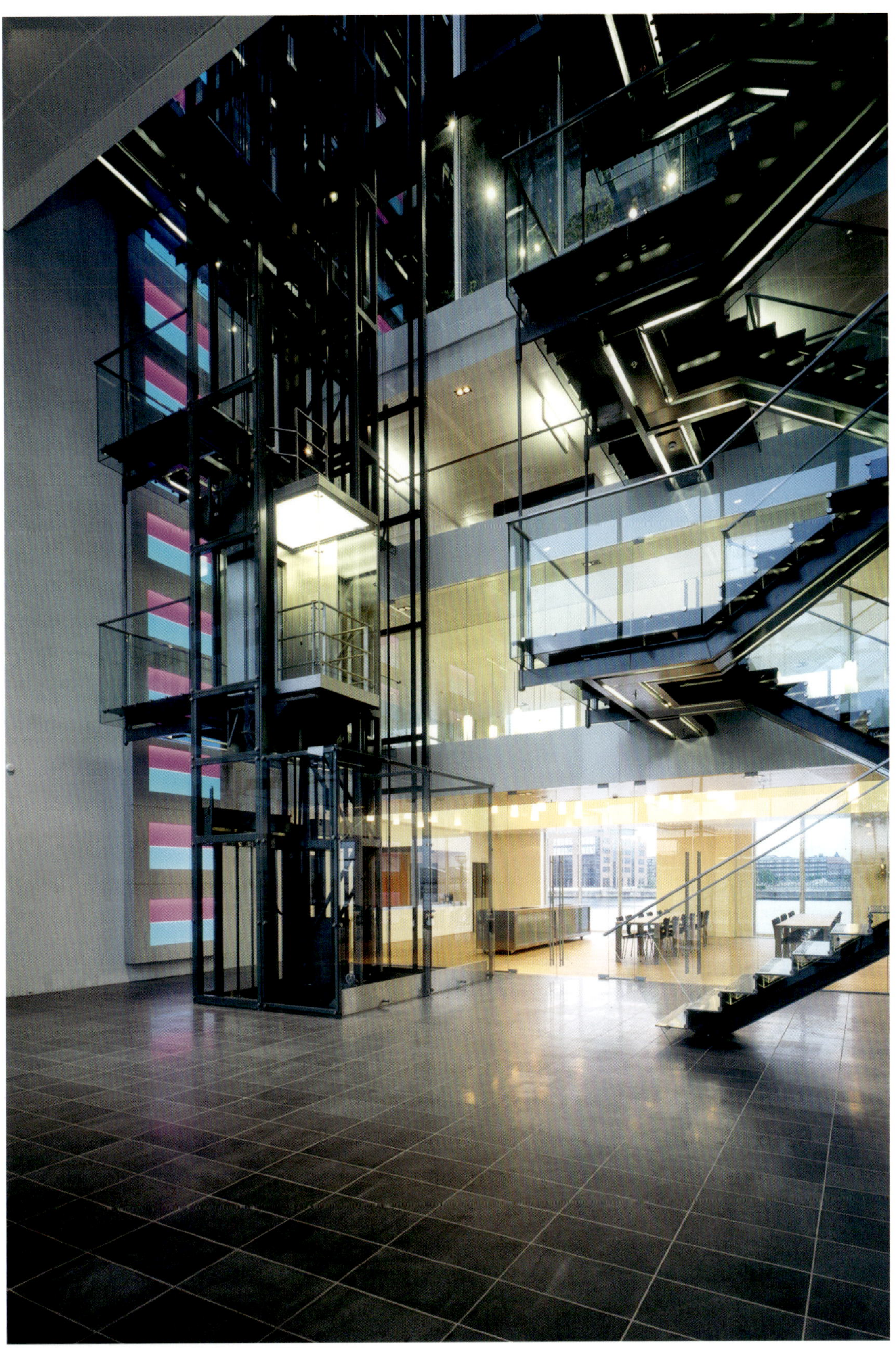

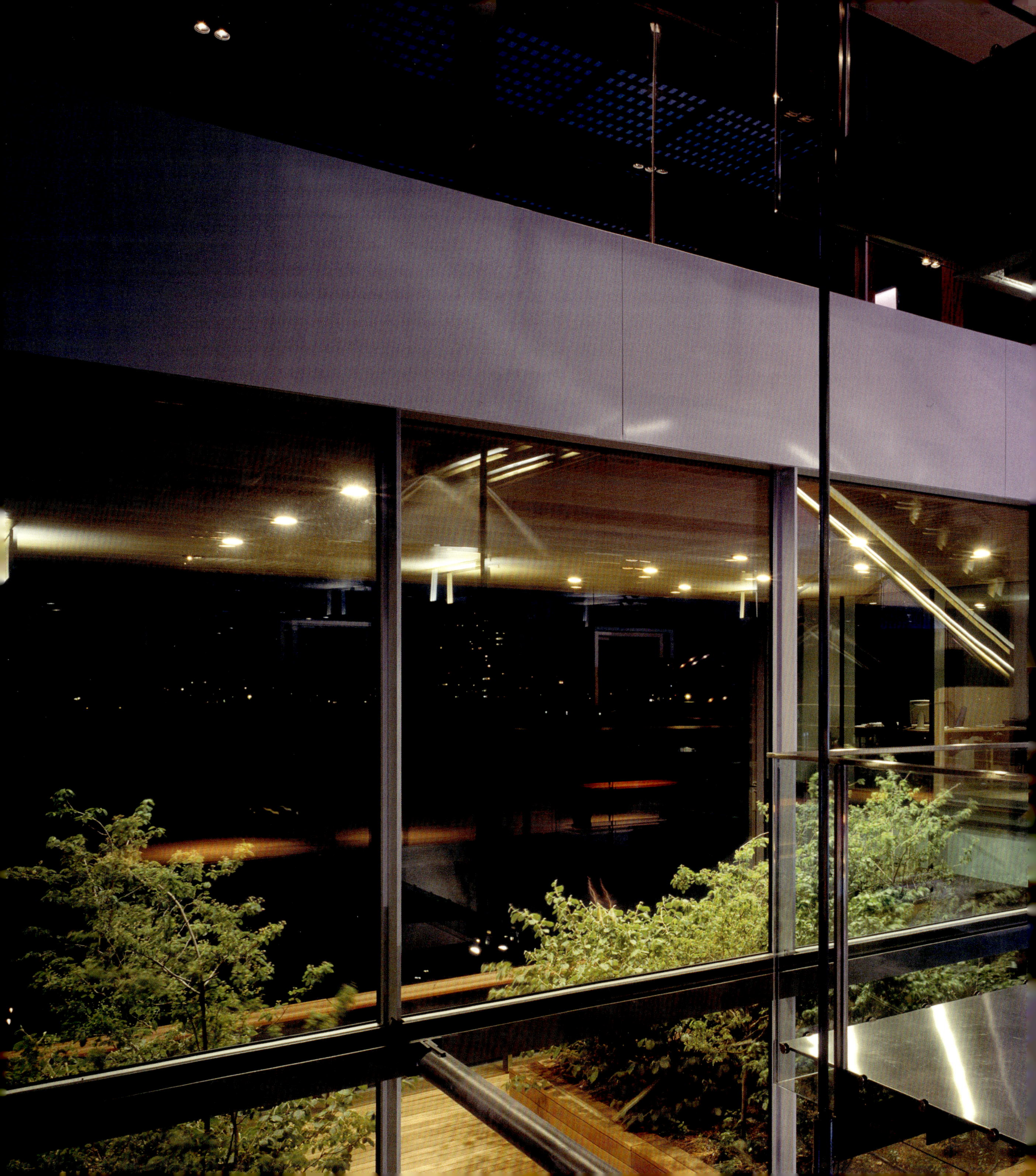

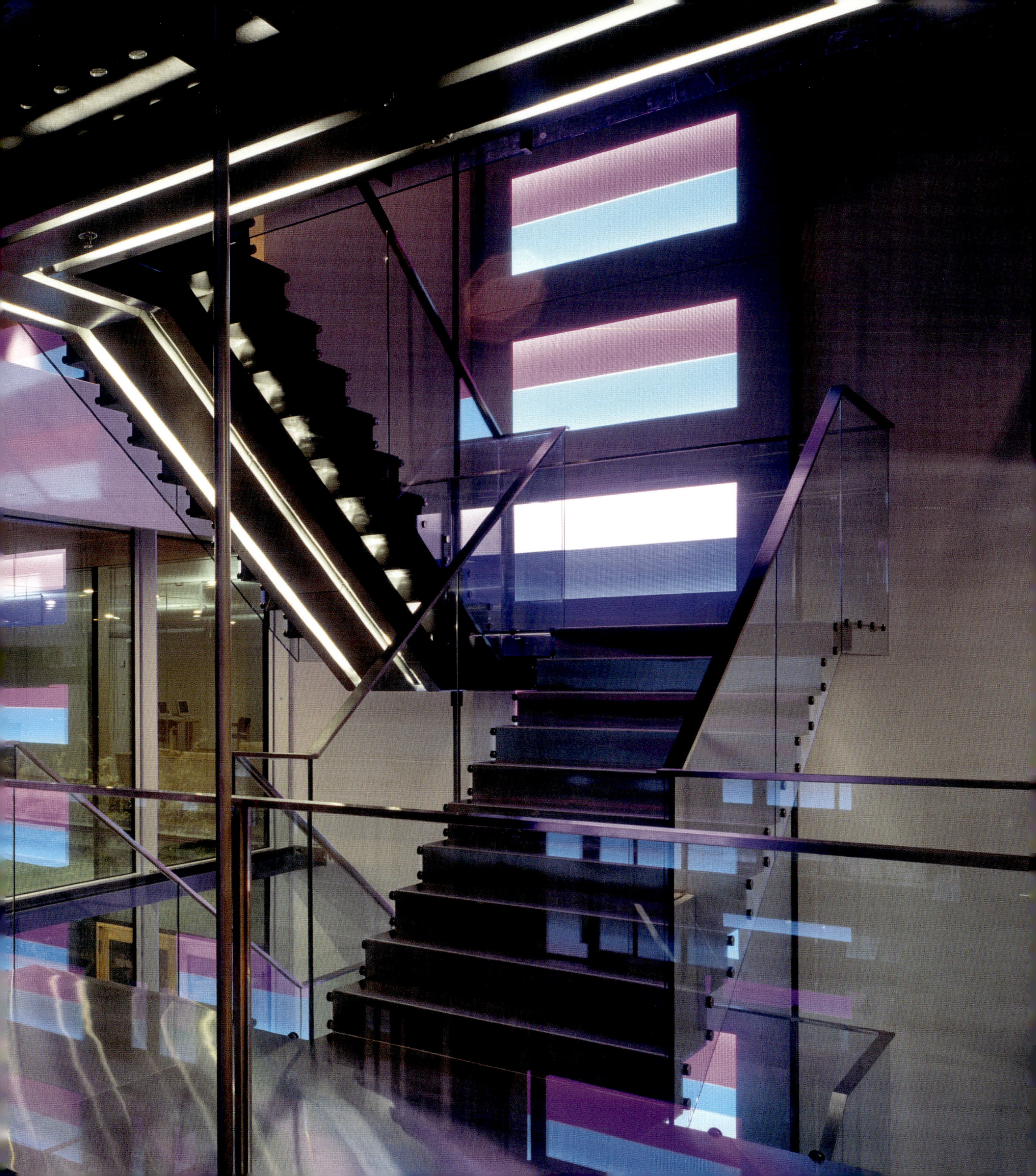

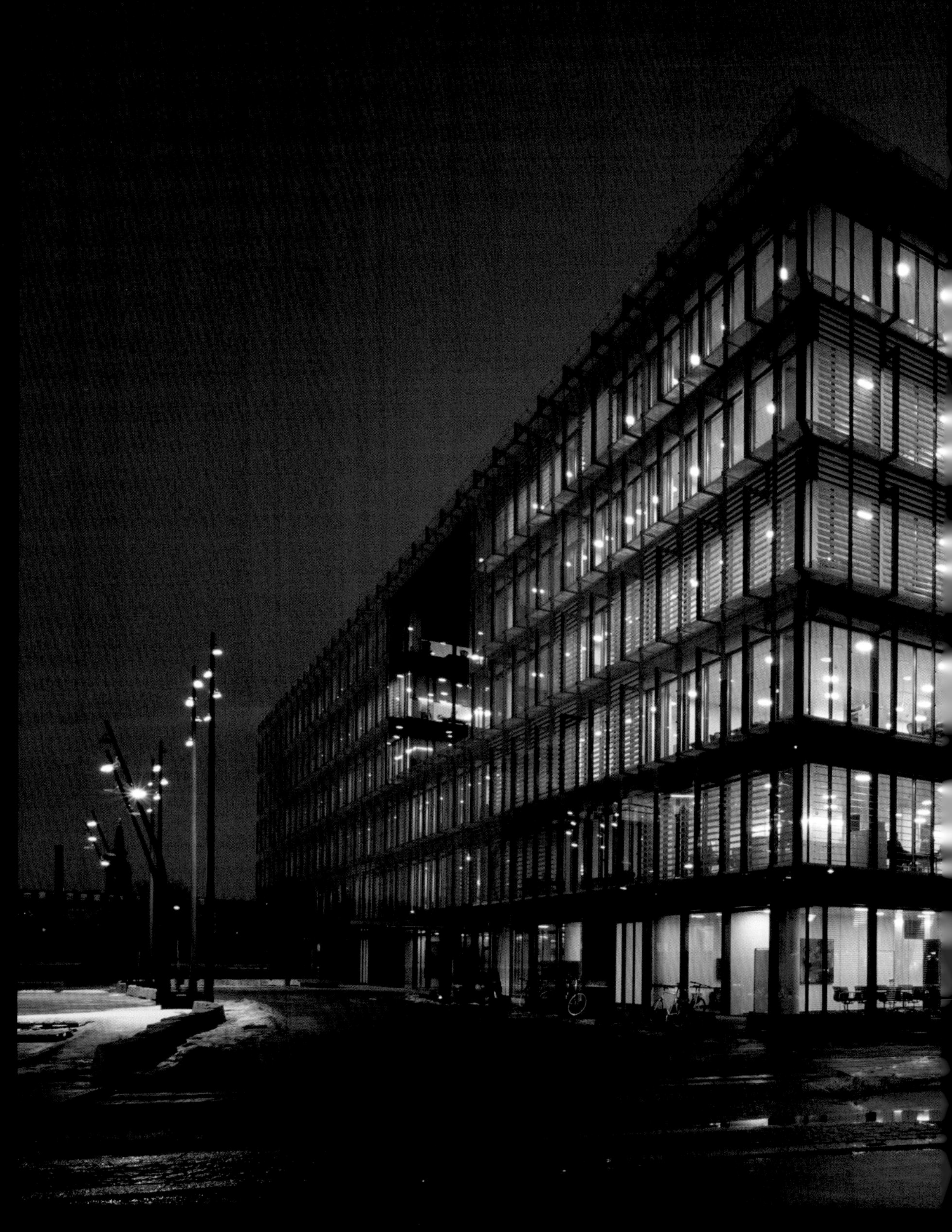

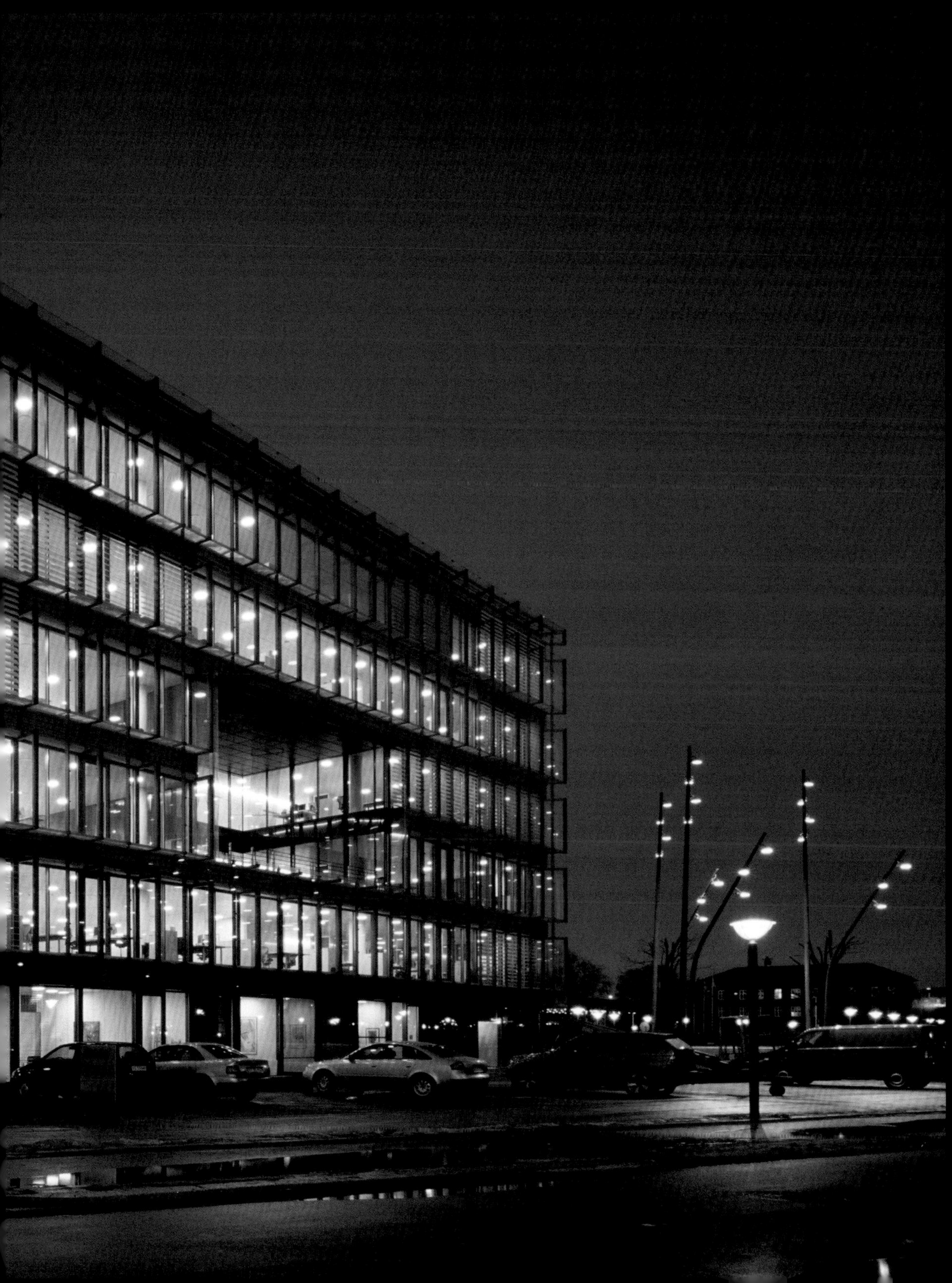

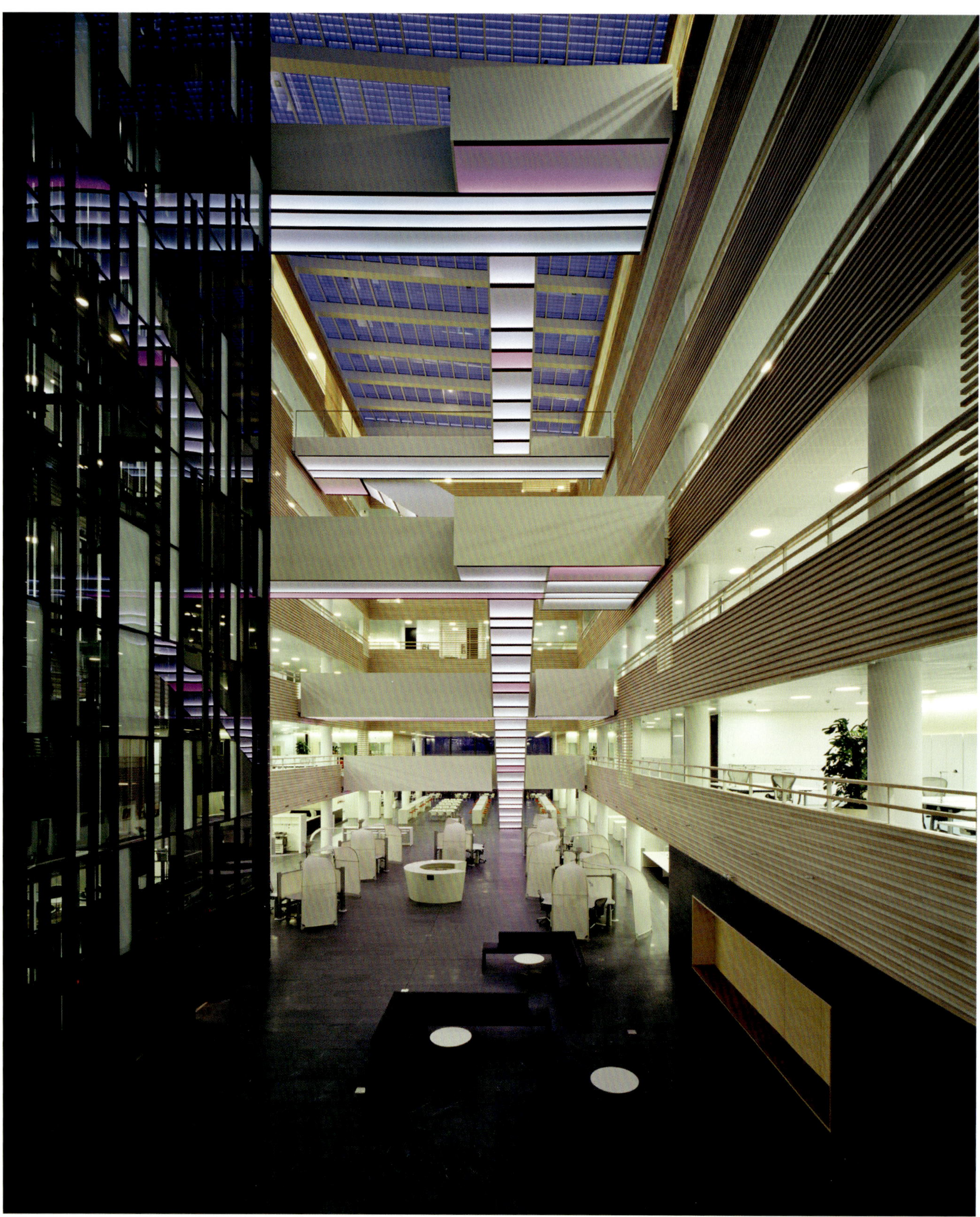

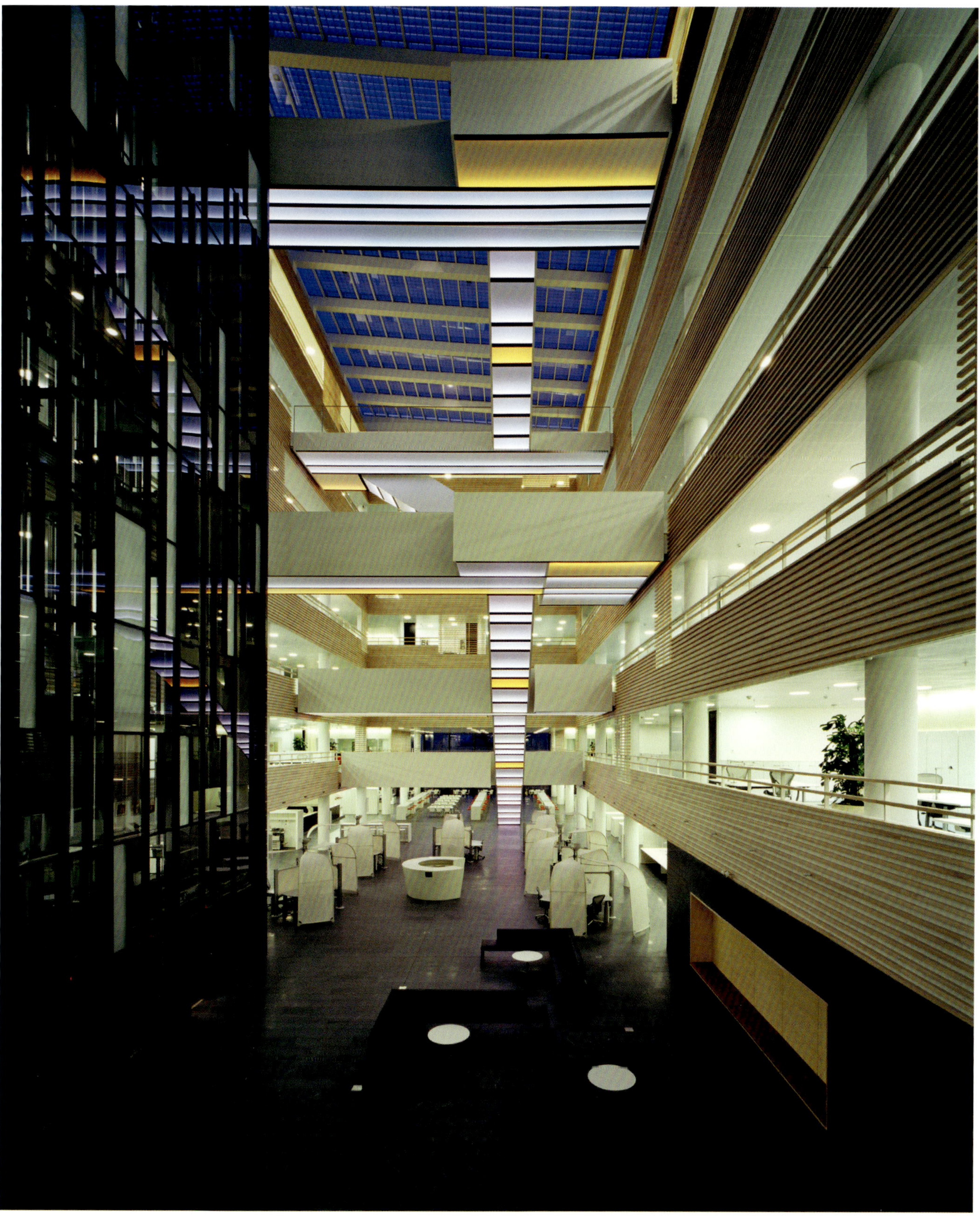

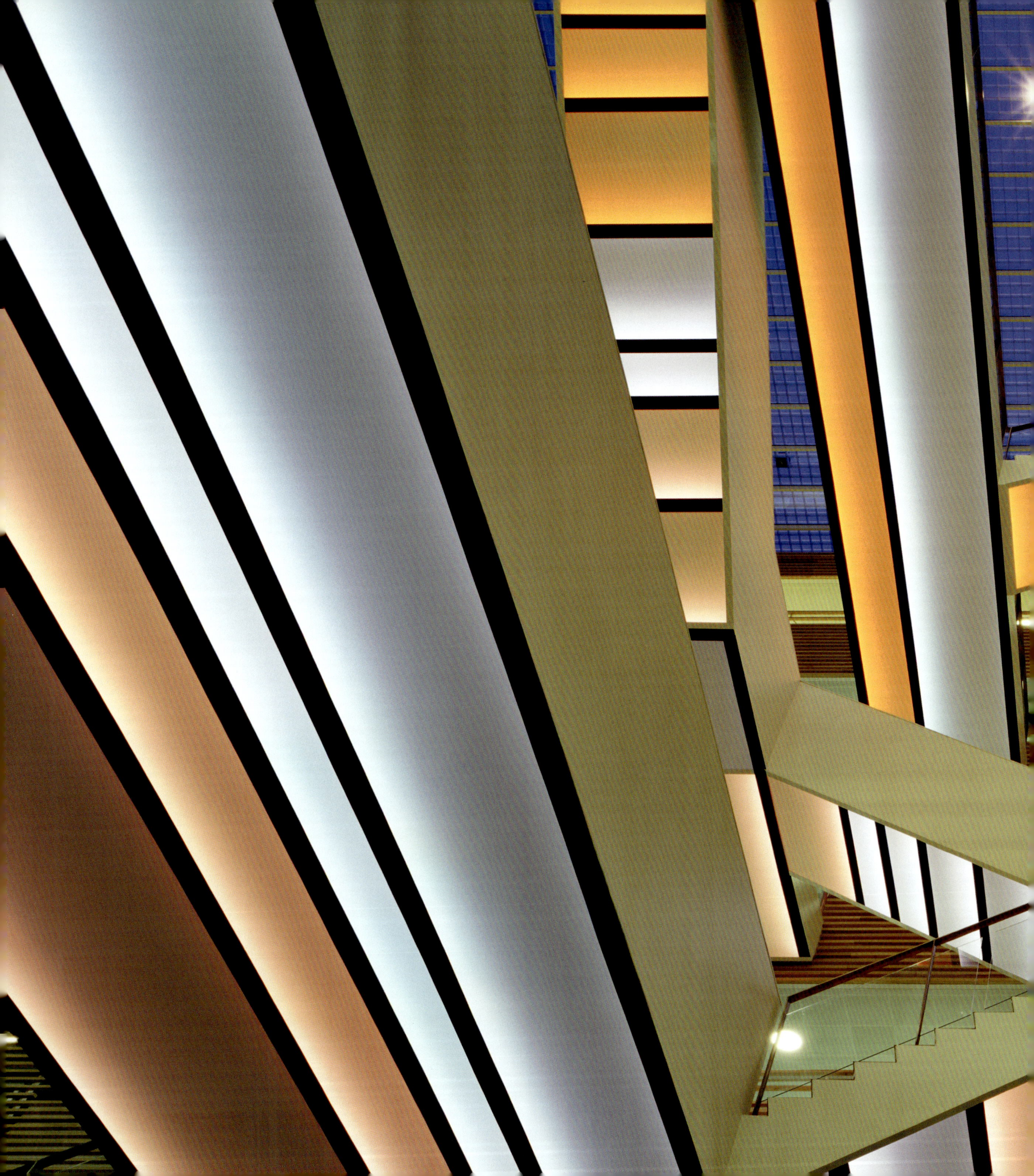

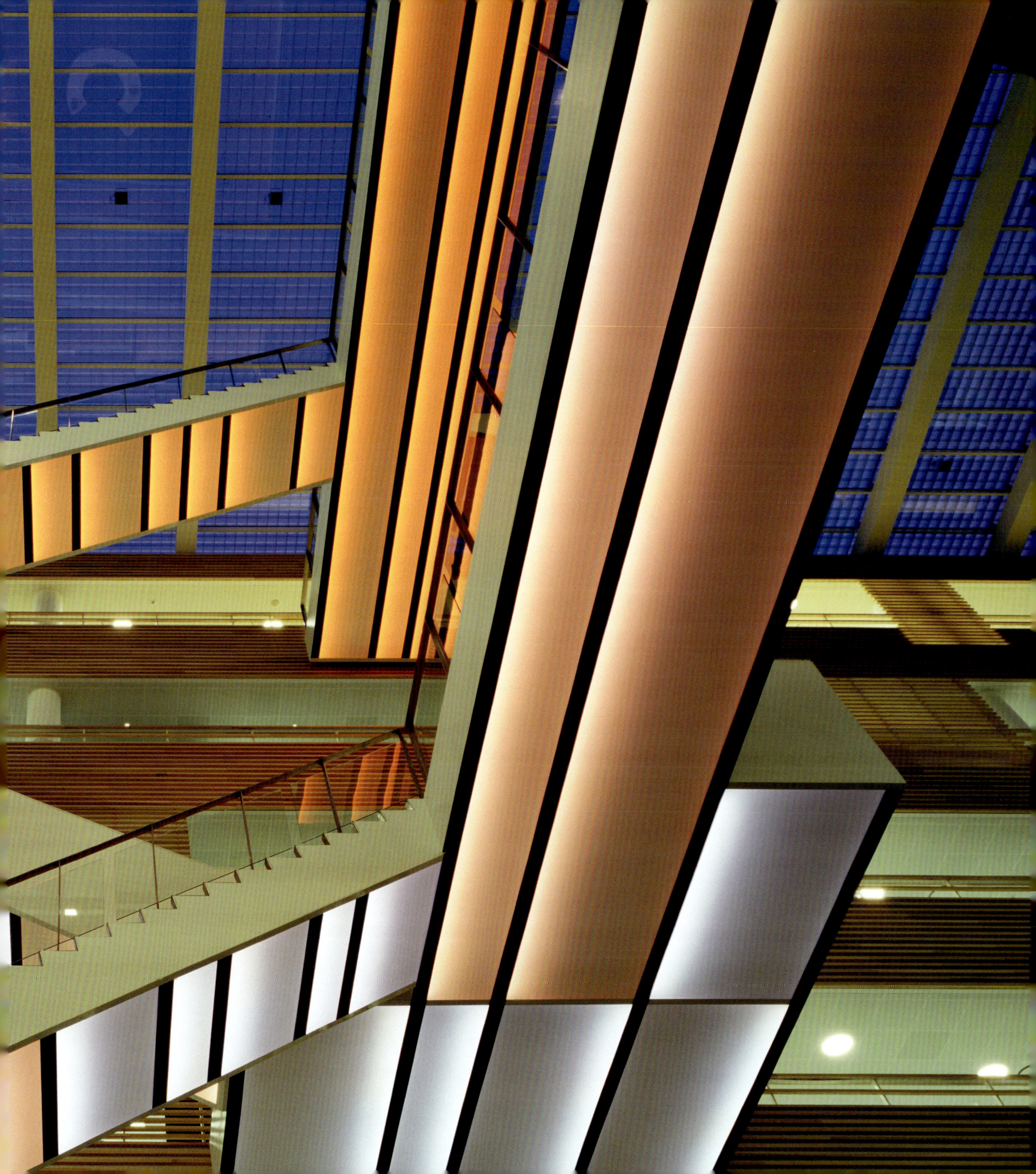

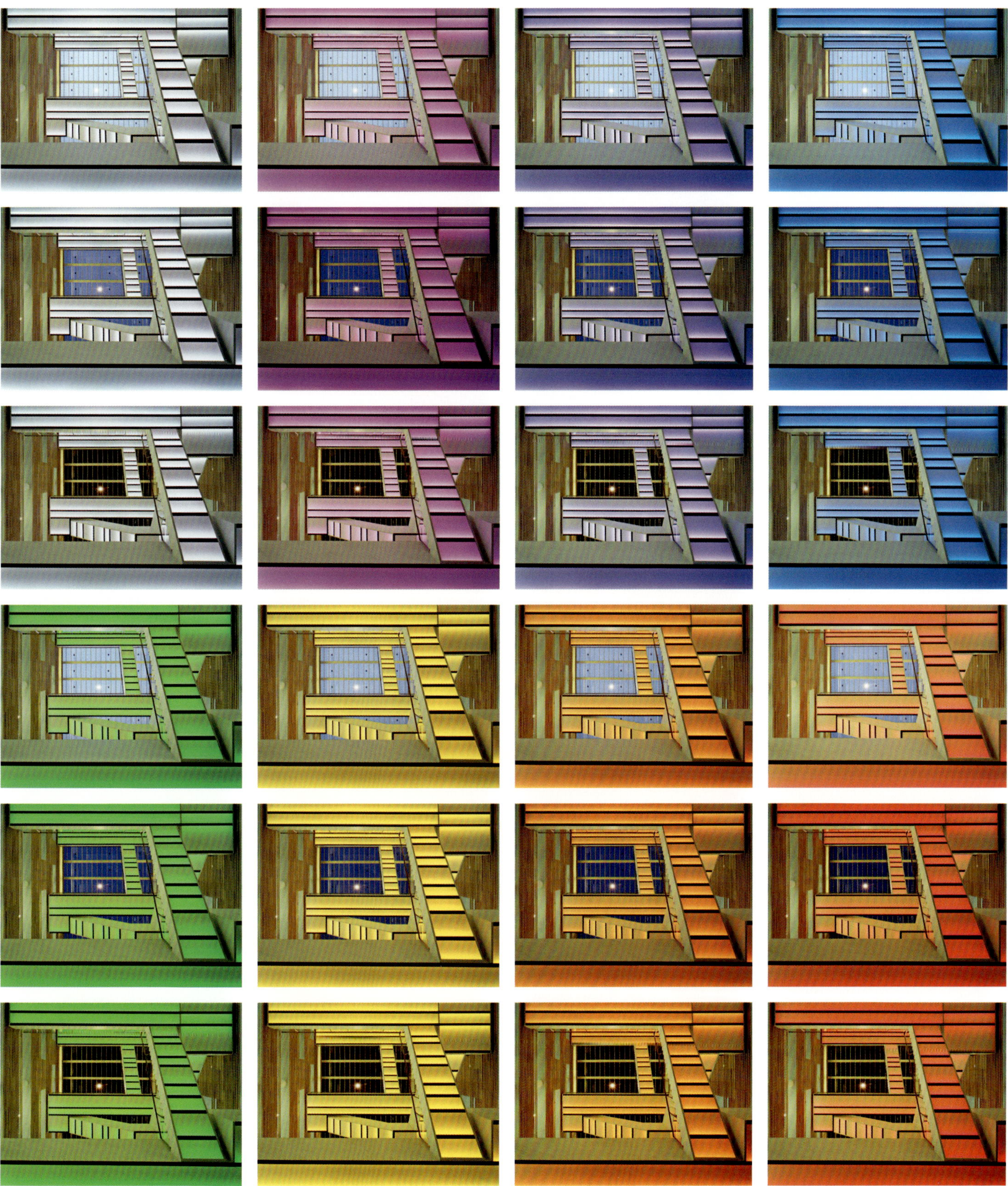

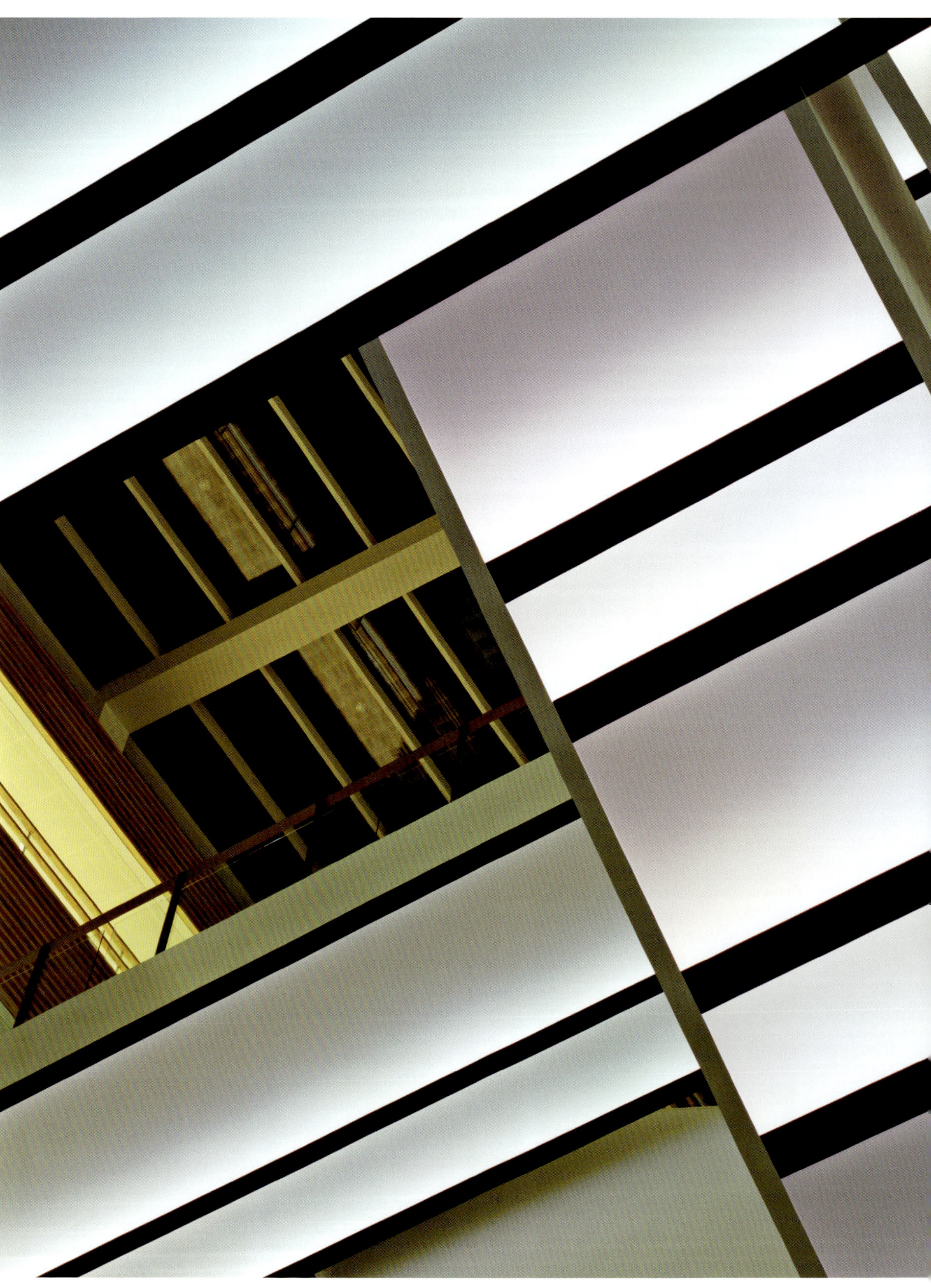

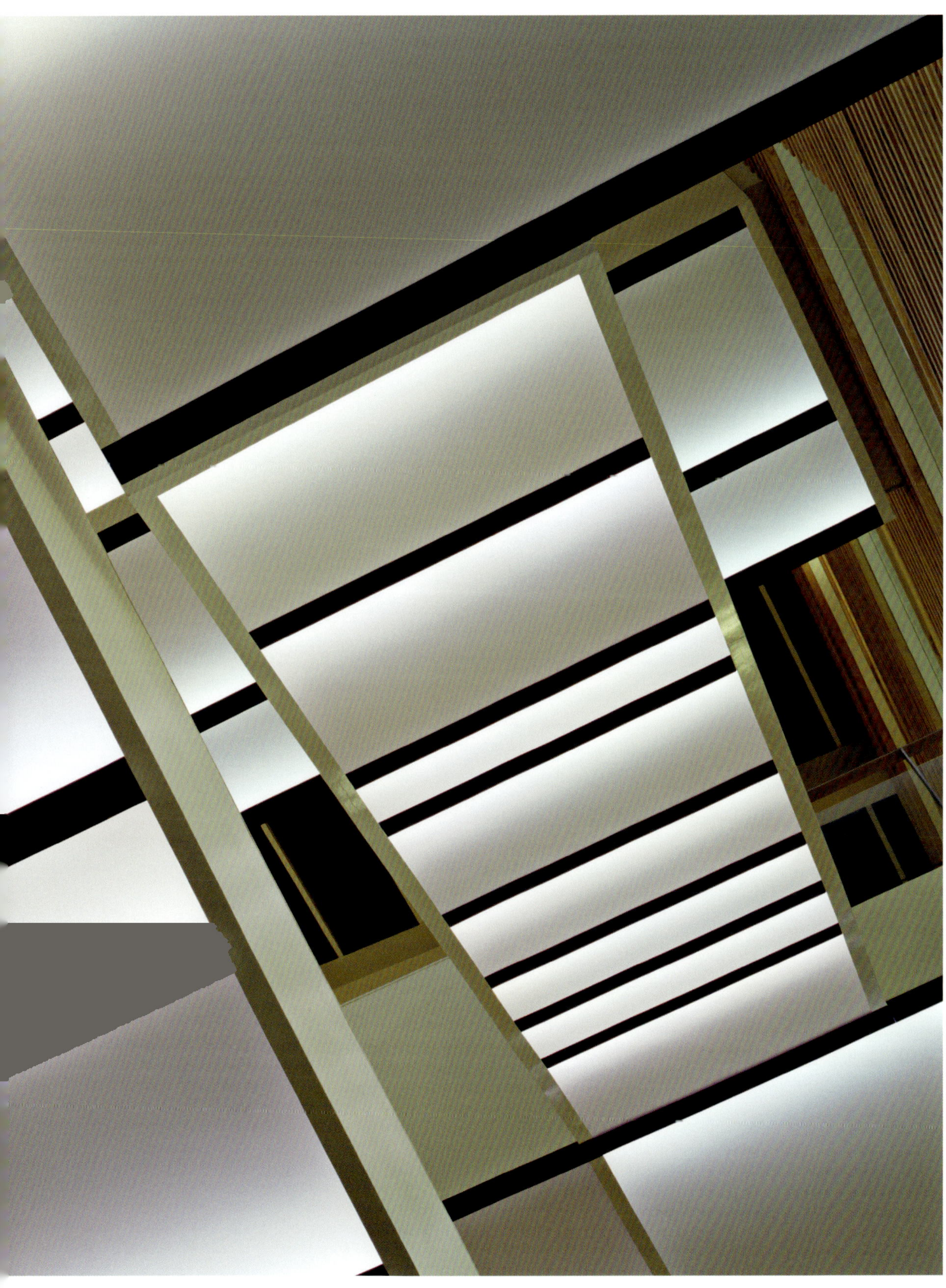

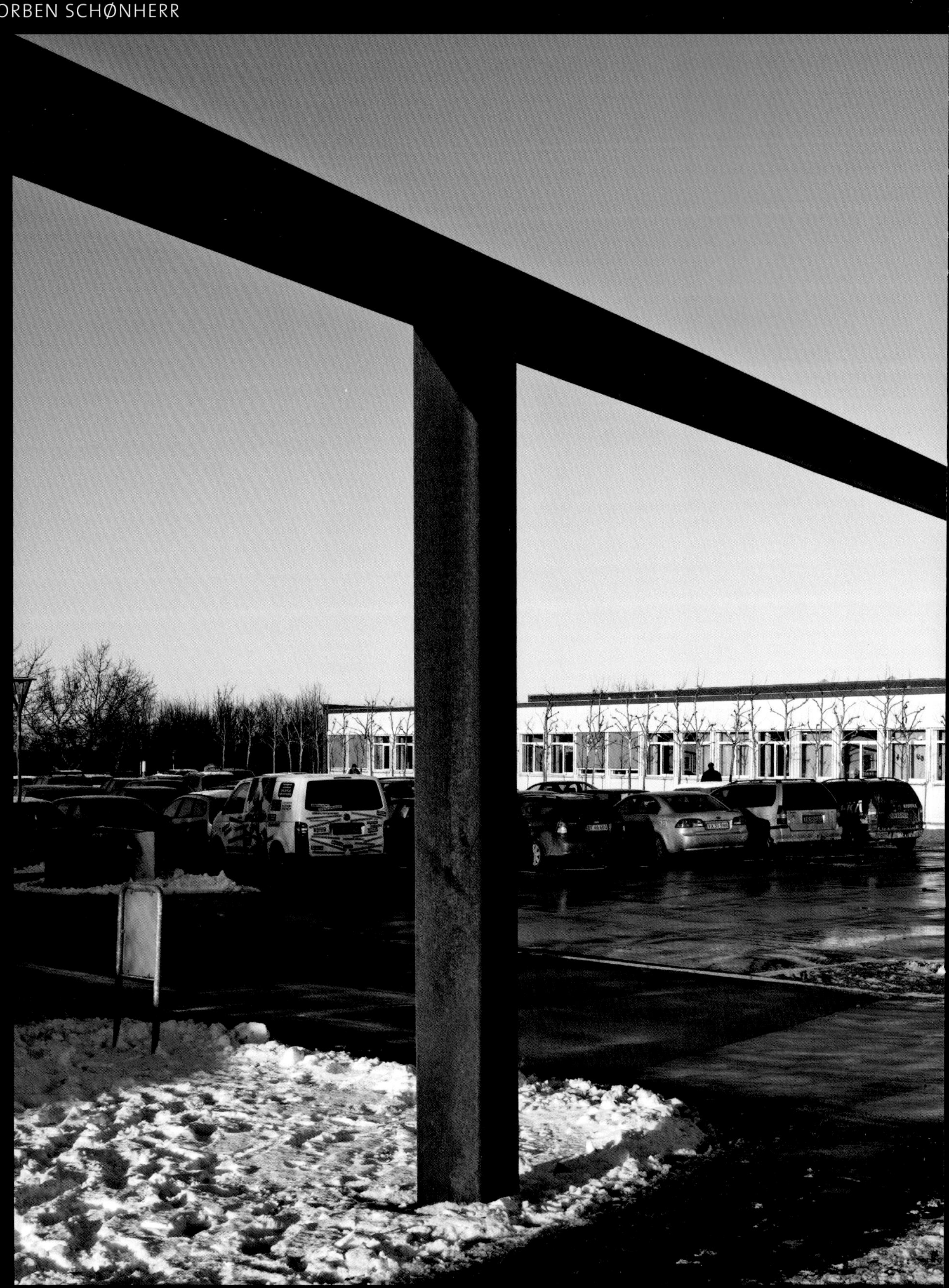

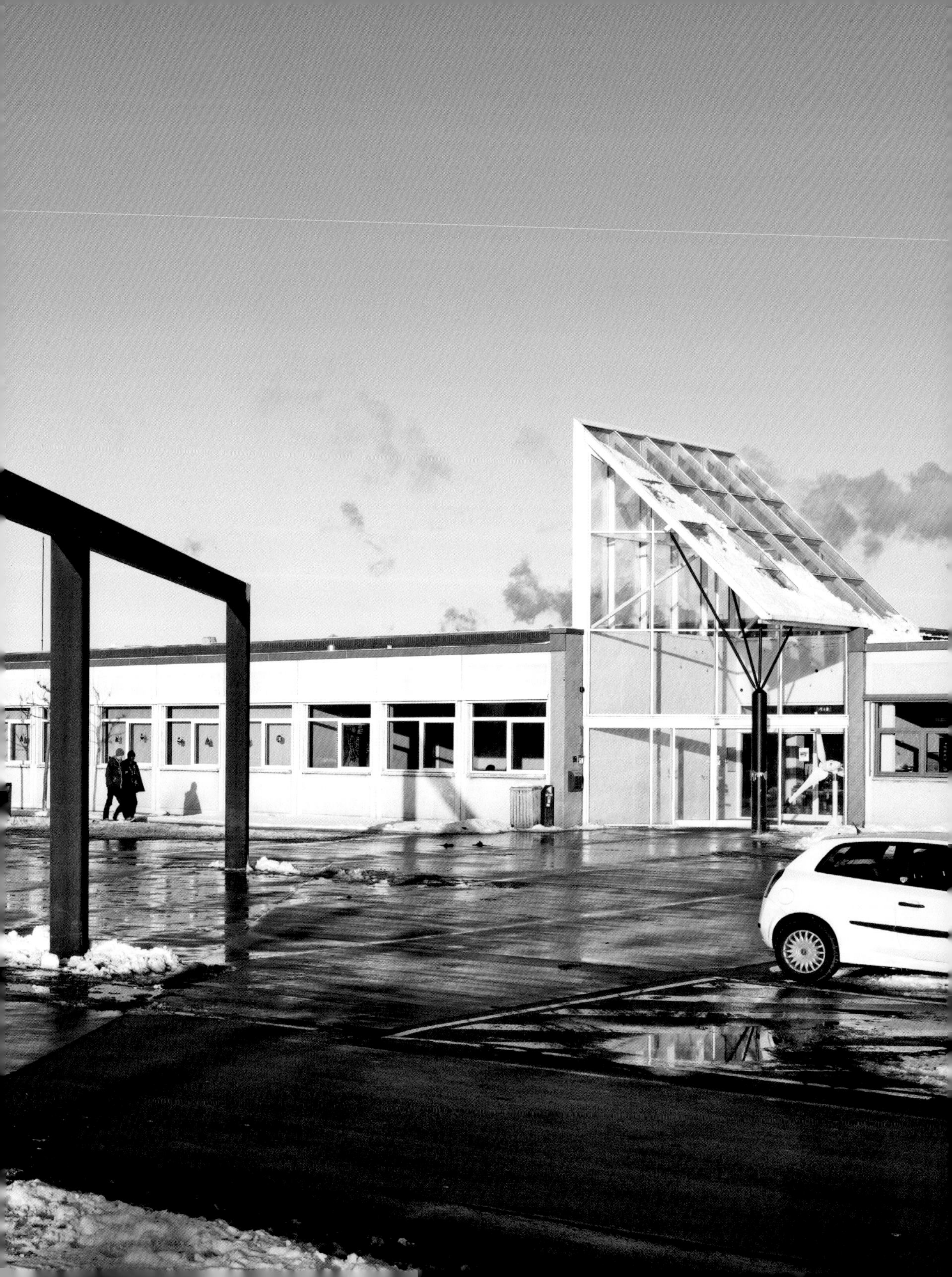

**BLADE OF LIGHT** | 5100 x 600 x 50 cm | 50 x 50 cm cor-ten steel section
TECH COLLEGE AALBORG | 200-YEAR ANNIVERSARY COMMISSION
IN COLLABORATION WITH TORBEN SCHØNHERR

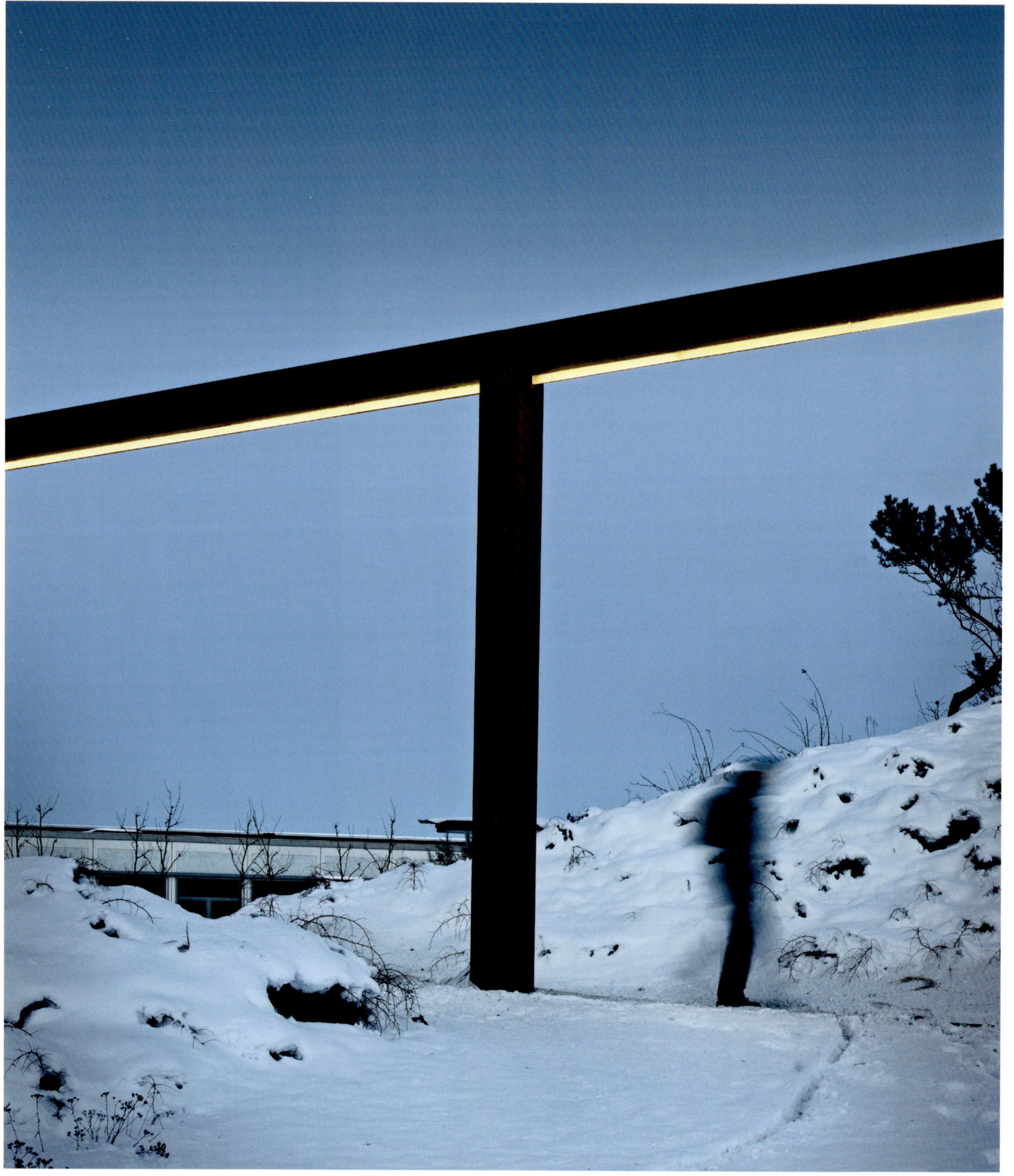

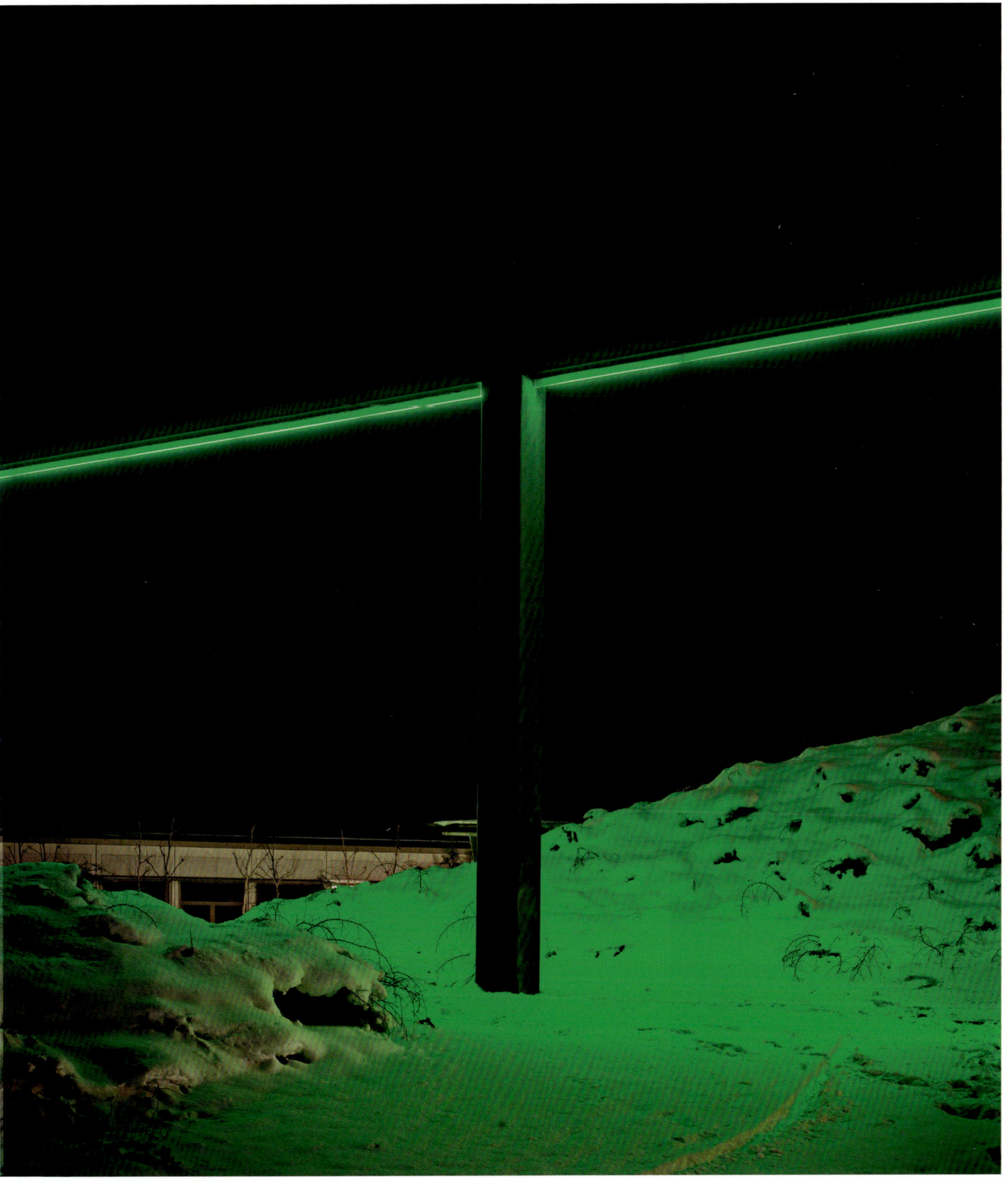

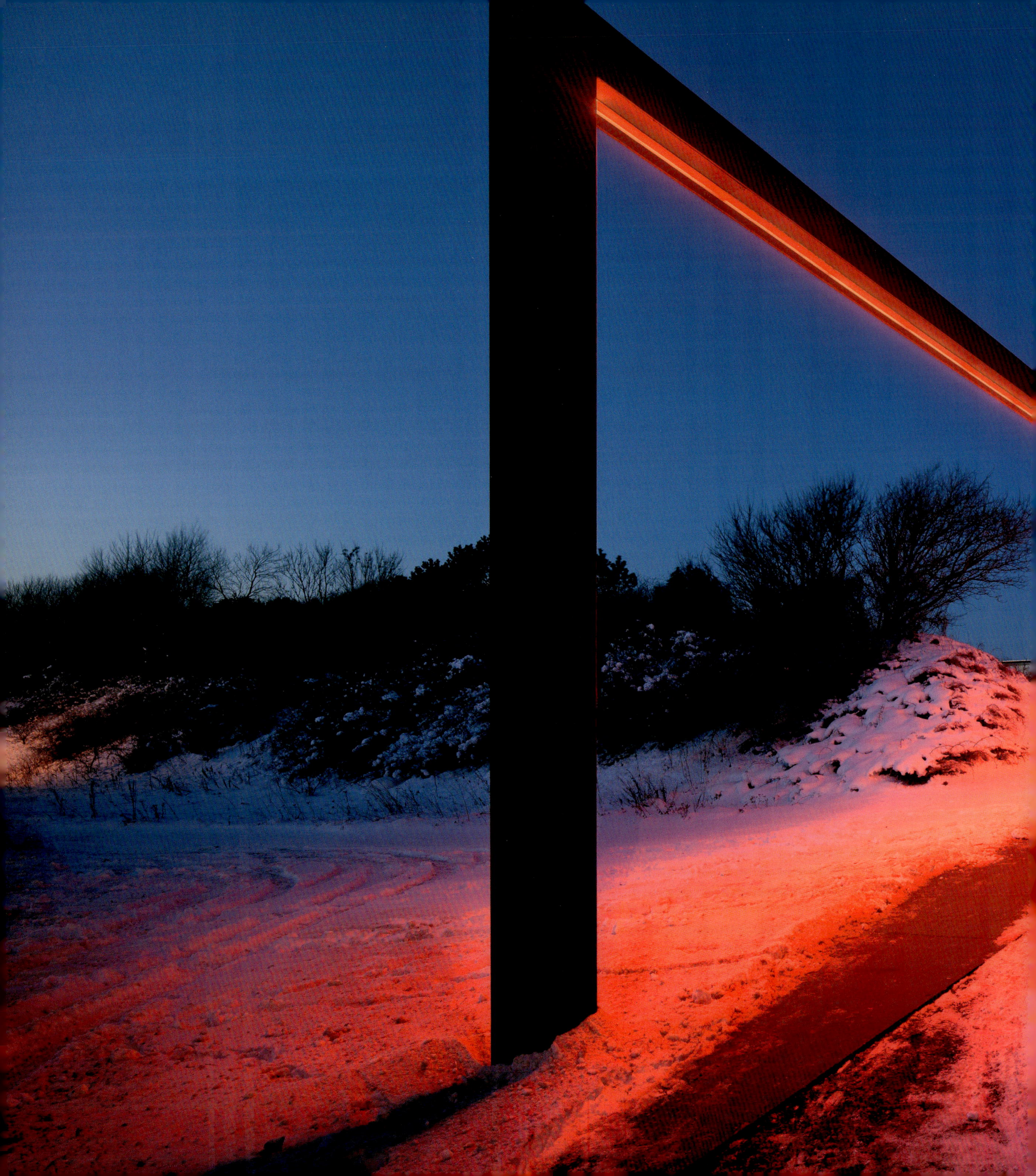

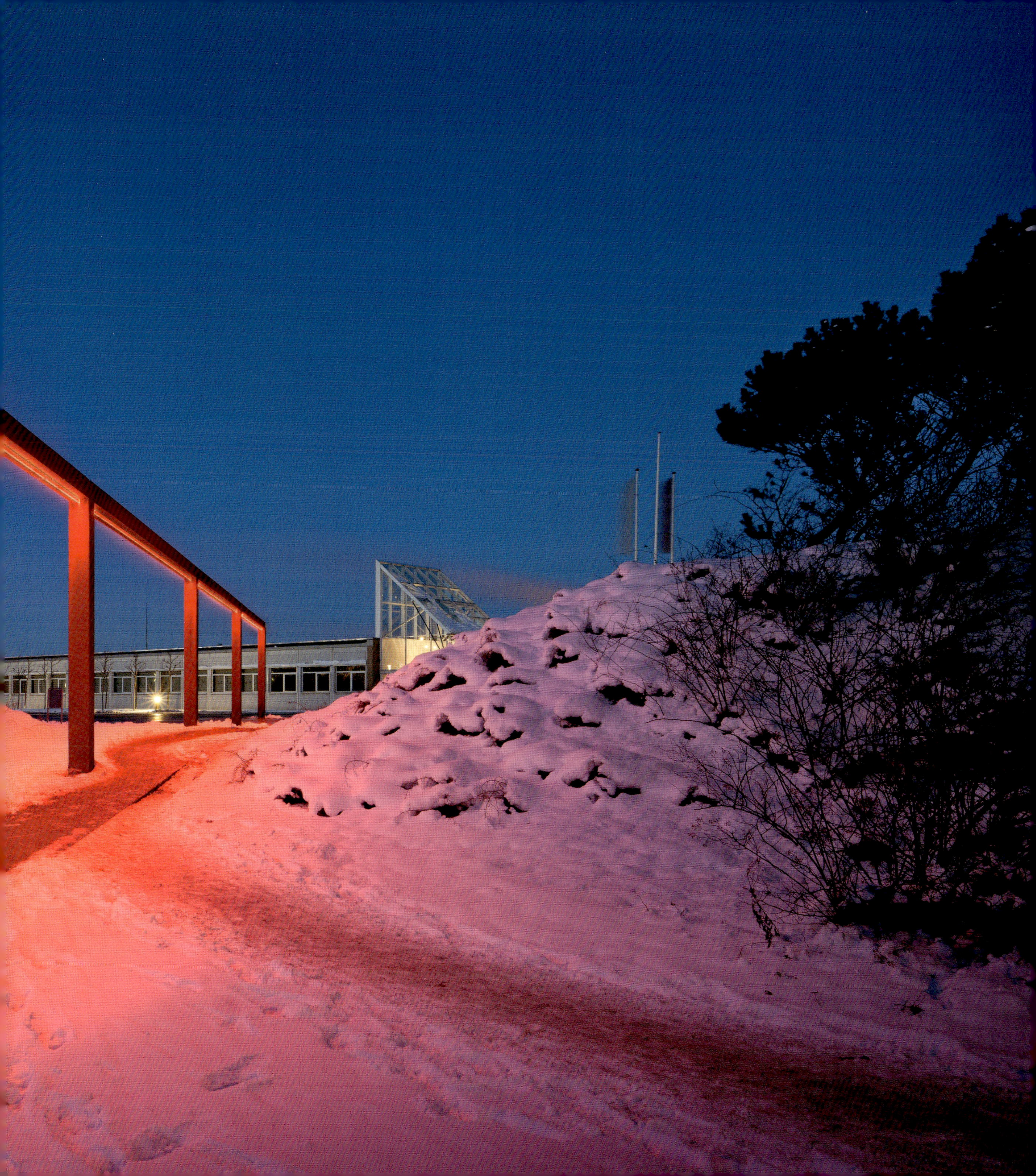

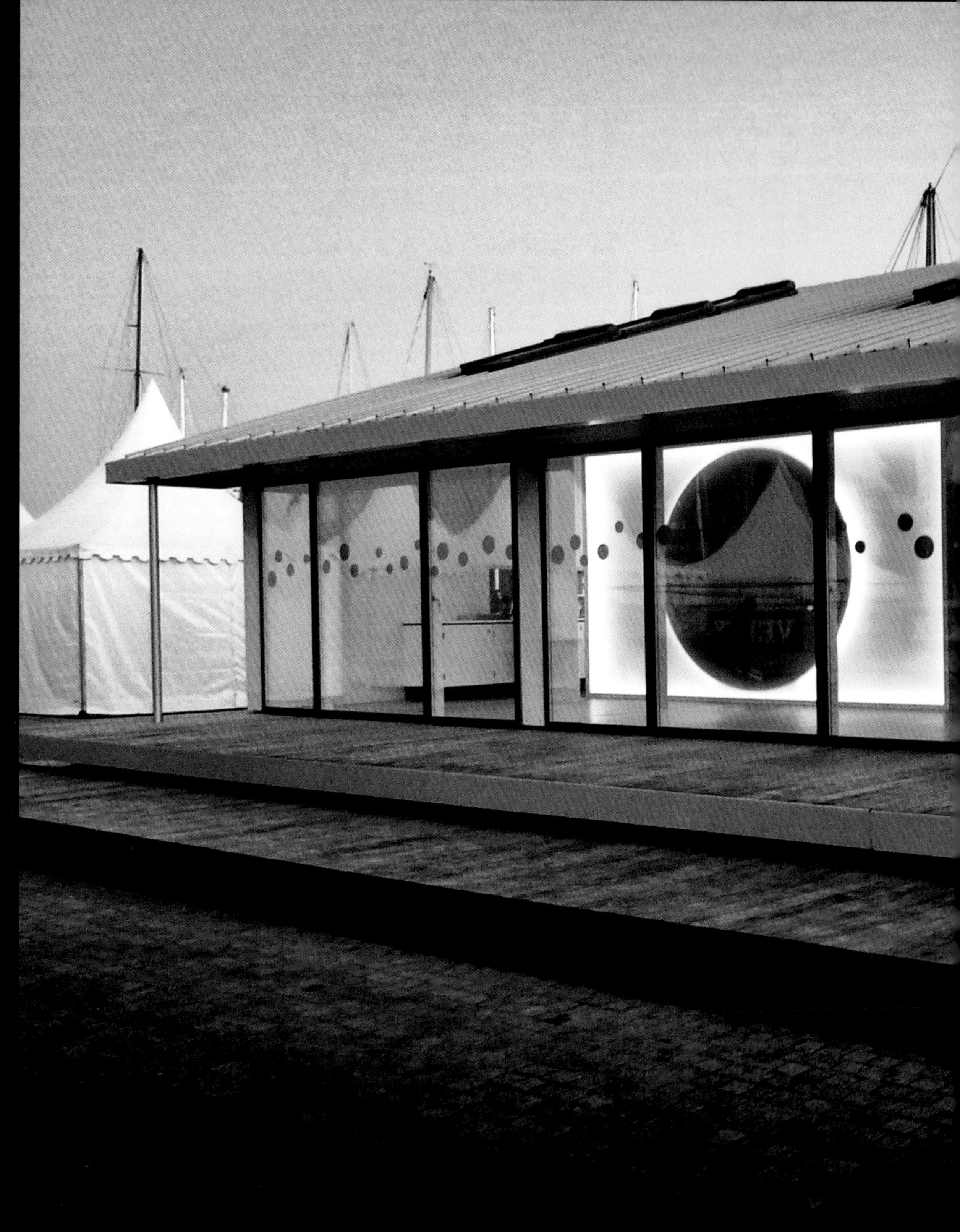

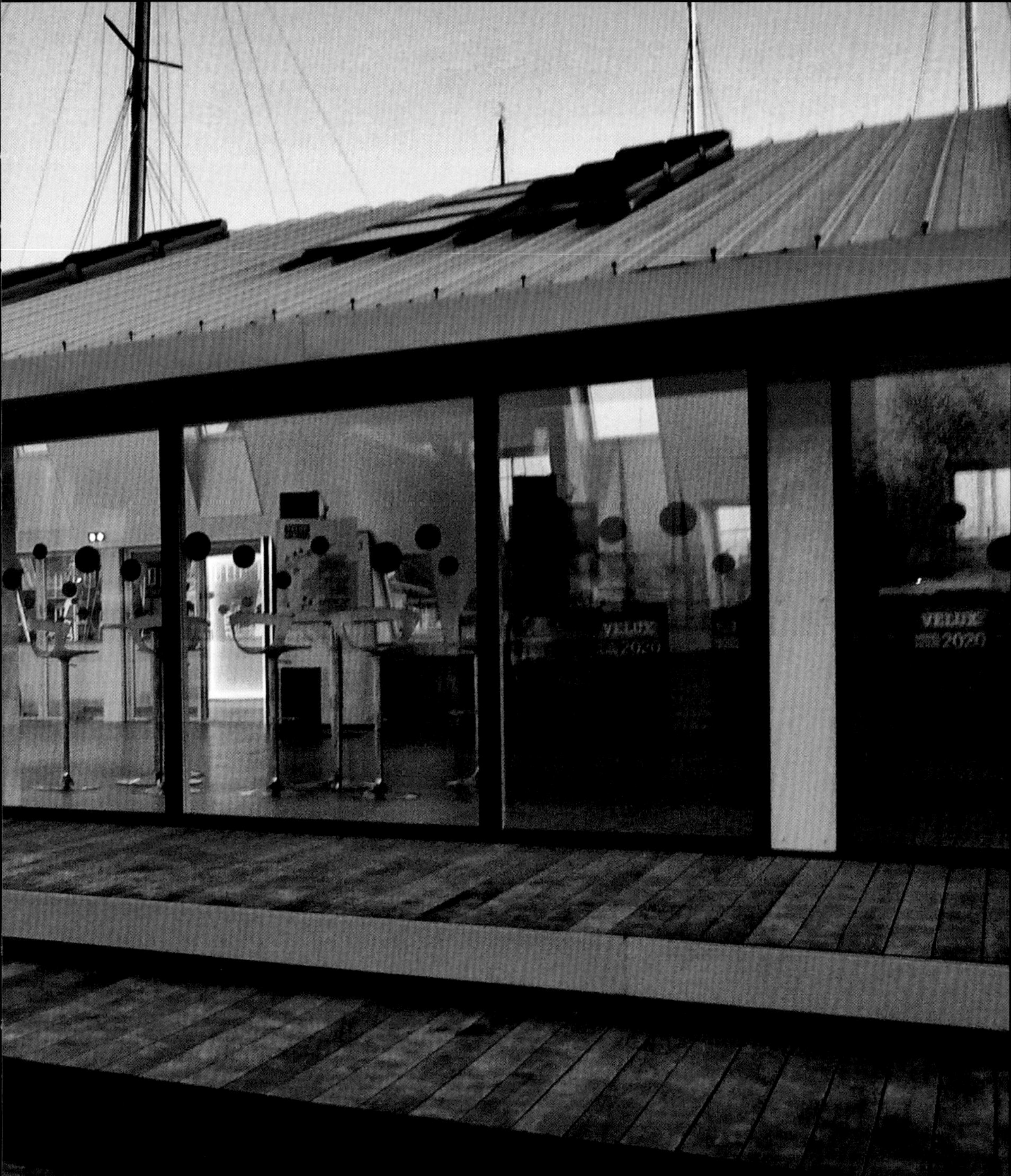

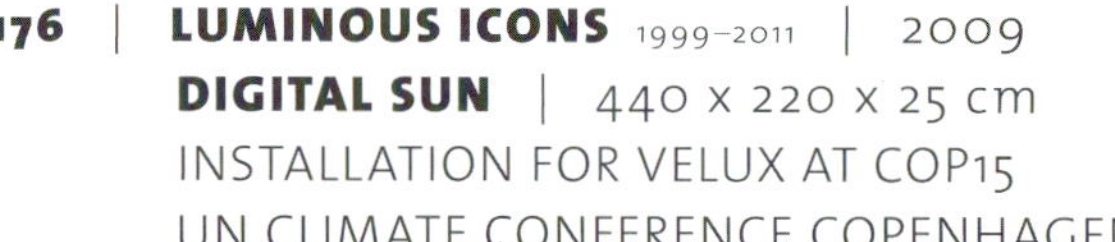
VELUX

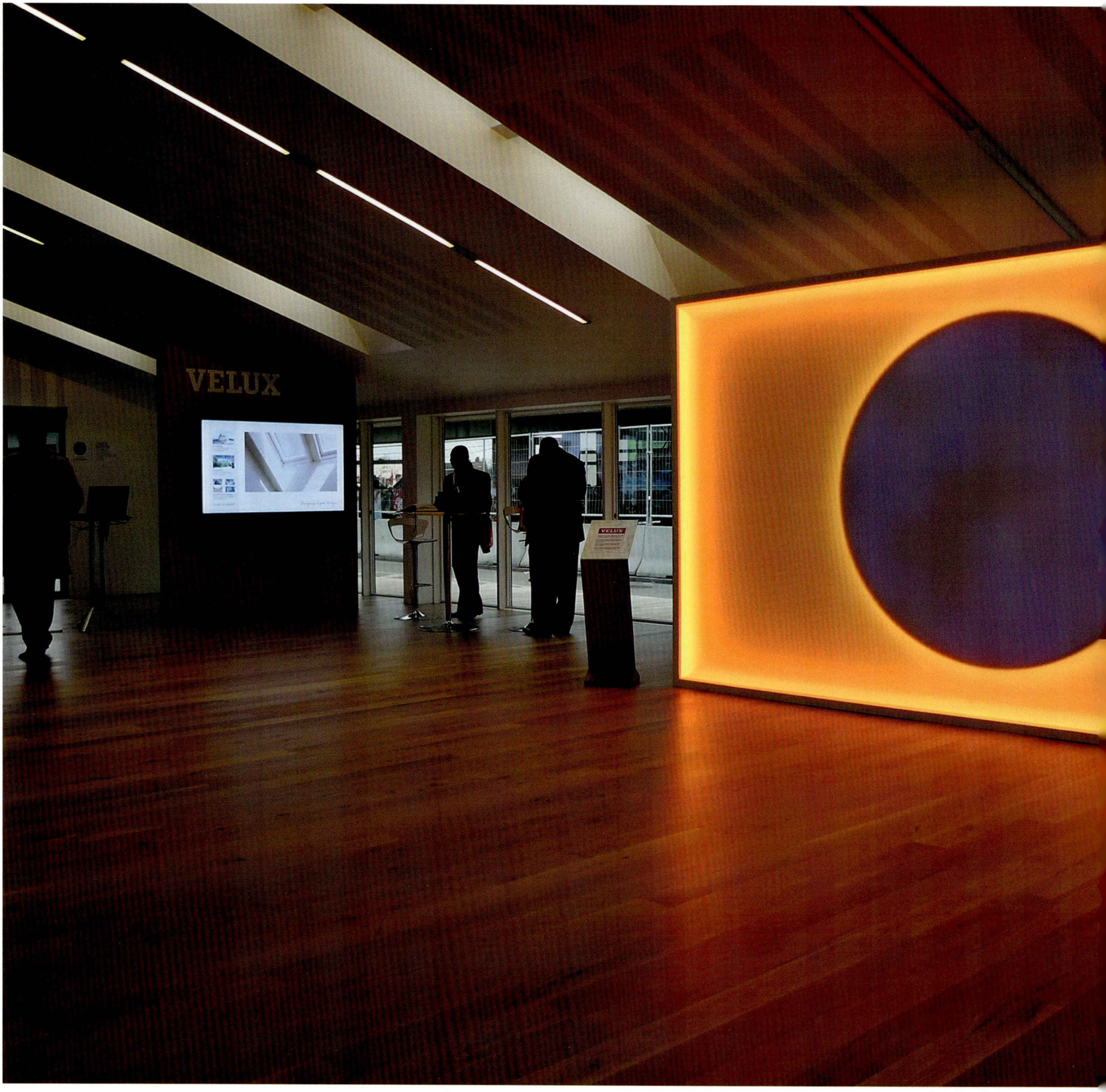

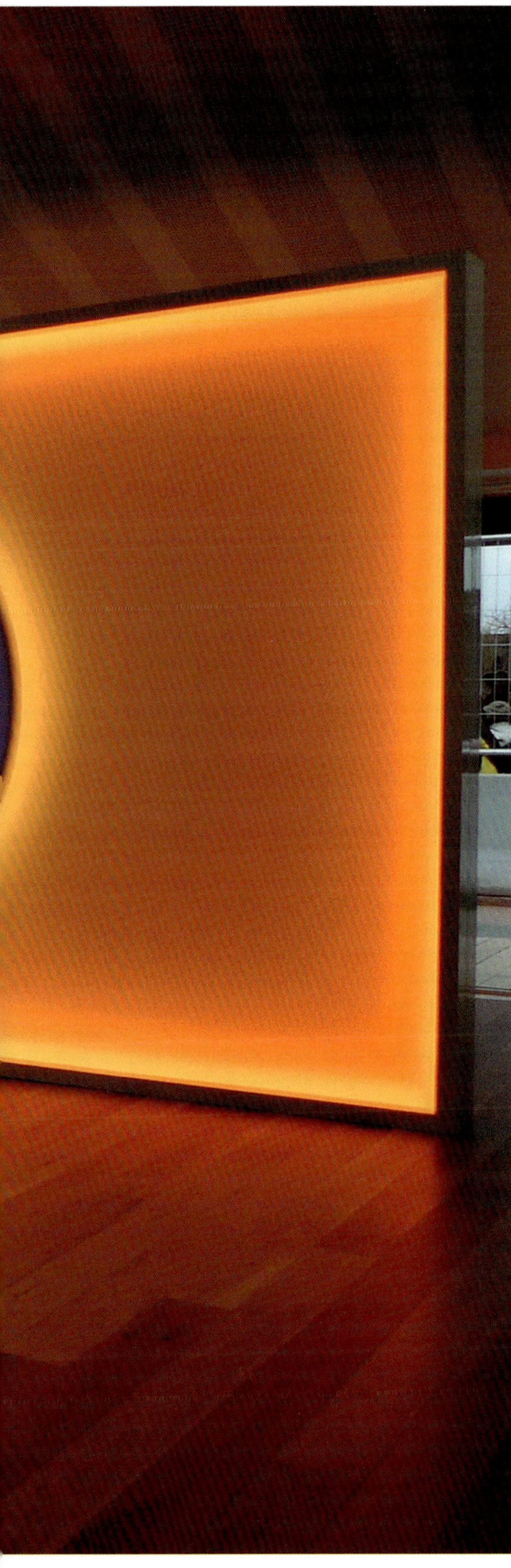

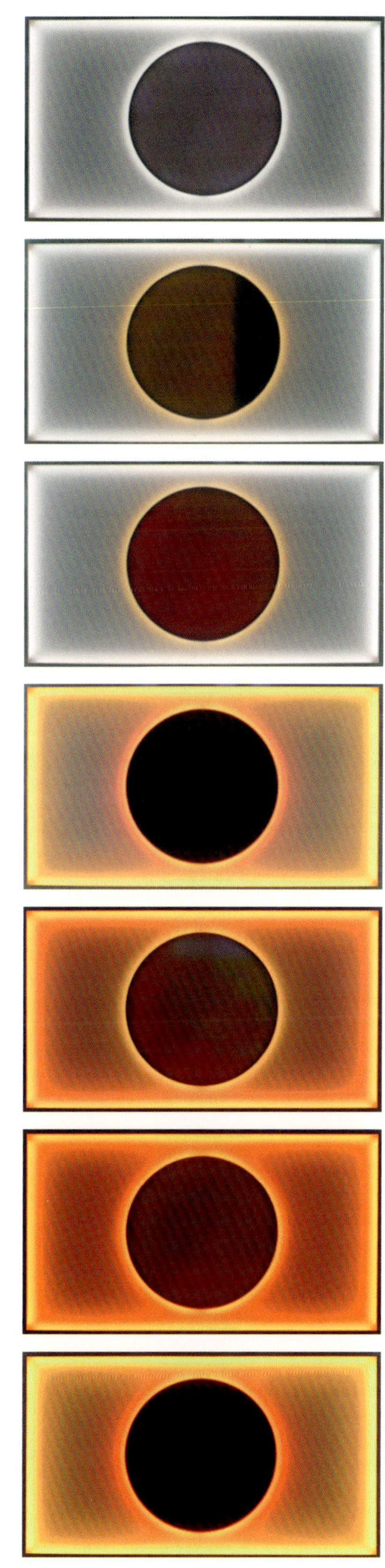

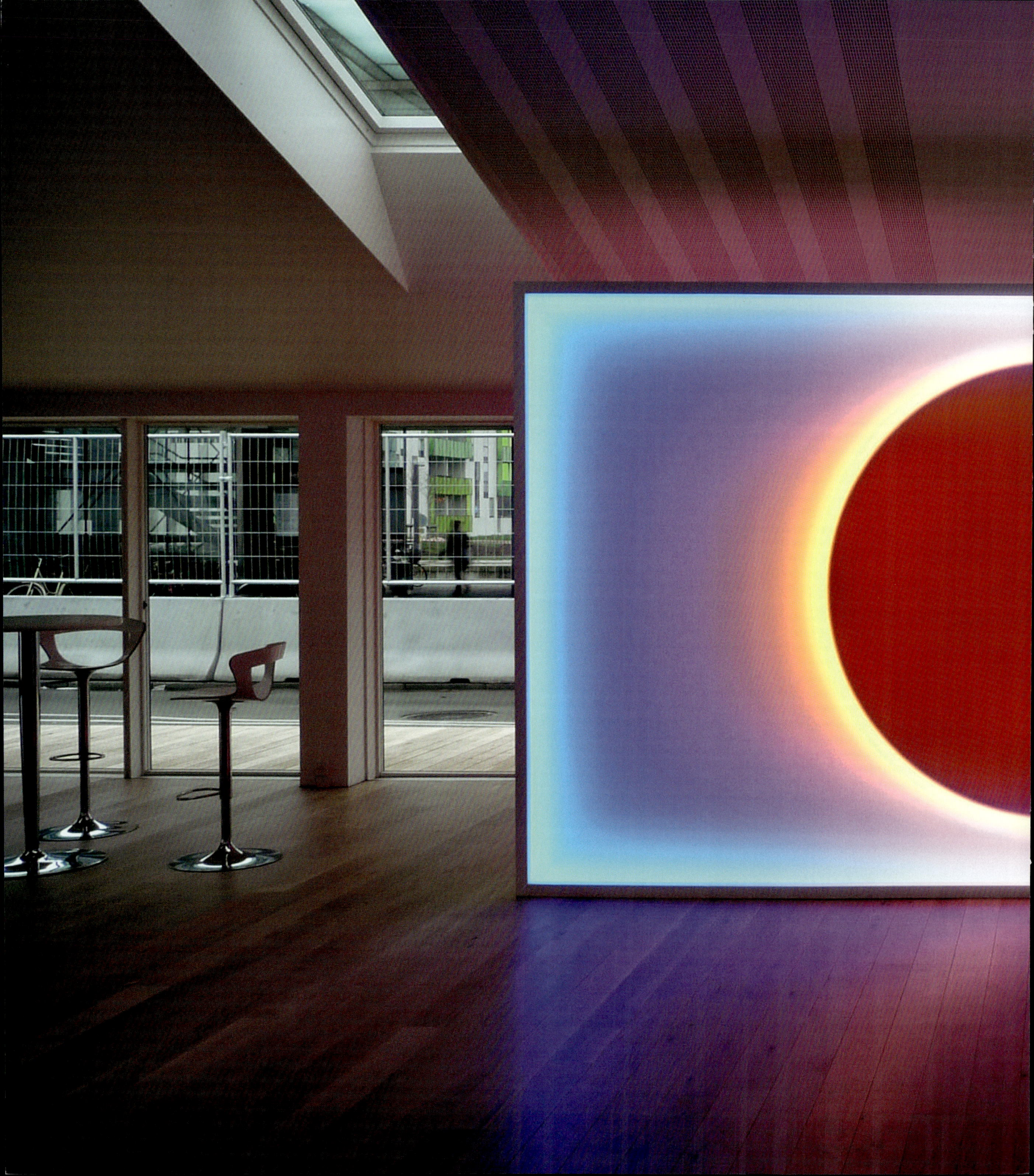

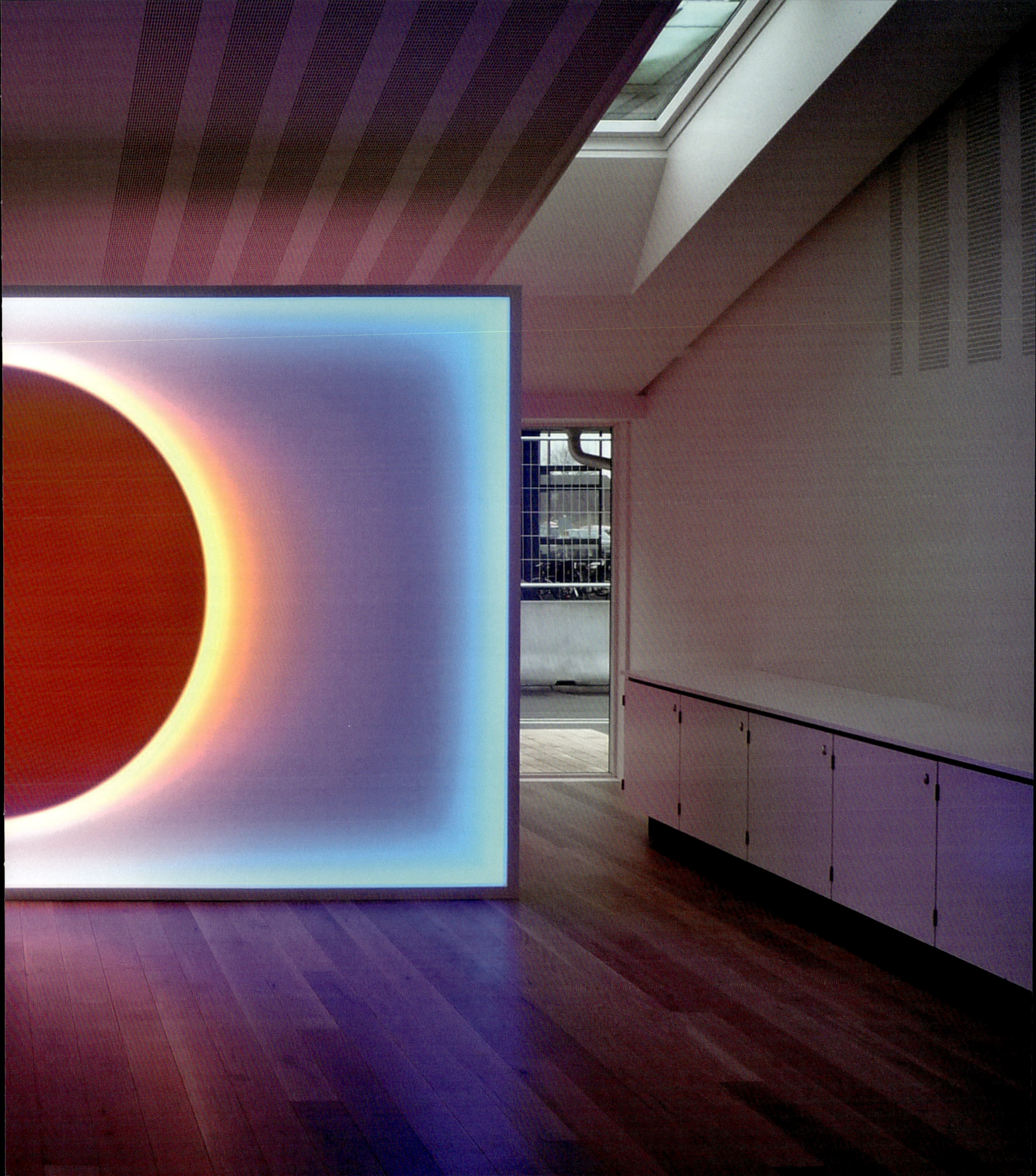

**DIGITAL SUN** | 440 x 220 x 25 cm
INSTALLATION FOR VELUX AT COP15
UN CLIMATE CONFERENCE COPENHAGEN

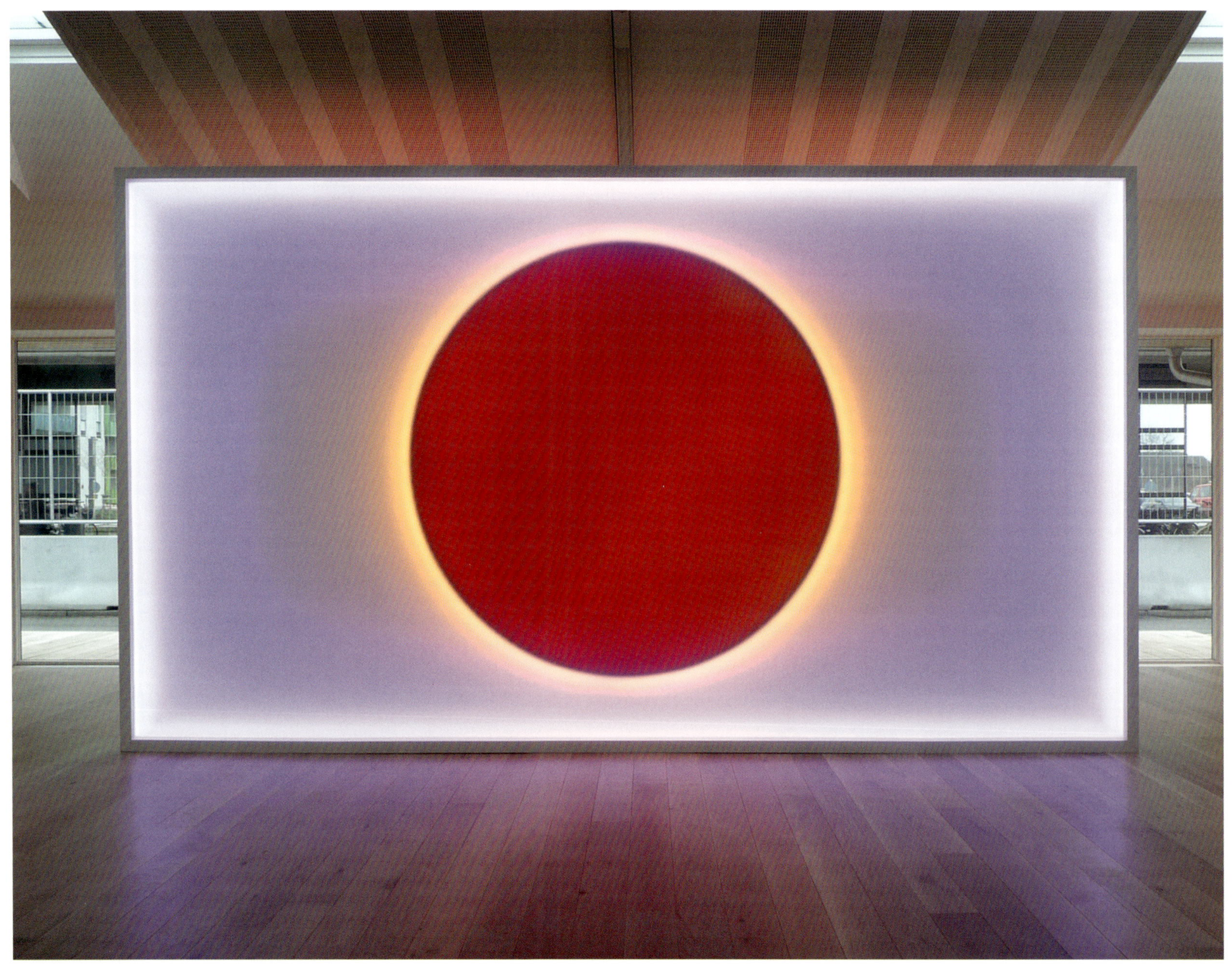

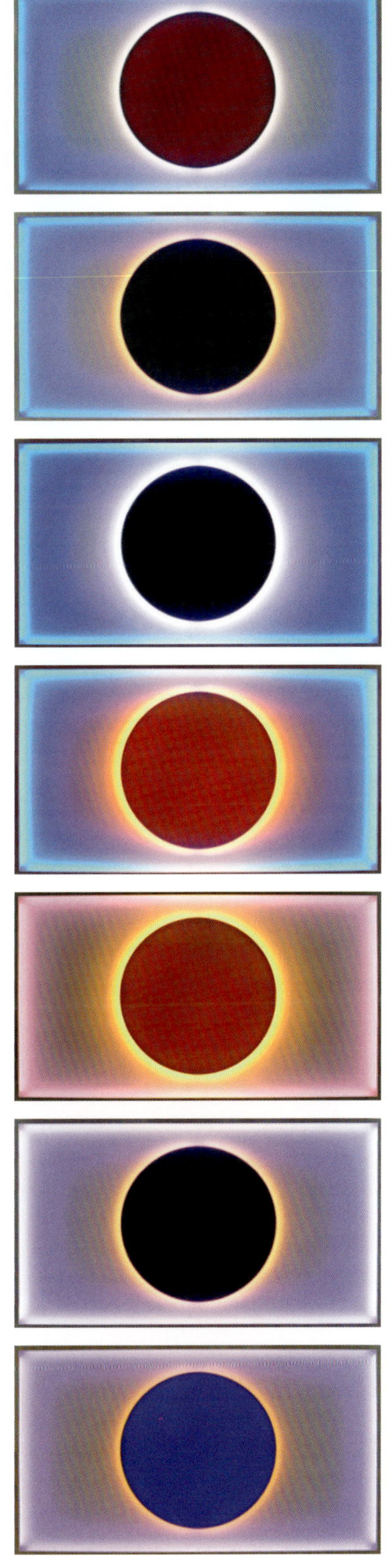

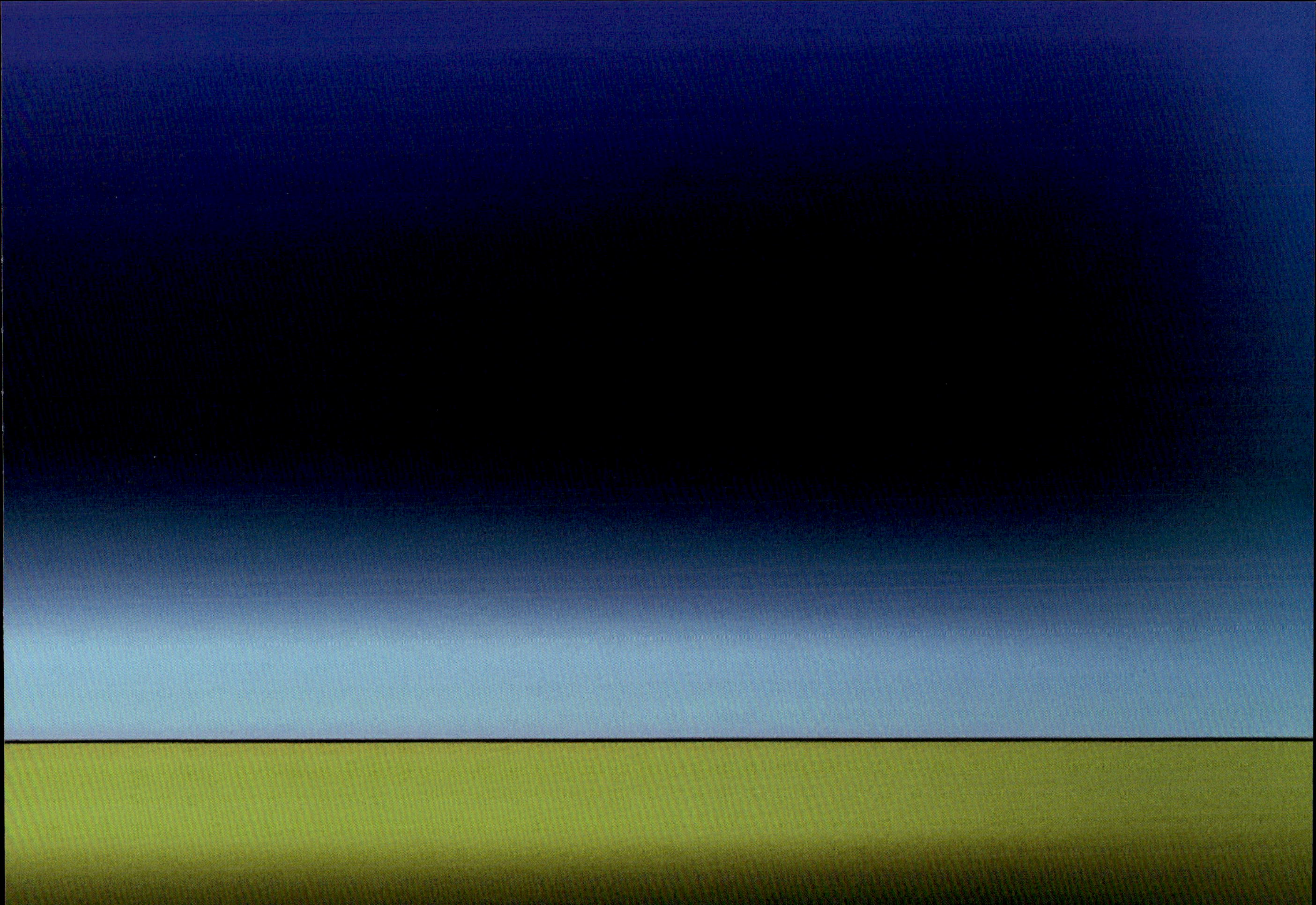

# SELECTED SOLO EXHIBITIONS

**2011**  Schaltwerk Kunst, Hamburg, Germany
Ecstasy Series

**2011**  Alingsås Museum of Light, Alingsås, Sweden
Subtle Waves of Emotions

**2011**  Galleri Weinberger, Copenhagen, Denmark
Light Works 2011

**2009**  La Rochelle, France and COP15,
UN Climate Conference, Copenhagen, Denmark
Digital Sun

**2008**  Galerie König, Berlin, Germany
Eclipse Series

**2007**  Galleri Weinberger, Copenhagen, Denmark
Shared Space 3 with Jon Groom

**2007**  Galerie König, Hanau, Frankfurt, Germany
Shared Space 2 with Jon Groom

**2006**  Kulturrum Hammenhog, Ystad, Sweden
Shared Space 1 with Peter Ch. Petersen

**2005**  Galleri Weinberger, Copenhagen, Denmark
Black Light

**2005**  Kunstforeningen, Gl. Strand, Copenhagen, Denmark
Labyrinth for H. C. Andersen.
A 6-room Installation of Light and Sound
Catalogue with a foreword by Helle Behrndt,
Director, Kunstforeningen Copenhagen
Barbara Schneider-Kempf,
Director General, Staatsbibliothek zu Berlin
Germany

**2004**  Galerie König, Hanau, Frankfurt, Germany
Light and Glass Works

**2003**  Galleri Weinberger, Copenhagen, Denmark
Montanalight

**2001**  Vaerket Art Centre, Randers, Denmark
Light Works 2 2001

**2001**  Galleri Weinberger, Copenhagen, Denmark
Light Works 2001

## SELECTED GROUP EXHIBITIONS

**2010**  Galleri Weinberger, Copenhagen, Denmark
Black & White
Michael Goldberg, Trevor Sutton, Jon Groom,
Eduardo Chillida, Linda Levit, Richard Serra,
Cathrine Lee, Ted Stamm, Ian McKeever

**2009**  Glowing Planet COP15
Copenhagen, Denmark

**2008**  Galleri Weinberger, Copenhagen, Denmark
Michael Goldberg, Catherine Lee, Leif Kath,
Kresten Havgaard, Torben Ebbesen,
Margrete Sørensen

**2007**  Galleri Weinberger, Copenhagen, Denmark
20th Anniversary Exhibition

**2007**  Days of Light Øksnehallen, Copenhagen, Denmark
Gun Gordillo, Viera Collaro, Thorbjørn Lausten

**2006**  Stadt Galerie, Prien, Bavaria, Germany
Stille Abstraktion
Stephen Westfall, Werner Haypeter,
Jon Groom, Dany Paal
Catalogue with a foreword by Robert C. Morgan

**2004**  Kunstverein Schloss Plön, Germany
Abstraktion III, 30 artists
Curator Jürgen Schweinebraden

**2004**  Mecklenburgisches Künstlerhaus, Plüschow,
Germany
Abstraktion III, 30 artists.
Curator Jurgen Schweinebraden

**2003**  Galleri Weinberger, Copenhagen, Denmark
Lone Arendal, Torben Ebbesen, Maja Lisa Engelhardt,
Linda Levit, Michael Goldberg

**2002**  Galleri Weinberger, Copenhagen, Denmark
Lone Arendal, Janne Mandrup, Mette Ussing,
Torgny Wilke,

**1997**  Zentralinstitut fur Kunstgeschichte, Munich, Germany
3 Installations Jon Groom, Andreas Horlitz
Catalogue with a foreword
by Dr. Michael F. Zimmermann

 | **LUMINOUS ICONS** 1999–2011 | SOLO EXHIBITION | 2011
**ECSTASY ONE** | 150 x 45 x 10 cm | **ECSTASY TWO** | 150 x 45 x 10 cm
**BROWN LIGHT** | 93 x 151 x 15 cm
BROWN LIGHT EDITION OF FOUR
BROWN LIGHT PRIVATE COLLECTIONS | DENMARK & SWEDEN
ALINGSÅS MUSEUM OF LIGHT    ALINGSÅS    SWEDEN

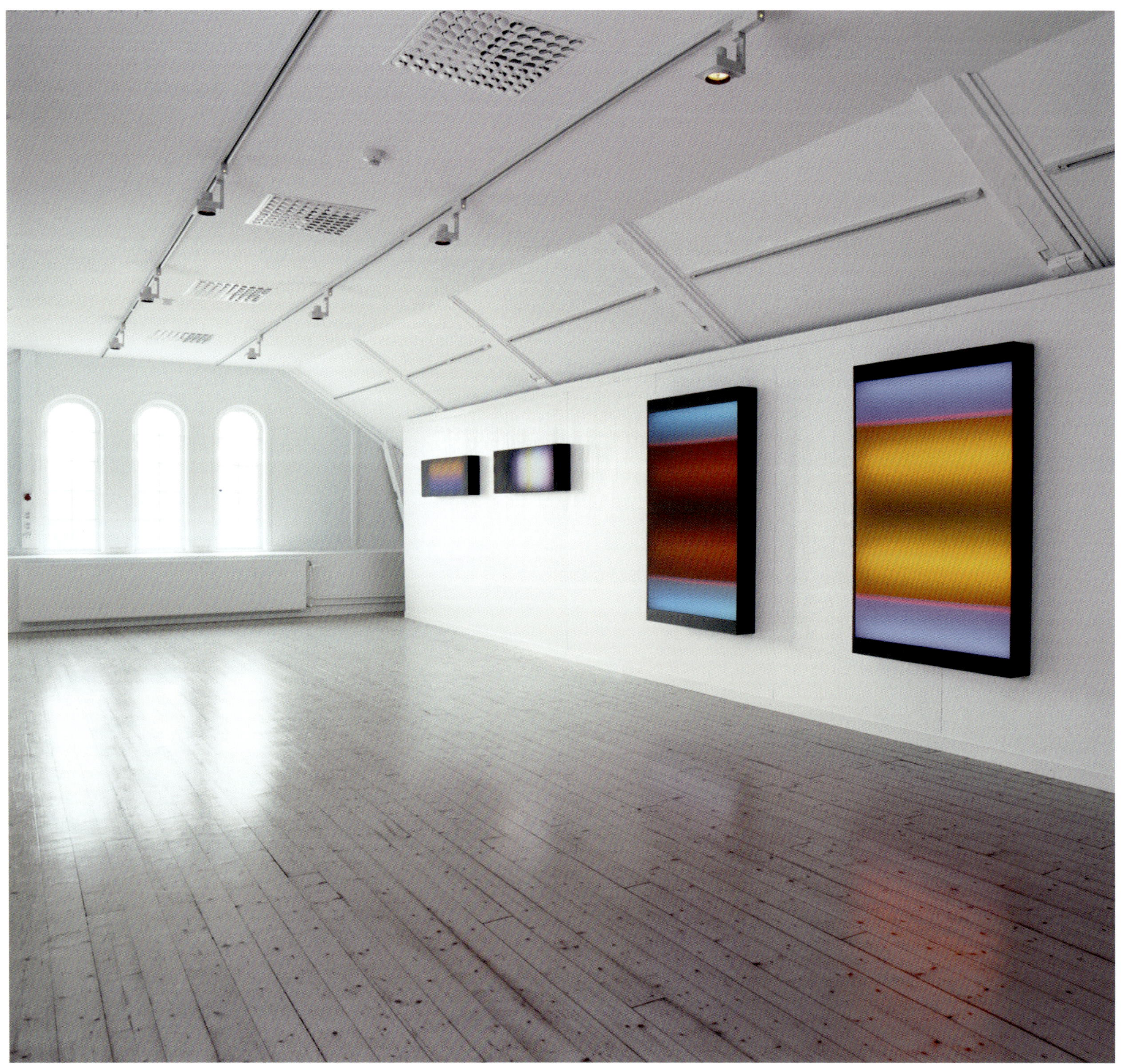

# PRIVATE & PUBLIC COLLECTIONS

Statens Kunstfond, Denmark

Velux Foundation, Hørsholm, Denmark

Tryg Foundation, Copenhagen, Denmark

Holch-Andersen & Sørensen, Copenhagen, Denmark

Deloitte Foundation, Copenhagen, Denmark

ING-DiBa Bank, Hanover, Germany

ING-DiBa Bank, Nuremberg, Germany

ING-DiBa Bank, Vienna, Austria

ING DiBa Bank, Frankfurt, Germany

Het Muziekgebouw, Concert Hall, Amsterdam, Holland

Aalborg Tech College, Aalborg, Denmark

Weldebrau Brewery, Heidelberg, Germany

Montana Foundation, Haarby, Denmark

Davids Samling, State Hospital, Copenhagen, Denmark

FIH Merchant Bank, Denmark

Værket Art Centre, Randers, Denmark

Museum of Light, Alingsås, Sweden

Alingsås Energy, Alingsås, Sweden

# SELECTED RECENT BIBLIOGRAPHY

**2010** Joachim Ritter, PLDA

**2010** Sara Engeln/Jesse Lilley
"we can change the weather"
Vrie University Brussels, Belgium

**2007** Ole Nørlyng "Lysets himmelstige"
Weekendavisen Kultur Nr. 51. 21.12.07

**2007** Christoph Schütte "Pulsierrende Farbräume"
Frankfurter Allgemeine Zeitung 9.5.2007

**2007** Jacob Schoof "Beneath" Interview 12
Daylight & Architecture, Magazine by Velux
Issue 5, spring 2007

**2007** Peter Michael Hornung, "farvernes forvandling"
Politiken 3.2.2007

**2006** Lie Madsen Interview/Heike Sütter Foreword
"Seventy Seven"
Deloitte Art Installation

**2006** Robert C. Morgan "Stille Abstraktion"
Stadt Galerie, Prien, Bavaria, Germany,
Exhibition catalogue

**2006** Light Art Het Muziekgebouw, Amsterdam,
The Plan # 12 2006, Italy

**2005** Trine Møller Madsen
"H. C. Andersen's Labyrinth"
Foreword Helle Behrndt/Barbara Schneider-Kempf
Kunstforeningen, Gammel Strand Copenhagen,
Exhibition catalogue

**2005** Merete Madsen
"Perception of Colour and What Makes White Light"
Arkitekten 9/2005

**2005** Ole Nørlyng, "Kunstforeningen,
H. C. Andersen Review", Denmark
Berlingske Tidende 16.3.2005

## ROBERT C. MORGAN
PROFESSOR OF ART HISTORY

Robert C. Morgan lives in New York and is an international critic, curator, lecturer, poet and occasional artist. The first critic to receive the Arcale award in Salamanca (1999), Professor Morgan holds an advanced degree in studio art and a doctorate in aesthetics and art history. In addition to his many books and extensive list of essays, Morgan is Visiting Professor of Graduate Fine Arts at Pratt Institute in Brooklyn, Professor Emeritus in Art History at the Rochester Institute of Technology and a consulting editor to The *Brooklyn Rail, Sculpture Magazine* and *Asian Art News* in Hong Kong. In 2005, he was a Fulbright Senior Scholar in the Republic of Korea.

## OLE NØRLYNG
ART HISTORIAN AND DANCE CRITIC

Born in 1946, Ole Nørlyng graduated from the University of Copenhagen in art history and music. He won a research scholarship to study the music of the Bournonville ballets and later became a teacher (in music, art history and ballet history) at the university and the Royal Danish Ballet. Since 1983, he has been art and dance critic for the newspapers *Berlingske Tidende* and *Weekendavisen*. Ole Nørlyng has reworked versions of the score for *La Sylphide* and *A Folk Tale,* and served as dramaturgic advisor. He has published extensively, writing several books on ballet: *Balletbogen* (1992), *Dance Is an Art* (2005), *Springkraft og danseglæde* (2007) and *Silja* (2009), as well as books on art and architecture, including *Apollons mange masker* (1998).

## JAN GJØNNES MØLLER
GRAPHIC DESIGN

Jan Gjønnes Møller graduated in graphic communication in 1999 from the Graphic Arts Institute of Denmark. He has worked in advertising, publishing and fashion as an art director and a graphic designer. Co-founder of the international men's fashion magazine HE. Specialised in corporate identity, magazine and book design for both public, private and commercial clients. Based in Christianshavn, Copenhagen. He has worked with Steven Scott on different projects since 2005 and designed the book *Seventy Seven* in 2006.

## ELI LAJBOSCHITZ
RETOUCH

ELI Digital Imaging is an image processing company that offers a range of services. We focus on creating images that have photographic authenticity.

A close dialogue with the client and photographer is a natural part of our operation, as we guide our clients all the way from the initial idea to the finished product. The company ELI Digital Imaging was founded in 2002 by Eli Leibo, who has many years of experience in the image processing and reproduction business.

## ADAM MØRK
PHOTOGRAPHY

Adam Mørk graduated as an architect in 1997 from The Royal Danish Academy of Fine Arts, School of Architecture. He worked for five years as an architect doing competitions at Dissing+Weitling Architects.
Based with a studio in Copenhagen, he has since 2002 worked worldwide as an architectural photographer.
In all his work, Adam Mørk shows a special attention and sensitivity to light – and how light sculptures create space in harmony with materials.
Adam Mørk is chosen by leading architects to portrait their works. They include: 3XN, Behnisch Architekten, Henning Larsen Architects and schmidt/hammer/lassen architects/.
www.adammork.dk

## MATTHEW McCONNELL
PHOTOGRAPHY

Matthew McConnell has had a wide-ranging career both as a photographer and as a technical/production manager in theatre, opera, dance and exhibitions. He has collaborated on many projects involving the integration of art installations into architectural contexts. He was project manager for James Turrell's light space *Night Rain* in the Millennium Dome in London in 2000.
He has been an associate and friend of Steven Scott since they first worked together at Riverside Studios in London in the early 1980s, and has, since then, been part of the studio team on many occasions.
Now based in Barcelona, he is concentrating on photographic and documentary projects.

## PER MORTEN ABRAHAMSEN
PHOTOGRAPHY

Per Morten Abrahamsen is an award-winning photographer whose 20-year career spans fashion, advertising and portrait photography. His work is known for avoiding staged formality in favour of a looser approach that enables his subjects to become active contributors to the process. Per Morten Abrahamsen's work continues to be shown worldwide in art museums and galleries, most recently at the Christina Wilson Gallery in Copenhagen.

## HENRIK STENBERG
PHOTOGRAPHY

Photographer Henrik Stenberg has a long history of creating artistic images, portraits and dance images. With his Danish background and international carrier, he is well known for his timeless, honest and graphic style. For more than 10 years, Henrik Stenberg has been commissioned by The Royal Danish Ballet and several modern dance companies. Prior to this, Henrik Stenberg worked out of New York City, where he lived for more than a decade.

**WHOLE TWO** | 63 x 38 x 12 cm
ALINGSÅS MUSEUM OF LIGHT   ALINGSÅS   SWEDEN
PRIVATE COLLECTION DENMARK

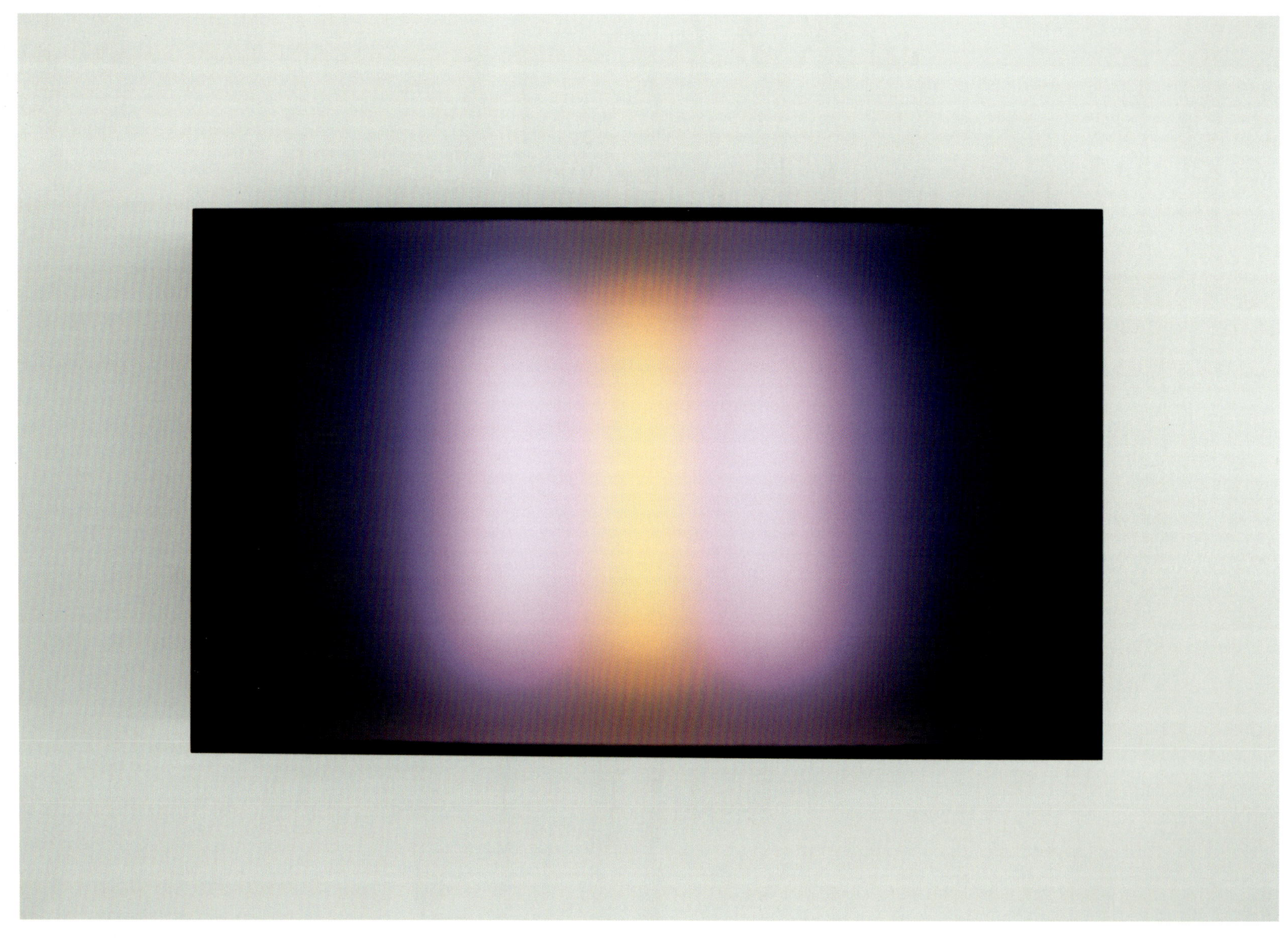

*With my work I have never sought to underline things too heavily. The intangible softness of light defies hard-edged, literal interpretations. The aim instead is to open up the viewer's imagination and allow him to find his own expression. The works are an invitation to observe the complexities of colour for as long as the viewer has time. Working with imperceptibly slow changes does require the observer to spend time with the pieces. I slow time down in order to bring the viewer back into a contemplative mood as if looking at a landscape or painting. Time is the central theme of all my works. The works are about creating time and space for people to see the world around them.*

STEVEN SCOTT

## CREDITS

Copyright **STEVEN SCOTT** ©

Publisher and copyright **HIRMER VERLAG** ©

Hirmer Verlag GmbH

Nymphenburger Straße 84

80636 Munich

www.hirmerverlag.de

www.hirmerpublishers.com

ISBN 978-3-7774-4631-8

Printer and binder **AUMÜLLER DRUCK REGENSBURG**

Aumüller Druck GmbH & Co. KG, Regensburg

Printed in Germany

## ARTISTS' ACKNOWLEDGEMENTS

Kim Herforth Nielsen and Staff of 3xN for making projects happen with light as a relevant material.
Peter Weinberger and Dorthe Budtz of Galleri Weinberger for 10 years of exhibitions.
Uschi and Hans König of Galerie König in Frankfurt and Berlin.
Dr. Nanna Preussners of Schaltwerk Kunst in Hamburg.
Jörg Paal of Galerie Thomas in Munich.
Søren Jensen and Martin Sidelmann of Scenetek for years of support in the production of all artworks and installations.
Adam Mørk and Matthew McConnell for their dedication and eye for the work over many years.
Thanks to my lifelong friend Jon Groom the painter.
Thanks for many years of work together with ELI Lajboschitz and his team.
Jan Gjønnes Møller and his partner Rikke Tvilum for our second book together.
Thanks to Jesse Lilley, who has joined this group of close collaborators on the realisation of this book.
Ole Nørlyng has kept a constant eye on my work since the mid-eighties in both theatre and fine art and his wisdom is greatly appreciated.
A special thanks goes to Thomas Zuhr and his team at Hirmer Verlag Munich for taking on the publication of this book with such an incredible energy and spirit.
Thanks to the staff at Aumüller Druck Regensburg.
Finally to Robert C. Morgan for a fantastic week In Copenhagen, which led to the essay titled Luminous Icons, which became the title of this book.
Thank you.

## PUBLICATION CONTRIBUTORS:

Essay titled Luminous Icons by **ROBERT C. MORGAN** ©

Foreword by **OLE NØRLYNG** ©

Graphic design by **JAN GJØNNES MØLLER** ©

Front cover photo by **ADAM MØRK** ©

Requiem, Sylphide, Deloitte, FIH, Alborg, Amsterdam finished building, Black Light, Flood, Brown Light, 3XN room shot, Light Works 2011 room shot, Nominal Twenty One (detail). Pages 10. 13. 14. 17. 19. 21. 22./50. 51. 52. 54. 55. 56. 57. 58. 59. 61. 62. 63. 64. 65. 67. 68. 69. 70. 71. 72. 73./82. 83. 84. 85. 86. 87. 88. 89. 90. 91. 92. 93. 100. 108. 109. 118. 119. /136. 137. 143. 144. 145. 146. 147. 148. 149. 151. 152. 153. 155. 156. 157. 158. 159. 160. 161. 162. 163. 165. 166. 167. 168. 169. 170. 171. 172. 173. ©

Chapter dividing photo by **MATTHEW McCONNELL** © Prototype Amsterdam, Horizon, Open Box, Nominal Eight and Nominal Twenty One, Ecstasy One and Ecstasy Two, Icon 2.0 and Icon 2.1 , Horizon One (detail). Pages 39. 40. 41. 43. 44. 45. 47. 48. 49. 53./94. 95. 97. 99. 102. 103. 105. 107. 110. 111. 113. 114. 115. 117. 120. 121. 123. 124. 125. 127./138. 139. 140. 141. 186. 190. ©

Digital Sun photo by **STEVEN SCOTT** ©

Pages 174. 175. 176. 177. 178. 179. 180. 181. ©

Sylphide photo by **PER MORTEN ABRAHAMSEN** ©

Pages 18. 20. 23. ©

Requiem photo by **HENRIK STENBERG** ©

Pages 11. 12. 15. 16. ©

Digital imaging by ELI: **ELI LAJBOSCHITZ, MOGENS WITTRUP, BENJAMIN LAJBOSCHITZ** & **NINA SCOTT**

Text editing by **JESSE LILLEY**

Proof-reading by **DANKO SZABÓ**

*I wish to dedicate this book to Vanja, Scarlett, Nina, Georgia and Sophia and to all friends and family involved in Georgia's Arabian Summer Adventure of 2011.*